AN INVITATION TO
ITALIAN
COOKING

Antonio Carluccio

AN INVITATION TO
ITALIAN
COOKING

Food photography by Christine Hanscomb
Illustrations by Flo Bayley
Location photography by Carey More

PAVILION

Dedico questo libro con profonda riconoscenza
a mia madre, unica e involontaria maestra
e a mia moglie Priscilla per tutto l'affettuoso
incoraggiamento necessario ad iniziare e
terminare quest opera
Londra Ottobre 1986

This edition first published in Great Britain in 1991

First published in hardback in 1986 by
Pavilion Books Limited
26, Upper Ground, London SE1 9PD

Text © Antonio Carluccio 1986
Illustrations © Flo Bayley 1986
Location photographs © Carey More 1986
and by Antonio and Priscilla Carluccio
Designed by Bernard Higton

A CIP catalogue record for this book is
available from the British Library

ISBN 1 85145 074 2 (hbk)
ISBN 1 85145 547 7 (pbk)

Printed in Singapore by Kyodo Printing Co. (S'pore) Pte Ltd

6 8 10 9 7 5

**Measurements in this book are given in metric
quantities with imperial and American
equivalents in brackets. When measuring
ingredients, follow one system throughout.**

Title page and jacket show clockwise from left to
right: Red mullet in red wine, Dandelion and violet
salad, Capellacci with mushroom sauce, Quail with
grappa raisins, Roast pepper salad, Elsbeth's cake.

CONTENTS

INTRODUCTION

My passion for food developed very early in my life. I used to spend hours in the kitchen, watching my mother cooking – I found it fascinating. But it wasn't until I was around twenty, that I discovered the excitement of cooking for myself.

The food I ate during my childhood was very, very good indeed. Even in wartime when there were severe food shortages, we were lucky. My father was station master in Castelnuovo Belbo, a little town near Alessandria in the north of Italy. On one occasion the Germans destroyed two bridges, one on either side of the village, while there was a goods train pulled up at the station. It was full of provisions such as rice and oil which we shared with the villagers and exchanged for fresh bread and salami and cheese. But that lasted only so long, and there were times when we had to live by our wits. I remember watching a group of partisans on the move. A big man was running along with a huge side of beef over his shoulder and there was my father right behind him with a knife saying, 'Wait a minute. That's too heavy for you,' and slicing a piece off for us.

Later, we moved to Borgofranco d'Ivrea, situated in the Aosta valley, north of Turin. My happiest memories of those schooldays were the lunches. I went to school in Ivrea, which is about seven kilometres from Borgofranco. Since it was too far to go home in the middle of the day, my mother used to send my lunch via a goods train. Everyday I would wait in the Ivrea station, impatient for the moment when the guard handed me that wonderful little basket. Inside there would be a complete meal – hot soup, a little meat or fish with vegetables, some cheese, bread, and a piece of fruit. The menu changed every day! In summer I used to eat it sitting on a pile of sleepers, completely alone. I could really concentrate on my lunch, it was so peaceful. When you grow up with pleasant experiences like that, you can't help but love food.

After I finished school I joined the navy and was sent to Sardinia. The navy food was plain but rather monotonous and I used to write letters home describing what I was eating and imagining what my family was having. For some reason, the navy cooks used very little local food. When we went out to sea we saw wonderful fish swimming around – it was frustrating thinking about how they would taste. But there were lighter moments. Sometimes we would go to Maddalena on leave and go to a café to eat the little almond and Anis biscuits called Anisettus, the local speciality, and drink Monica wine, a sort of Marsala, with them. And I had a brush with history when I was one of those chosen to take a birthday cake to Clelia Garibaldi. She was over ninety and she sat there in Caprera amongst all her memorabilia telling us stories about her father, the man who succeeded in unifying Italy.

But I didn't really enjoy life in the navy and only stayed about a year. Back in Borgofranco I worked as the local correspondent for a Turin newspaper. I found I could combine work with pleasure. I used to go to little trattorias which were renowned for particular specialities – one of my favourites served grapes and prunes preserved in alcohol that we ate at the bar – and, of course, they were good places to gather the local news!

I started cooking after I moved to Vienna. I used to telephone my mother to ask how to cook particular dishes. I remember one time I wanted the recipe for soffritto alla napoletana so that I could prove to a friend that the Viennese were not the only people who ate lung!

A few years later, when I lived in Germany, I found myself doing more and more cooking. I was reluctant to eat the local food, which I thought was too heavy. The Germans eat big, one-course meals. Or else they go to the other extreme, not having proper meals but eating an incredible amount of salami with bread, accompanied by tea or beer. I was not used to that. Even after I had lived there for ten years or more, the food I enjoyed most was the little titbits, such as pickled cucumbers and salami, and some pork dishes. What I was doing was cooking Italian food and adding a few German specialities – the best of these is herrings served with schnapps.

Now, even though I work with food every day, I still enjoy cooking. I love the challenge and excitement of transforming simple ingredients without losing their essential character, and creating something that tastes and looks and smells wonderful.

THE ITALIAN MEAL

One thing that becomes obvious if you travel around Italy is the enormous variety of local dishes. The food is distinctly regional in character and the raw ingredients are chosen with great care – quality and freshness are very important.

All Italians have been brought up to be knowledgeable about food. They can recognize good food and, even if they don't cook themselves, they know exactly how it should taste. This education starts at a very early age. If children – particularly boys who tend to be a bit spoilt – don't like the food they are given, they will be offered something else. And I remember that, like most Italian men, my father was very critical. The first thing he would say when he came to the table was 'It needs more salt,' or 'It's overcooked.' Compliments were given sparingly. So I learnt that food should be treated very seriously indeed. And I learnt later, when I started to cook myself, just how valuable compliments are!

There is no doubt Italians live for food. They think and talk about it constantly and they spend a lot of money on it. The high point of the day is the midday meal. Of course, this obsession with food is a very old one. The ancient Romans were famous for their gastronomic excesses. The Florentines and Venetians of Renaissance Italy held sumptuous banquets that were talked about the length and breadth of Europe. They were the gourmets of the Western world. Even the French learnt many of the basics from the Italians. When Catherina de Medici went to France to marry the future Henri II she took fifty cooks with her. They introduced cooking techniques and foods which were unknown in France. Béchamel sauce, for instance, and petits pois and artichokes.

Unlike the French chefs, the Italians never forgot the age-old principles of their cooking – it is always simple and straightforward, never overloaded with fancy sauces, and only the best ingredients are used. It is that approach which is found in the French provinces surrounding the Mediterranean. If you go to Provence, you will eat dishes that have a strong Italian influence – anchoïade, pissaladière (a version of pizza) and the lightly cooked vegetables sautéed in olive oil and garlic, for instance.

It is interesting that only a few 'avant-gardists' in Italy use la nouvelle cuisine. There is no need. The sophistication of Italian cooking lies exactly in the very simple preparation of a few ingredients, resulting in wonderful tastes and flavours. Nouvelle cuisine seems more concerned with adding a little green touch to a pretty pink sauce and painting a picture on the plate than with the real character of the food.

For most Italians in the towns and cities breakfast is just an espresso. Anyone who is hungry will have a panino (a bread roll with a savoury filling) at a café. Or they will eat brioche or little cakes – but usually nothing too salty. Children have hot sweetened milk and coffee into which they dip bread or biscuits. When I was young I remember the best time for breakfast was around Christmastime. My father used to be given panettone (Christmas cake) as presents from companies – there were always so many they would last until the middle of January. We would have a delicious slice with hot milk every morning.

The evening meal, like breakfast, is a fairly minor event. It is usually quite light, perhaps a little brodino or an omelette, and it is often eaten quite late, particularly in the south. There, when it is very hot, the people go out in the evening and meet their friends on the corso and have an espresso or an aperitif. They go home and eat about ten or eleven o'clock, just before going to bed. In the big industrial centres, some workers will have a three- or four-course meal at night if they haven't had the time to go home in the middle of the day.

Traditionally, lunch is the most important meal of the day. The first-time visitor to Italy is usually a little bewildered by the way everything stops in the middle of the day for two or three hours. The shops close, churches are locked, the museums are shut, streets empty and the only visible activity is in the restaurants and the cafés. This is the point, when the sun is at its zenith, that Italians focus all their attention on the glories of the table. Now, although that is changing in the big towns, most families still come home and eat their midday meal together. It is a leisurely, communal affair, with plenty of time to concentrate on the food and on the conversation.

Sometimes it will start with an antipasto – perhaps a few slices of salami, or some roasted peppers. Just a little thing. And then always a first course (il primo) – a pasta or a soup, or maybe risotto. After that there will be a small portion of meat or fish (il secondo), accompanied by either lightly cooked vegetables or a salad. Cheese, which is always eaten with bread, and fruit are served at the end, followed by an espresso. Local wine and mineral water will be drunk, and throughout the meal great quantities of bread will be consumed.

This meal demonstrates the true artistry of Italian cooking. It is planned so that each course is in harmony with all the others: the tastes, the textures, the richness and the quantities are all perfectly balanced. A slightly heavy antipasto, such as vitello tonnato or eggs with truffles, would be followed by a primo or first course such as a light soup, perhaps just a consommé. After a very light antipasto like bresaola della Valtellina or a mixture of pickles with salami, you would have a primo of pasta or risotto. A delicately flavoured food, asparagus risotto for example, is never preceded by something that will overwhelm it — carciofi sott'olio or porcini sott'olio would be ideal — just as two very rich foods would never be served at the same meal — you wouldn't follow a fish soup with venison, for example. There are so many perfect combinations it is hard to choose just one. But if I were cooking a very special meal, I might base it all on fish: baked stuffed anchovies as an antipasto, followed by tagliatelle nere — a pasta flavoured and coloured with cuttlefish ink — as a primo; then a simple fish dish as a secondo or main course, like trout with ginger accompanied by spinach with oil and lemon and carrot and celeriac purée (i vegetali). I would serve a little piece of stracchino for the cheese course and mango in lime syrup to finish. And I would choose Gavi dei Gavi, a very dry white wine, to drink throughout the meal.

Within all the formality there is a feeling of immediacy and of sheer passion for food. There is continuous variety, keeping the diner's appetite and imagination constantly stimulated.

It is extraordinary that there is only one type of measurement the human race manages to agree on: time. All the others need the so-called conversion tables, which should unify the world. Very reluctantly I agreed to use precise measurements in my recipes. I'd always tended to use a bunch of this, a handful of that, like all Italian cooks do. However, when I was testing the recipes, I did discover one useful aspect of measuring: I no longer produce the vast quantities of food that I used to. (On the other hand, it can be very useful to have some leftovers. I leave it to you to decide.)

You may notice that when I've given British and American equivalents for metric measures, the conversions sometimes vary. The ounce, for instance, which is literally an unwieldy 28.4 g, comes out as more practical amounts of 25 or 30 g as appropriate — but if you follow one system of measurements throughout, the proportions will be correct.

I don't want to be dictatorial about my recipes. You can use them as ideas, and adapt them as you wish, without deviating from the spirit of Italian cooking — using the freshest and best-quality ingredients with minimum fuss and maximum flair.

INGREDIENTS & EQUIPMENT

If I had to choose a few basic ingredients to take with me to a desert island to conjure up the flavours of Italian cooking, I wouldn't hesitate to plump for olive oil, tomatoes, hard-grain flour, Parmesan cheese, plus some garlic and basil. Without these basics, Italian cooking would lose its essential character and become unrecognizable. Of course, there would need to be eggs to make the pasta, and yeast for pizza dough, and pepper, and nutmeg; and a grater for the Parmesan, and my favourite knife, and perhaps a pasta machine … Perhaps I could grow my own tomatoes and herbs, and settle instead for a supply of Parma ham, and certainly plenty of fresh ricotta. Perhaps the island would have woods where I'd be able to find my favourite wild mushrooms, and doubtless there'd be plenty of first-class seafood. Then again, I would miss polenta, Arborio rice for risotto, and pecorino cheese … And what about wine?

The best solution might be to pick upon a desert island with a superb Italian delicatessen!

The desert island fantasy, in a sense, represents the challenge of cooking the Italian way in any country other than Italy. It's a question of choosing top-quality fresh ingredients, combining them with certain essential items from the store cupboard, and then preparing and cooking them in characteristic ways. By taking a look at Italian shopping tactics for fresh ingredients, seeing what's in the store cupboard, and surveying the equipment in an Italian kitchen, I hope that this chapter will provide a useful background for the actual recipes in the following chapters.

Oregano

Bay

salted capers

Basil

Rosemary

Garlic

CIRIO

Peeled Tomatoes

Tinned Tomato(es)

F lli DECECCO

Virgin olive oil

Badia
a
Coltibuono

Olio
d'Uliva

oliv extra vergine
de oliva

Dry Pasta

Parmesan

13

SHOPPING

Shoppers travelling by gondola to market in Venice

As a little boy I was almost always sent to do the shopping. My mother would give me the shopping list and inspect everything I brought back very carefully. She'd open the parcels and say, 'No, that is not good. You take it back.' That was really terrible because I'd have to go back to the shop and say, 'Sorry, my mother doesn't like it.' So I learnt the art of choosing immediately and well. This not only put me in my mother's good books, but also left me time to be with my playmates. Later it stood me in good stead when I grew up and had to shop for myself.

Many a time I have fallen into the trap of dutifully making out a shopping list and then finding that none of the ingredients I want is available. The lesson gradually sank in. Now when I am planning a meal I always leave the choice open in case I have to rethink the whole of the menu. So I usually tend to buy not what I had previously decided upon in the seclusion of the kitchen, but what look like good-quality offers in terms of freshness, appearance and price when I am actually at the market.

The ability to know at first sight whether meat is tender or peaches are fresh yet ripe comes from long experience, but is an insight that can easily be developed by someone who is really interested in obtaining excellent results. If you are going out to buy fruit and vegetables, take a basket rather than using plastic bags which, although they seem more convenient, can damage the more delicate fruit by not allowing them to breathe. It is always best to scout round first in order to find the best produce on offer and to compare prices. Although in many instances you may irritate the seller by seeming to be fussy, by knowing exactly what you want you may also gain his respect.

MEAT

You need to find a trustworthy butcher, who understands you and gives you exactly what you require. The shop should be immaculately clean and hygienic, and for that reason I prefer places where there is a separate person employed at the till handling all the money. An understanding butcher is one who will sell you the cut of meat most suitable for the dish you intend to prepare. In Italy meat, particularly that served in ordinary restaurants, often does not come up to the standards of tenderness that one expects, but shoppers in Britain and America are more fortunate in that respect.

Beef should be bright red, with the grain neither too swollen nor tight, and the fat should be pale yellow; this shows that the beef has been hung for some days after butchering, which relaxes the muscles and tenderizes the meat.

Veal is obtained from calf butchered when it is only ten weeks old and still feeding from its mother – the meat should be pale pink. If the calf is older, the meat will be redder.

Lamb is a meat that I hesitate to speak of in the presence of the British, because of the excellent quality produced in the pastures of Wales and Scotland. In Italy the best lamb comes from the Abruzzo. The animal should not be more than a year old when it is butchered, otherwise the meat acquires an intense taste like mutton. The colour of good lamb is dark pink and it should be firm to the touch. The tenderest parts are the legs and the saddle. Other cuts are excellent for stews and 'spezzatini'.

Pork should be pale red and firm. If you are buying either 'salumi' or 'insaccati misti' (meaning literally 'bagged pieces' like salami, sausages, etc), be sure to ascertain from the label that the amount of pork meat is greater than the other meats that may be included. Suckling pig meat is very pale, the animal being butchered at between eight and nine weeks old, when still feeding from its mother.

POULTRY

It is worth taking into account the origins of the bird and what food it has been fed on as well as choosing the type that suits your purpose.

Capon is a castrated cock and its meat is particularly tender. The skin is a pale colour, the spurs are not too long and the weight of the whole bird no more than 2 kg (4 lb).

Chickens and cocks The best are free-range, not battery-bred. They are usually quite old, containing a considerable quantity of fat and suitable for making broths and stocks.

Roasting chicken should not exceed 1.5 kg (3 lb) in weight. The meat must be tender, but not soft.

Chick or poussin This is a young bird ranging from eight to nine weeks old. It should weigh around 400 g (less than 1 lb).

Turkey sold in Britain or in America can weigh up to 15 or even 18 kg (30–33 lb), but in Italy you will never find a turkey of more than 10 kg (22 lb). The meat of a young and tender turkey is pale; if it is old, the meat will be considerably more stringy, and tougher.

Ducks and geese must not be too young, as the meat will not have developed enough good flavour, but neither should they be too old, when the meat becomes very fatty and tends to be leathery. Duck is usually to be found the whole year round, whereas goose is more a winter (and specifically a Christmas) fowl. You can recognize a good duck by the leanness and delicate quality of its wings and also the pale yellow colour and roughness of its skin. Wild duck is slightly smaller than the domestic breeds, and the meat is more intense in taste. Goose naturally contains more fat, and may weigh anything up to 4 kg (almost 9 lb). The fat on the breast should be transparent, the leg tender and the beak and feet yellow in colour.

Guinea fowl (Guinea hen) was until recently to be found in the wild as a game bird, but is now bred extensively for the table. It is about the same weight as a chicken, but can be hung for a few days before being plucked and dressed – which enhances the meat's darker colour and more definite taste.

Wild fowl include quail (though these birds are now bred for the table), male and female pheasant, wild pigeon, woodcock, partridge, thrush – not to forget the smallest, the sparrow. Italians attract much derision by their time-honoured hunting and consumption of such creatures: I myself prefer seeing them alive in the countryside, although I have to confess to having eaten them and found them delicious.

Hare and rabbit are popular in Italian cooking, especially in Tuscany. The meat of both animals is tender and white and often it is only the size of the bones that allow you to tell one from the other. When choosing a rabbit, be careful about its age: it should not be more than six or seven months old. The neck should be quite short and the legs long. Wild rabbit is smaller than the domestic variety.

FISH

Perhaps my most extravagant shopping expedition ever took place during the summer holidays of 1984. I was staying near Naples and was going to prepare an evening meal for about 10 guests. I decided to go to Salerno market which is renowned for the exceptional quality of its fish but unfortunately is 60 km from Naples. Undaunted by the heat (which was enough to turn any fish in a matter of hours) I bought enormous quantities of 'frutti di mare' – razor shells, scallops, mussels, sea truffles, and giant shrimps as well as cuttlefish to make a black risotto. As the heat got more intense I started to worry about how to preserve my purchases. Luckily some local restaurateurs took pity on me and found me enough ice to enable me to transport my fish back to the safety of the fridge. The food that evening turned out to be a great success.

When you are shopping for fish, the most important quality to look for is, naturally, freshness. Any fish will be delicious if it is eaten when very fresh. You can tell whether a fish is

fresh or not by its appearance. The eyes should be clear, transparent and without a red glazing; the gills should be a bright red and the scales shiny and slimy in texture. The final test, of course, is the smell of the fish, which should be indicative of the time that it has been out of the water.

When looking around for a trustworthy fishmonger, try and find one who always has very fresh-looking fish. When buying shellfish that are normally eaten raw (such as oysters, sea truffles, mussels and sea dates) be particularly careful to see that they come from non-contaminated waters. Ideally these shellfish should be served straight away or, if a delay is necessary, heaped with ice.

Nowadays frozen fish is becoming the norm in cities and inland towns. This convenient alternative to fresh fish can produce good results, but only if your supplier is really trustworthy. Indeed, to be really good, the fish should have been frozen immediately after being caught, and kept at a constant temperature of at least minus 25 degrees for no longer a period than is allowed.

VEGETABLES AND FRUIT

When shopping for fruit and vegetables, it is always a good idea to scout around first in order to sort out the best produce and to see what is newly in season. One of the pleasantest fruit and vegetable markets that I know takes place at Porta Palazzo in Turin. Here you can find an astounding variety of greens – northern specialities such as asparagus, peppers, wood fungi and peaches as well as olives, small green peppers, clusters of small cherry tomatoes, fennel and other wonderful vegetables introduced by southerners, especially those from Sicily and Calabria. Owing to the influx of immigrants bringing with them from the south the basic ingredients of their home cooking, the people of northern Italy have become accustomed to using vegetables that did not appear in traditional Piedmontese gastronomy. The same adaptability to local ingredients is, of course, being displayed by the immigrants. This phenomenon of interchanging ingredients is becoming increasingly noticeable in other big cosmopolitan communities, especially London, New York and Paris. In my view, the greater the choice of ingredients available, the more exciting and interesting the preparation of any meal becomes. If you choose your ingredients judiciously, the problem of cooking Italian meals outside Italy diminishes yearly.

Always try to buy only in the quantities to suit your immediate purposes. Don't expect miracles of the refrigerator, which can only temporarily suspend the gradual process of deterioration. Equally, buy vegetables and fruit that are currently in season rather than imported produce which, in any case, is both more expensive and less tasty since it is either grown in a greenhouse or picked immature and allowed to ripen in crates on the journey.

Perhaps I should apologize to those of you to whom I seem to be suggesting the obvious. However, I have suffered such misery on seeing excellent recipes and lengthy preparation work totally ruined by inadequate ingredients, that I take the risk of becoming a bore in my campaign to encourage intelligent and discriminating shopping.

GROCERIES

It is usually best to put yourself in the hands of a good Italian delicatessen. Most important for the smooth running of everyday cooking is to equip your larder or store cupboard with the basic ingredients that will allow you to cater for even the most unexpected of guests with good grace.

Groceries that you should never be without include: olive oil, rice, pasta, dried mushrooms, canned tomatoes, anchovies (preferably salted), capers (salted), dried and possibly canned beans (note that beans and tomatoes are the only acceptable canned goods in my book), polenta and hard-grain or all-purpose flour, salt and pepper and garlic. For herbs, I recommend that you keep (fresh if possible, grow them if you can): rosemary, basil, oregano, sage and bay leaves. Coffee beans keep better than already ground coffee.

But let's take a look at some of these basic

ingredients in more detail: others will be described as we come to them in individual recipes.

Olive Oil

Although it is one of the fundamental ingredients of Italian cooking, by no means all Italians use olive oil extensively in their cooking. Indeed, butter is more commonly used in northern Italy. However, all Italians do eat salads and certain other specialities dressed with olive oil, and for these recipes the real thing is indispensable. I suggest that you cook the recipes in this book only with genuine olive oil: I personally would never use an alternative. (If you must, choose bland neutral-flavoured peanut or sunflower oil – where the flavour is not positively detrimental!) Olive oil can become rancid if it is kept for a long time in an open container, and it will tend to solidify if kept in the refrigerator. White clouds in oil which has been refrigerated should disappear when the oil is brought back to room temperature without in any way altering the flavour.

There is a growing trend which subjects olive oil to sophisticated classification with a ticket indicating its origins similar to the DOC classification of many wines.

Extra Virgin Olive Oil The results of the first cold pressing of the olives, this oil is expensive

and should be used parsimoniously – literally a drop at a time is sufficient. It is very green in colour, slightly opaque and is viscous rather than fluid. It has a very pungent taste, and the full quality of its flavour and texture is best appreciated raw, which is why it is recommended for salads and uncooked sauces, as well as for the famous fresella and pinzimonio.

Virgin Olive Oil This is less green and more yellowish in colour, is runnier and can be used more generously. It is ideal for salads, mayonnaise and for general cooking purposes, but not for frying as the flavour is still too strong.

'Pure' Olive Oil Successive heated pressings of the olives produce oils which are more or less refined and blended, and can be used in all types of cooking. If the oil is of good quality, the flavour will still be distinctive, but bland enough to be used in frying.

Whenever 'oil' is mentioned in the ingredients of a recipe, use olive oil (the recipes specify if a superior quality is called for).

Cereals and Grains

Rice Arborio and Vialone rice indispensable for risottos is grown mostly on the Pianura Padana, on the plain of the Po between the provinces of Vercelli, Novara and Milan. The main characteristic that makes it ideal for risottos is the fatness and starchiness of the grain which enables it to swell to at least three times its original volume, while still retaining a firm al dente texture.

Flour The wheat grown in southern Italy, particularly Apulia, and on the plains of North America and Russia, is durum wheat, a hard-grained variety which when milled has a slightly granular texture as opposed to the softer powdery flour commonly used for bread-making

and other cooking. Commercially made pasta must (in Italy) be made from 'pura semola di grano duro': you can check this on the label. Pasta made from this flour stands up to cooking very well, swells in cooking to increase its volume by over 20 per cent, and is also both nutritious and easily digestible. For making home-made pasta and gnocchi, you may be able to find this semolina (which naturally must not be confused with the semolina used in puddings) in any store specializing in Italian products.

On the other hand, strong plain (all-purpose) flour, preferably unbleached, makes perfectly good home-made pasta all'uovo, if you follow the recipe proportions and quantities accurately and work the dough to the right texture; it is also perfect for pizza doughs. It needs no extra sifting.

When the recipes in this book call simply for 'flour', it is plain or all-purpose flour that is meant.

Polenta is made from coarsely ground cornmeal. This is less popular in the south of Italy than in the north, where it is one of the best-known specialities and is particularly suited to the cold winter months. It used to be the staple diet of the inhabitants of the Alpine valleys, who ate it with local produce such as butter, milk and cheese. Nowadays polenta has suffered a sharp decline in popularity, perhaps due to the lengthy preparation it needs. However, modern techniques have worked miracles to produce polenta called Valsugana or Star, both of which can be prepared in only five minutes.

Bread crumbs Every bread shop in Italy sells good bread crumbs, fresh and dry: they make their own. Dry crumbs for coating should be of good quality – not the luminous orange crust that often covers frozen food abroad. They are easy to make by toasting bread in the oven and then putting the golden rusks through a food processor. If you must buy packets, try to find makes imported from Austria, where they also care about the quality of this product.

Tomatoes The Italian 'pomodoro' meaning golden apple reflects the almost mythical veneration attached to this versatile fruit. When I first moved away from Italy and its cult of the golden apple used extensively in daily cooking, it was difficult to find satisfactory quantities of fresh tomatoes. I soon overcame my prejudice against the canned variety (for sauces, at least), however, provided that these are of good quality. Not all canned tomatoes are good. Look for deep red fruit, preferably of the 'fiaschetta' variety, which is plum shaped, meaty and has relatively few seeds. The surrounding liquid should be thick and not too watery. Ask for 'San Marzano' peeled tomatoes, named after the town in the province of Salerno where enormous quantities of tomatoes are grown exclusively for canning. Sometimes a can has 'with basil' on the label, when the herb has been added to enhance the flavour. (Please don't repeat the mistake of the lady who tried to get a refund on a can which she claimed was unhygienic because she had found a whole leaf on top of the tomatoes). Canned tomatoes are available already chopped up for use in sauces, but it is easy enough to chop them in the can with a long knife.

In the recipes the following tomato can sizes are used:

a small can	*226 g*
a medium can	*420 g*
a large can	*780 g*

Fresh tomatoes for sauces should always be fully ripened: canned ones are preferable to unripe fresh ones. Skin them (by immersing in boiling water for a minute) and deseed them. In the markets of southern Italy you can find a type of small round tomato with a tough skin; they are very sweet, meaty and juicy inside, and are among the best varieties for sauces.

For salads the Italians prefer a type of tomato known abroad as the 'beef' or 'beefsteak' tomato: a large, meaty kind which they delight in eating almost green, whereas I appreciate them better well ripened but still firm.

Dried tomatoes preserved in oil are now commercially exploited, and make an excellent antipasto: look for the recipe for regenerating air-dried tomatoes (Pomodori secchi sott'olio). There is even a paste derived from this product, which I personally find much to my taste, for adding in small quantities to sauces or simply serving with a knob of butter as a dressing for cooked pasta. A labour-saving product is Pomí, a purée available in cartons.

Herbs, Spices and Seasonings

The rule with herbs is to use them fresh whenever possible.

Oregano is the one exception that will keep well in a glass jar. This plant, closely related to thyme, has a minty flavour and can be found almost anywhere in the Italian hills. It is much beloved of the southern Italians, who use it mainly in pizzas, but also in dishes such as baked anchovies and meat cooked alla pizzaiola.

Basil In Italy we consider basil to be the king of aromatic herbs, and in my view its culinary value is far superior to all the others. It has a refreshing and distinctive quality which can perk up and enliven even the simplest of tomato sauces and other dressings. It is, of course, an essential of Pizza alla napoletana, and combines with garlic to reach its sublimest moment in Pesto alla genovese.

What a pity that this delightful herb can be found in abundance only in summer (though I know some green-fingered enthusiasts who increase its lifespan by careful indoor cultivation and parsimonious use). Dried basil is no substitute for fresh. There are two possibilities for preserving basil for use out of season. One is to preserve a good bunch of leaves in oil, to which they will impart their fragrance. The other method, ideal for sauces, consists of chopping the basil coarsely and incorporating it in a pat of soft butter, which is then frozen wrapped in silver foil. If you freeze the basil butter in a cylinder no thicker than a thin rolling pin, it will be easy to chip pieces off the block when the need arises rather than having to thaw the whole lot.

There is a third method, which is to preserve basil in the form of Pesto.

Rosemary This plant is typical of the Mediterranean, but succeeds in growing almost anywhere. A twig will endow any roast with a distinctive yet delicate flavour, and will counterbalance fattier ingredients: but don't overdo the amount used. One of my (many) favourites is to add rosemary to potatoes and onions cooked in the oven.

Mint has its place as an excellent tea in North African and Arab countries, and is an institution in Britain in the sauce served with lamb. Italians generally attach less importance to it, simply sprinkling it raw over salads or Courgettes alla scapece. It's a favourite taste of mine, however, and I perhaps use it more in my recipes than do most of my countrymen.

Parsley is ubiquitous – the flat-leaved variety, whose flavour is richer and more pungent than the curly-leaved sort.

Sage is a significant ingredient in one or two distinctive recipes: it is indispensable with calves' liver, for instance.

Nutmeg A vital ingredient in many Italian dishes, particularly those containing spinach and ricotta, whether sweet or savoury. Don't buy ground nutmeg, always grate it freshly as you need it. This is why our recipes deliberately list among the ingredients the phrase '3 or 4 grates of nutmeg'.

Pepper As with nutmeg, our recipes always state 'freshly ground black pepper', and that is what it should be.

Garlic is indispensable in Italian cooking, a clove or two imparting subtle flavouring to countless soups and sauces, while greater quantities are responsible for the famous Bagna cauda and (with basil) Pesto alla genovese. In spite of its reputation in myth and medicine from the ancient Romans to the present day, one must not get carried away: garlic must be used above all in moderation, and at the right moment. If

you are preparing a dish that needs only a hint of the flavour, you can chop a couple of cloves finely and leave them to macerate in some olive oil; strain this oil to use in your recipe.

Onion Together with garlic, onions form the basis of many Italian sauces. While the cooking of garlic must always be moderate, even minimal (never must it be allowed to become brown or burnt), onions can be cooked even up to the point where they become slightly caramelized.

A trick to prevent crying while cutting up onions is to breathe only through the mouth, since the nerves that are sensitive to the smell are situated in the nasal cavity. Equally, if after slicing an onion you rub a little table salt on your hands, you will find that the pervasive smell disappears almost immediately.

Vinegar Always use good-quality wine vinegar; it can be flavoured with herbs such as tarragon or rosemary. I particularly recommend a new product – balsamic vinegar, which is a rich infusion of aromatic spices and herbs.

Capers Choose salted ones rather than those preserved in vinegar, which retain their vinegar flavour. You will need to desalt them before use by soaking for 30 minutes in water. Try to buy smallish ones.

Anchovies As well as being eaten as antipasti, preserved anchovies are an important constituent of sauces and a flavouring for other dishes. They reach their apotheosis in Bagna cauda. The best way to buy them is in their salted form: Italian delicatessens sell them in bulk from large tins. Soak them for 30 minutes to desalt them before use. If at this stage you dry them thoroughly, you can preserve them in oil for your own store cupboard to use at any moment. When you buy them, the flesh should be pink and fresh-smelling; and choose medium-sized ones – the larger ones have a grosser taste.

Mushrooms

For a few weeks in autumn wild mushrooms can be found in profusion by anyone who knows where to look, and the pleasure of cooking and eating favourite dishes competes with the pleasure of going into the country to search for the precious ingredients. Out of season their indispensable contribution to recipes has to be achieved by more roundabout means. While they are abundant, either preserve them (see Porcini sott'olio recipe); deep-freeze them, when their thawed texture will be acceptable in sauces; or dry them. Dried mushrooms are readily available from delicatessens, too; they are easily regenerated for use in sauces by being soaked in lukewarm water for 10–15 minutes before use. A small amount – just 25 g (1 oz) – of dried ceps or porcini will improve the flavour of 500 g (1 lb) ordinary field mushrooms. Keep some in the store cupboard.

Cheeses

Although cheeses are more fully described in a chapter of their own, a word or two about the ones you are likely to use for cooking.

Parmesan Always buy it in a piece, never pre-grated in tubs or packets. Choose Parmesan that is a fine pale yellow, wrap it in aluminium foil and it will keep in the refrigerator for several weeks.

Ricotta Always buy it perfectly sweet and fresh and use it straight away: if kept too long at home (or in the shop), it quickly acquires an acid taste.

Mozzarella This must always be kept cool and damp in its whey, which is why it is always sold floating in liquid. If you buy more than is needed, preserve it in the refrigerator in a small amount of lightly salted water. Buy good Italian brands, not northern European imitations.

Ceps Known in Italy as porcini, in France as cèpes; members of the genus *Boletus*. Most readily available dried; fresh in season in markets and stores.

Truffles These are a combination of all the smells and the tastes of the world put together. Indescribable. Something you either love or you hate. So intense and so remarkable and so completely different from anything that you know. White truffles, which grow around Alba and Piedmont, are more powerful than the black ones. You couldn't travel on a train with a truffle, so intense is the smell. It would disturb the other passengers too much – because it wasn't theirs.

I remember when I was little in Castelnuevo Belbo I used to go out with the truffle hunter. It was very misty, around 5 o'clock in the morning. I can still see the old man, the little dog, the trees. Wonderful. The dog would get wild with the smell and would search all of us. Then all of a sudden he would locate a truffle. Immediately the old man would come and put the dog aside, and dig with a little trowel. The truffles grow in the ground by the roots of some trees. The best ones are those which grow near the hazelnut.

EQUIPMENT

In an Italian kitchen, successful cooking does not depend on the tools you use, but tasks are made simpler with the aid of certain utensils and gadgets. An absolute essential in all kitchens is a set of good knives: they should be very sharp so that they cut cleanly, and you need a selection suitable for various purposes: a vegetable knife, and one for cleaning and peeling carrots, asparagus and sometimes potatoes. Another essential knife is for removing cores. Tomatoes are rather difficult to cut, and there is a special knife for the purpose. You need an all-purpose knife, and one for cutting meat which I sometimes use as an all-purpose knife.

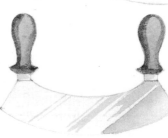

In Italy we use the mezzaluna (half-moon) knife for chopping finely. Its use has declined with the advent of food processors, but I think that the food processor is not always ideal, as it tends to chop too finely and too quickly, so that it is difficult to get the exact thickness required.

The Parmesan knife does not exactly cut, but allows you to put pressure on a certain point so that the desired piece is broken off.

Another useful implement is a knife for opening shellfish and oysters. The bread knife, naturally, has a serrated edge. It is a great pity that carbon steel knives are not widely available nowadays. They keep a very sharp edge but have the disadvantage of turning black after cutting acidic matter. The only really good ones are made of stainless steel and are very expensive.

Other cutting instruments are the wheel for cutting out square ravioli and other filled pasta shapes.

The knife for cutting pizza is more suitable for use in a pizzeria than in the kitchen of an ordinary home. These curved serrated scissors, however, are a typically Italian gadget used to cut up roast chicken and poultry.

Pasta requires a special set of utensils, and it goes without saying that a whole series of gadgets has been developed for this purpose. The pan should be made of steel, with a rounded base and a lid. The wide base is necessary to keep all the pasta at an even temperature while it is being cooked.

The colander should be large. For cooking sauces, especially meat ones that need long slow cooking, a terracotta pan like this one is suitable.

There are many tools for making pastry, such as the

rolling pin. Apart from rolling out pastry, it is essential for rolling across the top of a 'raviolatrice' or ravioli grid to cut out the shapes. The small manual pasta machine is very convenient; it is the only concession to progress that I care to make. Using electric pasta machines takes all the fun out of it.

A special machine for making spaghetti comes from Abruzzo and is called 'la chitarra' — the guitar. It has a number of taut steel strings stretched over a rectangular frame. A sheet of pasta is placed over the top, a rolling pin is rolled over the sheet and pieces of square-section pasta fall through into the container below.

Other essential pieces of pasta equipment are a large spoon and fork for stirring pasta while cooking.

For removing spaghetti from the pan there is a 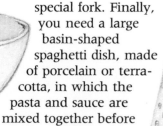 special fork. Finally, you need a large basin-shaped spaghetti dish, made of porcelain or terra-cotta, in which the pasta and sauce are mixed together before serving, and a grater for the Parmesan.

For making an individual pizza you need a round iron pan, not too thick, with a shallow rim and with a diameter of about 20–27 cm (8–11 inches), I suggest you have about four. If you want to make pizza in grand style, then I suggest you use a large baking sheet. Another useful utensil for pizza making, and for pouring salad dressing, is an oil can, usually made of metal.

This copper pan and a wooden spoon are the classic ingredients for making polenta. A special pan with automatic stirring facility has been invented, which is very useful if you are making polenta in the old-fashioned way that requires over half an hour of cooking and continuous stirring. The polenta is cut with steel wire on a wooden board.

The garlic press that squeezes out the juice, leaving the flesh behind, is useful, although I prefer to chop garlic with a knife. The old-fashioned mincer (grinder) has been replaced by the food processor, but I still find it useful for certain operations, such as mincing beef. Another useful item is the vegetable mouli used for sieving tomatoes for sauces and vegetables for soups and purées.

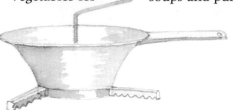

Important, too, is a dish for cooking timballi and for roasts. A terracotta pan for cooking beans is not only attractive, but beans cooked in this way really do have more flavour. In my opinion, the best type of pan is still one made of iron, even though it blackens with age.

For pesto alla genovese, it is a joy to use a mortar and pestle, especially one made of marble. The grid iron is especially important for char-grilling (broiling) steak or fish, and for picnics.

A very useful gadget is the salad drainer which can be seen hanging in many an Italian window keeping things fresh.

If you are making zabaglione, you need a round copper pan which, when placed in a bain marie, conducts all the heat needed to cook this speciality.

For making Cannoli alla siciliana you need bamboo or metal tubular moulds on which to form the pastry before frying; half a dozen would be sufficient.

One machine I consider an absolute must is a coffee-maker. There are many excellent small espresso machines for the home, although I think the best coffee is made in a bar from a well-oiled machine. For the home there are two kinds of coffee-maker. One is the Moka express which uses steam pressure to force the water through the ground coffee into the top of the pot. The other is the classic Neapolitan coffee-maker that filters the coffee downwards and produces an excellent coffee if you have used a good blend. I use this type in my restaurant, much to the satisfaction of my customers.

Of course, you will need a few extra pots and pans, but if you have all the ones that I have described, then all you need to be successful in your kitchen is to use good ingredients carefully.

ANTIPASTI

──────── STARTERS ────────

There is a popular misconception that the word antipasto means the course that is eaten before the pasta dish. Rather, it is the food served before the pasto, or meal, begins and its purpose is to stuzzicare l'appetito, to stimulate the appetite. The attitude to the antipasto course varies enormously from region to region. The southern Italians tend to miss it out altogether, preferring to jump straight into il primo, while in the north, and particularly in Piedmont where I grew up, there are literally thousands of local variations.

You might have one or two thin slices of salami or Parma ham with pickles (my own favourite is Porcini sott'olio), or a selection of meats and sausages – perhaps salame felino from Emilia, prosciutto San Daniele, a pork sausage called sopressata from Calabria, and mucetta from the Aosta valley. Mortadella will be served in its native Bologna, and bresaola in the Valtellina in Lombardy. By the sea you'll find tiny fish fried in oil or marinated raw like my Acciughe marinate; in Tuscany a plate of young beans will be seasoned with a fruity olive oil or there will be all sorts of crostini, and up in the mountains there will be autumn salads of raw porcini or fine slices of wild boar served with a little olive oil and lemon juice. Usually the antipasto will be mildly acidic in order to stimulate the gastric juices.

All the recipes I have given here can be eaten by themselves. (Some, of course, can be expanded into a main course by increasing the quantities; vegetable antipasti often make good accompaniments to the fish and meat dishes in il primo – there is no hard-and-fast rule, and the chapters overlap.) If you particularly want to impress, you can combine three or four antipasto dishes. In either case, the quantities served will be small. I have never understood why, in Italian restaurants abroad, the antipasto dal carrello is almost a meal in itself. How are you expected to enjoy the next course?

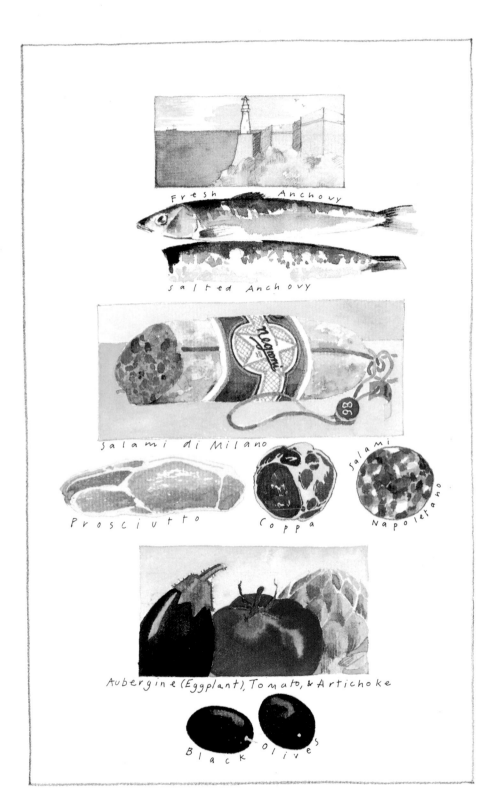

Fresh Anchovy

salted Anchovy

Salami di Milano

Prosciutto

Coppa

Salami Napoletano

Aubergine (Eggplant), Tomato, & Artichoke

Black Olives

ACCIUGHE RIPIENE AL FORNO
Baked Stuffed Anchovies

The fresh anchovy is undoubtedly one of the most popular fish in Italy. Each of the many coastal villages and cities has its own recipe, and rapid transportation means that even inland you can buy very fresh fish. In countries where fresh anchovies are not available, it's possible to use frozen ones instead: combined in this recipe with fresh herbs, they make a very unusual and appetizing dish. Fresh or frozen sardines offer another alternative, but since these are larger than anchovies, you will need only half as many.

Two anchovy 'sandwiches' per person make an antipasto; four would be sufficient for a main course.

Makes 12 'sandwiches'

24 fresh anchovies
1 tbs chopped fresh dill
1 tbs chopped fresh parsley
1 tbs chopped fresh chives
1 tbs chopped fresh rosemary
a few sage leaves, finely chopped
1 clove garlic, chopped
25 g (1 oz) pine nuts, or chopped walnuts
2 tbs olive oil
salt and freshly ground black pepper
a few drops of lemon juice
10 g (about ½ oz or ⅓ US cup) fresh bread crumbs

Preheat the oven to 220°C (425°F or gas mark 7). With a pair of kitchen scissors, cut off the head, tail and lower part of the fish, and discard the insides. Using your thumb, loosen the backbone from the flesh, leaving the two fillets still attached by the upper skin. Wash and dry the fish. Chop the herbs and garlic finely together and mix with the pine nuts and a tablespoon of olive oil. Grease a baking tray with a little olive oil and lay 12 of the anchovies skin side down next to each other on the tray. Spread a little of the herb mixture on each, season with salt and pepper, sprinkle with lemon juice and cover with another anchovy, skin side up, to make a 'sandwich'. Sprinkle with bread crumbs and pour on the remaining olive oil in a thin stream. Bake for 8–10 minutes until golden. Serve hot or cold.

ACCIUGHE IN SALSA VERDE
Anchovy Fillets in Green Sauce

This recipe, perhaps more than any other, reminds me of certain happy days of my youth when I would set out with my friends into the mountains or into near-by villages on outings which would invariably end in a small inn or café. Here we would consume vast quantities of anchovies in green sauce, slices of home-made salami and succulent fresh bread, all doused by a locally produced Barbera wine. Few meals can surpass this excellent, if rustic, menu.

For this antipasto the ideal anchovies would be the salted kind that need soaking and filleting. However, this would cause the dish to be unnecessarily complicated, and equally good results can be obtained by using canned fillets in oil. Two or three fillets per person will be sufficient as a starter with fresh bread. The jar can be kept in the refrigerator and used whenever the occasion arises.

Makes a 500 ml (1 pt) preserving jar

345 g (12 oz) can of anchovy fillets in oil
1 clove garlic
a large bunch of parsley
2 dried red chili peppers
the inside of a white bread roll, or 25 g (1 oz or ⅔ US cup) fresh bread crumbs
1 tbs wine vinegar
enough olive oil to cover – at least 150 ml (¼ pt or ¾ US cup)

Open the can of anchovies, and drain off the oil. Finely chop the garlic, parsley and chilis. Soak the bread in the vinegar, squeeze and finely chop. Mix these ingredients together. In a glass jar with a rubber seal, place first a layer of the herb mixture and then a layer of anchovies; cover with oil and press down. Repeat until the jar is full. Pour some olive oil over the top and keep in the refrigerator until required.

Right: Baked stuffed anchovies surrounded by the ingredients used in the filling

ACCIUGHE MARINATE
Marinated Fresh Anchovies

For best results, this dish must be prepared with the freshest of anchovies – if you can buy them when they have just been caught all the better, as they will marinate quickly leaving the meat firm and tasty. This is a Neapolitan speciality but is popular wherever there is a good fresh fish market.

Serves 4–6

350 g (¾ lb) very fresh anchovies
For the marinade:
3 tbs olive oil
the juice of 1½ lemons
1 clove garlic, finely chopped
1 tbs finely chopped parsley
1 small dried red chili pepper, chopped
salt and freshly ground black pepper

Clean and fillet the anchovies well, taking good care to shave off all the bristles and fins. Wash and dry the separated fillets and arrange them in a flat dish. Prepare a marinade from the olive oil, lemon juice, garlic, parsley, chili, salt and pepper. Leave to marinate for at least four hours before serving. Marinated anchovies can be kept refrigerated for a couple of days.

ANGUILLA IN CARPIONE
Marinated Eel

The most typical Christmas dish of the Romans is marinated capitone. The capitone is a type of large eel that is first roasted, usually on a grill

Live eels

(broiler), and then marinated. The fresh eels that are normally found in the markets are generally quite small, and are rather tastier.

Serves 4

500 g (1 lb) eel, cleaned and skinned: ask the fishmonger to do this for you
olive oil for brushing on the eel
salt and freshly ground black pepper
For the marinade:
2 tbs olive oil
1 tbs white wine vinegar
salt and freshly ground black pepper
1 clove garlic, coarsely chopped
6 fresh bay leaves

Cut the eel up into chunks 10 cm (4 inches) long, brush with olive oil and season with salt and pepper. Grill (broil), preferably on embers, until cooked or even slightly burned on the outside, making sure the flesh remains firm. While the eel is cooling, prepare the marinade with oil, vinegar, salt and pepper, garlic and bay leaves. Turn the pieces of eel over in the marinade so that they are well covered. Leave to marinate for at least 24 hours in order to improve the flavour. Marinated eel can be kept in the refrigerator for a couple of days or more.

ARINGA ALLA CASALINGA
Pickled Herring with Apple and Onion

I first encountered this delicious northern antipasto when I was living in Germany and have since adopted it as one of my favourite dishes. If I were to include it in Italian regional dishes, it would have to be in the region of the Alto-Adige, where German and Austrian influences are to be found, even in local culinary specialities. If the herrings are to be served by themselves as an hors-d'œuvre, they are best accompanied by a distilled kümmel schnapps in a chilled glass: a single glass of Aalborg Aquavit straight from the freezer is quite enough!

Serves 4

2 large pickled herrings of the 'Matjes herring' or Dutch variety
8 new potatoes
1 red onion
1 cooking apple
8 tbs double cream
1 tsp chopped parsley

Fillet the herrings and leave them to soak in cold water for about 1 hour in order to take away some of the salt (Matjes herrings are usually pickled in brine). Meanwhile, cook the potatoes and peel them. Peel the onion and cut thinly into rings. Peel the apple and cut it into fine slices; chop the parsley. Drain and pat dry the herrings. Put one large herring fillet on to each plate and spread two spoonfuls of the cream over it, then arrange the apple slices, potatoes and onions around it. Sprinkle with parsley and serve.

COZZE AL FORNO
Mussels au Gratin

This recipe is popular in many Italian regions, and is a tasty dish that is relatively easy to prepare. It can also be served as a main course merely by increasing the quantity of mussels. Cooking the mussels with oil allows you to eat them hot or cold.

Try and choose the biggest and freshest mussels, making sure that they are tightly closed and are quite heavy.

Serves 4

500 g (1 lb) fresh mussels – about 12 per person
1 clove garlic, finely chopped
2 tbs finely chopped parsley
salt and freshly ground black pepper
2 tbs dry bread crumbs or 25 g (1 oz or ⅔ US cup) fresh bread crumbs
1 tbs olive oil

Clean the mussels under running tap water. Throw away any that are open or that float to the surface. Place the mussels in a lidded saucepan with a wineglass of water and bring to the boil. Shake the pan: the steam will open the mussels in a few minutes. (At this point throw away any that have *not* opened.) Put aside to cool.

Preheat the oven to 220°C (425°F or gas mark 7). Next, take off the top half of each shell. Loosen the mussels and arrange the lower shells one next to the other in a baking dish. Sprinkle them with garlic and parsley mixed together, then with the bread crumbs, and season with salt and pepper. Finally pour a thin trickle of olive oil over each mussel. Then place the dish in a hot oven for about 10 minutes.

FAGOTTELLI DI GRANCHIO
Crab Parcels

This was the recipe that I invented when I first became manager of the Neal Street Restaurant, using fresh crab from Cornwall. This crab is particularly fleshy, with a sweet and fragrant taste. In Italy they use grancevole – spider crabs. The most important single factor in this recipe, however, is the freshness of the crab. Even after several years this dish is still a favourite among my clients. It owes its popularity, perhaps, to its curious presentation. This recipe is well worth the effort involved in its making.

Serves 4

1 medium-sized crab, preferably already cooked, or 300–350 g (about ¾ lb) white crabmeat
150 g (6 fl oz or ¾ US cup) fresh mayonnaise (half the quantity given in the next recipe) plus 1 extra tsp lemon juice
1 tsp brandy
500 g (1 lb) fresh spinach
250 g (½ lb) broccoli
1 tbs fresh cream
salt, freshly ground black pepper and nutmeg
a few strands of cooked spaghetti
1 tsp chopped parsley for decoration
For the pancakes:
1 large egg
50 g (2 oz or ½ US cup) flour
150 ml (5 fl oz or ⅔ US cup) milk
salt and freshly ground black pepper
oil for frying

Remove all the meat from the cooked crab, mixing the brown flesh with the white. Add the mayonnaise, brandy and salt and pepper then mix well. Cook the spinach and the broccoli, drain thoroughly and pass them through the mincer, adding the cream, salt and pepper and nutmeg. Reduce the mixture to a liquid sauce which should not be too runny and keep in a cool place. (This should make enough for 2 tablespoons per serving.) For the pancakes, stir the flour together with the egg, milk, salt and pepper and blend until you obtain a thin paste. Heat the pancake pan then add a couple of drops of olive oil. Use the batter to make four thin pancakes about 20 cm (7 inches) in diameter. Leave to cool.

On each pancake place a small amount of crab then proceed to wrap it into a parcel, tying with strings of cooked spaghetti which (with a bit of patience) you can make into a bow. Spread the spinach sauce on each plate so that it covers the bottom. In the middle of the dish place the parcel of crab decorated with a sprinkling of chopped parsley.

MAIONESE
Mayonnaise

The amount of lemon juice alters the consistency of the mayonnaise. In some recipes where mayonnaise is used I suggest you add more lemon to this basic formula.

Makes 300 g (12 fl oz or 1½ US cups) of mayonnaise

2 egg yolks
250 ml (9 fl oz or 1 US cup) olive oil
juice of half a lemon
salt and freshly ground black pepper

In a heavy bowl stir the egg yolks together, then slowly add the olive oil dribble by dribble. Stir continuously until you have added all the oil: the mayonnaise will become very thick and sticky. At the end stir in the lemon juice which should liquefy the sauce a little. Season with salt and pepper.

FRITTELLE DI GIANCHETTI
Fish Fritters

Gianchetti are minute fish, only 2 cm (½ inch) long, particularly well known in Liguria and in Sicily, where they are called 'neonati', or new-born. They are generally prepared in the normal way – boiled, then dressed with oil, lemon and parsley. This fritter recipe was a favourite of my mother's. Even though it is virtually impossible to find gianchetti outside Italy (I myself have never seen them in markets abroad), you can easily substitute whitebait or smelts, as long as you choose the very tiny ones.

Serves 4

250 g (½ lb) gianchetti or other tiny fish
olive oil for frying
1 lemon for serving
For the batter:
1 egg
2 tbs flour
salt and freshly ground black pepper

Beat the egg, add the flour and stir until you get a creamy consistency, add a pinch of salt and pepper, then finally add the fish and mix together gently. Heat about 1 cm (½ inch) of oil in a heavy pan. Put a spoonful of the fish mixture into the hot oil and fry, turning over once. They literally take a few seconds: the colour should be golden. Drain on kitchen paper and sprinkle with a little salt and squeezed lemon. This mixture makes 16 frittelle.

GAMBERONI IN CAMICIA
Prawns in Pastry Cases

Gamberoni are enormous red and orange prawns found in the fish markets of Italy, and I was reminded of them – and inspired to develop this particular recipe at the Neal Street Restaurant – by the wonderful fresh Dublin Bay prawns that are available in London. Italian scampi, French langoustines or American saltwater crayfish could be used with much the same result.

Serves 4

8 large Dublin Bay prawns, peeled
85 g (3 oz) puff pastry (the frozen kind is fine)
1 egg
1 tbs finely chopped parsley
1 tsp chopped fresh dill
salt and freshly ground black pepper
50 g (2 oz or ¼ US cup) ricotta or curd cheese

Preheat the oven to 220°C (425°F or gas mark 7). Roll out the pastry as thin as possible and cut it into eight 10 cm (4 inch) squares. Beat the egg lightly and set a teaspoon or so aside for sealing the pastry. Add to the egg the chopped herbs, salt and pepper and finally the ricotta cheese. Mix well. Place one prawn on the diagonal of each pastry square and add a spoonful of the egg, cheese and herb mixture. Roll over and fold in the points to form a sealed envelope. Brush the seals with raw egg. Oil a baking sheet, lay the envelopes on it side by side and bake in a hot oven for 15 minutes.

Summer antipasto.
Clockwise from the top: Marinated eel, Carrot and coriander
salad (page 183), Crudité with virgin olive oil (page 182),
French (green) beans with tomato (page 158), Marinated fresh
anchovies, Ox tongue in green sauce, Parma ham and
mozarella fingers and Fried courgette (zucchini) salad.

Fresh squid

INSALATA DI MARE
Seafood Salad

A variety of fish can appear in this salad, preferably a shellfish of some kind, and some prawns or shrimps. Squid, cuttlefish or octopus is the essential ingredient, for both looks and texture. All should be very fresh – frozen will not do. Look in your market for inspiration.

Serves 4

500 g (1 lb) mussels in their shells
350 g (¾ lb) squid
150 g (6 oz) giant prawns (jumbo shrimp)
2 scallops weighing about 120 g (about 5 oz) without shells
1 tbs chopped parsley
a small bunch of chives, chopped
the juice of a lemon
3 tbs olive oil
salt and freshly ground black pepper

Scrub the mussels thoroughly, discarding any that are open or have broken shells. Put a wine glass of water in a saucepan with a lid, add the mussels and steam them over a strong flame, shaking the pan from time to time, for a minute or two. Put the pan aside to cool, and then remove the mussels from their shells. Clean the squid by removing the transparent bone and cutting off the head. Keep the tentacles whole in bunches and do not cut the body at this point.

Bring a saucepan of water to the boil and add some salt. Put in the squid, the prawn tails and the scallops. The cooking time of all these fish is largely to do with their size, but should not take more than 10–15 minutes: remove the prawn tails after 5 minutes; the squid, too (if they are small ones), will be cooked in 5 minutes. Test for tenderness and drain the fish when cooked. Cut the scallops in half and large squid into 1.5 cm (¾ inch) slices. Cut the prawn tails into four. Mix the mussels with the other seafood and leave to cool. Dress with the lemon juice and olive oil, season with salt, pepper and parsley and scatter the chives over the top. Serve along with other antipasti as a light summer main course.

TARTARA DI SALMONE CRUDO
Raw Salmon Tartare

This recipe was developed in my restaurant one day when I tasted a piece of raw salmon and found it so tender and fresh that I thought it could be cured instantly with lemon juice and spices to provide a wonderful alternative to steak tartare. It isn't necessarily Italian, because fresh salmon, which is essential, is rarely obtainable in Italy. I would say it is one of the recipes developed abroad using local ingredients but with an Italian touch. You can eat it by itself with toast or make it part of a mixed antipasto together with other fishy things.

Serves 4

500 g (1 lb) fresh salmon, preferably from the tail, which is less bony
a bunch of fresh dill, or a pinch of dried
2 tsp green peppercorns preserved in brine
2 tsp olive oil
2 egg yolks
10 drops of Tabasco (hot pepper sauce)
juice of 2 lemons
sliced cucumber for decoration

Discard all the skin from the salmon and remove all the bones. Chop the raw salmon finely (you can blend it, but I prefer to chop it by hand). Chop the dill finely and coarsely crush half the peppercorns, leaving the other half whole. Add the oil, egg yolks, Tabasco, lemon juice and the remaining green peppercorns and mix well together. Add salt and pepper to taste. Decorate with some slices of cucumber and serve with toast.

VITELLO TONNATO
Veal in Tuna Fish Sauce

This is rather an unusual combination of meat and fish, but which results in a very tasty dish. It is popular in all regions of Italy – perhaps the Piedmontese version is the easiest of all to make. My idea of incorporating the chopped vegetables which have been cooked in the meat broth, I think, adds some extra interest to this dish. The cut of veal used in Italy is the girello or eye of silverside which provides very fine, close-textured slices when cut across the grain.

Serves 12 or more

a piece of veal steak weighing about 1 kg (2 lb)
1 carrot, chopped
some celery stalks, cut in pieces
1 onion
170 g (6 oz) tuna fish in oil
2 tbs capers, plus a few extra for decoration
6 anchovy fillets
150 g (6 fl oz or 1½ US cups) fresh mayonnaise (half the quantity on page 32)
a dozen or so gherkin pickles for decoration
salt and freshly ground black pepper

Boil the meat together with the pieces of carrot, celery and onion and a pinch of salt for around 1 hour. Leave to cool, then cut into very thin slices and arrange on a dish. Put the vegetables together with the tuna, capers and anchovies through the food processor to produce a smooth paste, the consistency of thick cream, which can then be incorporated with the mayonnaise. Add salt and pepper, spread the paste over the veal slices and decorate with gherkins and capers.

INSALATA DI CARNE CRUDA
Raw Beef Salad

This is a typically Piedmontese recipe – indeed, hardly any antipasto is served in this region that does not include a raw beef salad. It differs from a steak tartare, which is usually prepared immediately before the meal, in that it is prepared the day before, allowing the meat to absorb the flavour of the spices. It is usually served in the form of little balls of meat on the plate. In Piedmont it is generally recognized that the best raw meat salad is made from fillets of horse meat. However, in this recipe I will not risk offending your sensibilities, and will suggest using fillets of beef.

Serves 4

250 g (½ lb) fillet beef steak
1 tbs chopped parsley
1 small clove garlic
1 tbs olive oil
juice of a lemon
salt and freshly ground black pepper

Chop the meat finely by hand, along with the parsley and garlic. Add the olive oil, lemon juice, salt and freshly ground pepper to flavour and mix well. Keep in the refrigerator for 24 hours, then take spoonfuls of the mixture and roll into little balls just before serving.

Different types of sausage

Mixed antipasto of salami with ceps.
Clockwise from the top: bresaola, felino, Parma ham, coppa,
speck, arista, salame abruzzese (centre)

BRESAOLA DELLA VALTELLINA
Dried Beef with Oil and Lemon

This antipasto is a popular dish in the Alps just north of Milan and can be compared with the German Bundnerfleisch or the Swiss viande de Grisons. The main ingredient is Bresaola, a piece of lean and tender beef silverside which has been pickled in a salt brine for 6 to 7 days and then left to stand in a well-ventilated spot for at least six months. It is usually eaten on its own (very finely machine-sliced) or with a mild dressing. In Tuscany wild boar fillet is served in the same way. A few slices added to a mixed salami antipasto will give the dish a wonderful deep red colour. The flavour of this dish is enhanced if eaten with grissini sticks.

Serves 4

160 g (6 oz) finely sliced Bresaola
juice of a lemon
4 tsp olive oil
freshly ground black pepper

Arrange the Bresaola carefully and decoratively

on a plate. Pour the lemon juice and olive oil over the slices and sprinkle with some freshly ground black pepper.

INVOLTINI DI CARNE CRUDA
Raw Beef Rolls

The difference between these rolls and the raw beef salad lies in the fact that this recipe is based upon slices of meat. You will probably need the help of your butcher in obtaining machine-sliced fillet of beef without any fat.

Serves 4

4 slices raw beef fillet, each about 30 g (a good 1 oz)
For the marinade:
juice of half a large lemon
2 tbs virgin olive oil
1 tsp brandy
salt and freshly ground black pepper
For the filling:
1 tbs chopped parsley
1 tbs chopped capers

36

Flatten each slice of beef by beating with a batticarne or meat-beater between two sheets of see-through strong plastic. Leave the slices of meat to steep for 30 minutes in the marinade of lemon juice, olive oil, brandy and salt and pepper. In the meantime coarsely chop the parsley and the capers. Cut the beef slices into rectangular pieces, place a little herb mixture in the centre of each piece and roll them up.

LINGUA IN SALSA VERDE
Ox Tongue in Green Sauce

This is a typical speciality of the Piedmont region. The green sauce is similar to the one used in the anchovy antipasto, but is particularly adapted to flavour meats that have only a mild taste. This dish can be described as being spicy yet delicate at the same time. As an antipasto one tongue will serve 8–10: as a main course, 6.

If you buy a tongue that has been pickled in brine, it will keep its pinkish colour when cooked.

Serves 8–10

1 ox (beef) tongue weighing approx 1 kg (2 lb)
salt
3 celery stalks
1 onion with a few cloves stuck in it
2 carrots, cut in pieces
For the green sauce:
75 g (2½ oz or 2 US cups) finely chopped parsley
1 clove garlic, finely chopped
50 g (2 oz) pickled gherkins, finely chopped
50 g (2 oz) capers, finely chopped
4 anchovy fillets, chopped
10 tbs olive oil
a few gherkins, for decoration

Clean and trim the ox tongue, then boil it for about two hours or more in slightly salted water with the celery, onion and carrots. Allow it to cool. Make the sauce by chopping together the parsley, garlic, gherkins and capers, add the chopped anchovy and finally add the olive oil. Once the tongue has cooled, proceed to peel it and cut into thin slices. Arrange the slices on a dish and cover with the sauce. Decorate with gherkins sliced as flowers.

POLPETTINE DI CARNE E MELANZANE
Meat and Aubergine (Eggplant) Rissoles

This is another simple recipe which relies on the interesting combination of the meat texture and the strong spicy flavour of the vegetable.

Serves 6

350 g (¾ lb) aubergines (eggplants)
1 egg
1 tbs finely chopped parsley
½ clove garlic, finely chopped
4 tbs freshly grated Parmesan cheese
salt and freshly ground black pepper
350 g (¾ lb) minced (ground) lean beef
3 grates of nutmeg

Peel the aubergines, slice them and cook in slightly salted boiling water for about 8 minutes. Leave to cool, then squeeze to remove any excess water. Cut them roughly into pieces. Lightly beat the egg and add the parsley, finely chopped garlic, grated Parmesan cheese, a little nutmeg, salt and pepper. Mix this with the meat and aubergine pieces to form a homogeneous paste. Shape the mixture into about 12 little golf balls and fry, turning them once, in 1 cm (½ inch) of hot oil until they are brown and the garlic is cooked: about 5 minutes on each side. These rissoles can be served hot or cold.

INVOLTINI DI PROSCIUTTO E MOZZARELLA
Parma Ham and Mozzarella Fingers

I really think this is the easiest recipe to prepare. It doesn't need to be cooked and it is ready in minutes. Wonderful for parties.

Makes 24 involtini

12 slices of Parma ham
1 mozzarella
2–3 dried sage leaves, crumbled
1 tsp thyme
1 tsp dried rosemary
pepper

Cut each slice of Parma ham in two halves. Cut the mozzarella first into thick slices and then into fingers. Chop the herbs finely together, making sure they are all mixed, then sprinkle the herbs over the mozzarella fingers. Roll each finger in a piece of ham and serve.

UOVA DI QUAGLIE NEL NIDO
Quail's Eggs in the Nest

This is another recipe created specially for my restaurant at about the same time as the parcels of crab. I am always amused at how my clients, made up mostly of important business and media people and politicians, always tend to recommend this antipasto to their guests. It is indeed a very tasty and spectacular dish to start a meal with.

Serves 4

24 quail's eggs (6 per person)

12 tbs mayonnaise (see recipe on page 32) mixed with 1 extra tbs fresh lemon juice

2 baskets of mustard and cress, or alfalfa sprouts, or some shredded lettuce

celery salt for serving

Immerse the eggs in boiling water for 2 minutes and then put them to cool under running water so that the yolks stay runny. Shell the eggs. Spread in the centre of each plate 2 spoonfuls of mayonnaise and arrange on it 6 shelled eggs. Scatter a circle of herbs or shredded lettuce around the eggs so as to create the effect of a nest. Serve with celery salt.

UOVA RIPIENE DI TONNO
Stuffed Eggs

A favourite recipe of my mother's, which does not take much time to make. It is also a very versatile dish, which can be eaten, for instance, in a cold buffet or as an appetizer.

Serves 4

4 fresh eggs

100 g (4 oz) canned tuna fish

1 tbs chopped parsley

2 tbs capers

1 tbs mayonnaise

freshly ground black pepper

Boil the fresh eggs for around 15 minutes, then leave them to cool. Drain the oil from the tuna, chop it finely with the parsley and capers (leave some capers whole for decoration) and mix with the mayonnaise. Shell the eggs and cut lengthwise into two. Take out the yolk, being careful to leave the white intact. Mash the yolks and incorporate with the tuna mixture, adding

the ground black pepper. Stir well so as to form a thick paste. Wet your fingers and shape the paste into little balls and place one in each half of egg. Arrange on a dish and decorate with capers.

CARCIOFINI SOTT'OLIO
Pickled Artichokes

This dish is a typically Italian speciality, popular throughout the whole country. Even though the cultivation of artichokes is mainly in the Southern provinces of Campania and Lazio, the Northern Italians are more enthusiastic about the vegetable, using them in starters like the antipasto misto. If you are lucky enough to come across some small artichokes (which sadly are rarely to be found abroad), I would heartily recommend that you preserve them.

Makes a 1 litre (2 pt) jar

1.5 kg (3 lb) fresh artichokes (if using large ones, cut them into quarters)

1 litre (2 pt) white wine vinegar

500 ml (1 pt) white wine

15 cloves

6 cloves garlic

3 sprigs fresh rosemary

½ lemon

3 dried red chili peppers

salt

500 ml (1 pt) olive oil

Wash the artichokes, and prepare as shown in the illustration (opposite). Trim the stalk, peel off all the tough outside leaves, cut off the tops and if they are large ones cut in half and cut away the choke. Put in a bowl of water with a piece of lemon in it, to prevent the cut artichokes from discolouring.

Put the vinegar, wine, cloves, 2 rosemary sprigs and the salt in a saucepan large enough to take the artichokes and bring to the boil. Drop the garlic cloves in the boiling vinegar for a few seconds, remove them and set aside. Put in the artichokes and cook until al dente: they should take 20–25 minutes. Drain upside down on a clean cloth until absolutely dry. When the artichokes are dry, take care not to touch them with your hands. Sterilize a preserving jar and put in it a rosemary sprig. Pour a little olive oil into the jar and then spoon in a layer of artichokes, pushing them into the corners with the end of the spoon so as to avoid air being

One way to clean artichokes, leaving the tender heart

trapped. Pour in more oil, add a little crumbled chili and a clove of garlic then proceed up the jar with another layer of artichokes, oil, etc. The artichokes must be completely covered with the oil before sealing the jar. Use after two months.

CARCIOFINI RIFATTI
Pickled Artichokes with Parsley

This simple preparation will enhance and freshen the flavour of bought pickled artichokes.

Serves 4

250 g (½ lb) pickled artichokes
a squeeze of lemon juice
coarsely ground black pepper
1 tbs chopped parsley
½ dried red chili pepper, chopped (optional)
1 tbs olive oil

Take the artichokes out of their oil and put them into a bowl along with the lemon juice, pepper, chopped parsley and, for those who like piquancy, the chili. Dress with fresh olive oil and serve alongside other antipasti.

FONDI DI CARCIOFI CON SALSA OLANDESE
Artichoke Hearts with Hollandaise Sauce

This is a recipe which is slightly more tricky to prepare but which can produce excellent results. If you are to incorporate this dish as part of an antipasto, it is best to use the smaller artichokes, otherwise the dish becomes a meal in itself.

Serves 4

1 artichoke per person
the juice of half a lemon
hollandaise sauce (see next recipe)

Clean the artichokes and prepare as shown in the first four steps (top of page). Boil them in salted water with the juice of half a lemon until cooked, for approximately 25 minutes. Remove the centre choke with a spoon, leaving only the outside ring of leaves, then keep hot.

Make the hollandaise sauce (see recipe). Put the artichokes on to a plate and pour the sauce into the centre of each heart. Serve immediately.

SALSA OLANDESE
Hollandaise Sauce

The best way to make hollandaise is to use a double boiler or a very thick round-bottomed copper pan. The heat has to be so gentle to prevent the egg yolks from cooking. A good light whisk is also important. I always use clarified butter for my hollandaise.

Makes 300 ml (12 fl oz or 1½ US cups) hollandaise

2 egg yolks
200 ml (7 fl oz or 1 US cup) clarified butter
the juice of one lemon
salt and freshly ground black pepper

To make clarified butter, gently heat up 250 g (½ lb or 1 US cup) of unsalted butter and remove the foam which rises to the top until the butter is clear. Allow to cool a little before using to make the hollandaise: the clarified butter should be warm, not hot.

Whisk the egg yolks in the double boiler over the lowest heat possible (on no account should the water be boiling). Start to add the clarified butter in little dribbles, whisking all the time. Continue slowly to add the butter; the sauce begins almost immediately to thicken. If you are unlucky and the eggs begin to curdle and separate from the butter, stir in a tablespoon of warm water drop by drop. I remove the pan from the heat from time to time so that there is no chance of the pan getting too hot. When you have added all the butter and the sauce is very thick, equally slowly add the juice of the lemon. Finally season with salt and pepper to taste.

CIPOLLINE IN AGRODOLCE
Sweet and Sour Baby Onions

This delicacy can be used to complement other antipasto dishes, or even meat dishes requiring the addition of a piquant contrast.

The onions you would use in Italy are sold in bunches, like bulbous spring onions (scallions), and are the size of the small onions used for pickling in Britain and the USA: about the size of a hazelnut. If you can't find the Italian variety, try using small fresh pickling onions for this dish.

Serves 4

350 g (¾ lb) small white onions
2 tbs olive oil
1 tbs white wine vinegar
salt
1 tbs sugar

Peel the onions and put them into boiling water for 2–3 minutes. Drain and fry in the oil over a moderate heat for about 15 minutes or until a golden colour. When they are more or less cooked, add the vinegar, salt and sugar and continue frying for another 5 minutes. Can be served cold or hot.

FUNGHI RIPIENI
Stuffed Mushrooms

For this recipe you can use open cultivated mushrooms or field mushrooms. The stuffing need not be exactly as I suggest, but can be diversified according to your imagination and to the ingredients at hand.

Serves 4

4 large open mushrooms
1 egg
1 small ripe tomato, skinned and chopped
25 g (1 oz) fresh bread
4 tbs freshly grated Parmesan cheese
1 clove garlic, chopped
1 tbs finely chopped parsley
salt and freshly ground black pepper
1 tbs dry bread crumbs
3 tsp olive oil

Preheat the oven to 220°C (425°F or gas mark 7). Clean the mushrooms. Detach the stalks and chop them coarsely. Prepare the filling: first beat the egg and add to it the chopped mushroom stalks, the chopped tomato, the roughly broken up bread, the Parmesan, chopped garlic, parsley, salt and pepper and finally 1 tsp olive oil. Mix well together and fill the mushroom cups with the mixture. Oil a baking dish and on it place the mushrooms side by side. Sprinkle the dry bread crumbs over the mushrooms and trickle with a little olive oil. Bake in a hot oven for 20 minutes until golden brown on top. Eat hot or cold.

FIORI DI ZUCCHINI RIPIENI
Stuffed Courgette (Zucchini) Flowers

This is above all a summer recipe, summer being the time when these vegetables are in flower. In Italy, especially, it is a well-known and easily prepared dish, as the flowers are sold in all the markets tied together with a willow branch. Usually it is little old ladies who sell these flowers in special baskets called cavagne along with herbs and other garden produce. If you have no vegetable garden yourself, try to persuade a gardening friend to let you have a few flowers.

Serves 4

12 courgette (zucchini) flowers
4 tbs olive oil, for frying
For the stuffing:
280 g (9 oz or 1½ US cups) fresh ricotta cheese
salt and freshly ground black pepper
3 grates of nutmeg
1 bunch chives, chopped
1 egg, beaten
4 tbs freshly grated Parmesan cheese
For the batter:
2 eggs
50 g (2 oz or ½ US cup) flour
4 tbs cold water

First make the batter. Beat the eggs, stir in the flour evenly, then gradually add the water to make a smooth consistency. Put it aside.

Meanwhile, clean the flowers carefully: gently wash and dry the outside, and make sure there are no insects inside. Prepare the filling by mixing thoroughly together the ricotta, salt, pepper, nutmeg, chopped chives, beaten egg and the grated Parmesan cheese. Use spoonfuls of this mixture to fill the flowers. Then dip the flowers into the batter and proceed to fry in hot oil until golden-brown. Drain on kitchen paper briefly before serving.

Winter antipasto.
Clockwise from the top: Pickled artichokes, Anchovy fillets in green sauce, Mussels au gratin, Ceps in oil, Stuffed dried tomatoes in oil, Yellow peppers with bagna cauda; centre: Leeks in vinaigrette (see page 176).

FUNGHI SOTT'OLIO
Mushrooms in Oil

Imagine a fine autumn day when you have just returned from gathering wild mushrooms. You have managed to pick 10 kg (over 20 lb) or so of beautiful, small, good quality ceps. Most of them will be used right away, perhaps in a risotto; some of them might be given away to friends; another batch can be sliced and dried. My suggestion for the remainder would be to cook them in vinegar and water, preserve them in oil and serve as an hors d'œuvre at Christmas time. This is the ambition of many a mushroom lover!

Those of you who are not mushroom connoisseurs, and those of you who are but can't go out looking for them, can buy them (if they can be found). Or you can buy canned ones. The most practical way, however, is to buy ordinary champignon mushrooms and preserve these. They will not be as good as the ceps, but will still be delicious.

Makes a 1 litre (2 pt) preserving jar

1 kg (2 lb) button mushrooms or ceps
700 ml (1¼ pt or 3¼ US cups) white wine vinegar
100 ml (¼ pt or ½ US cup) white wine
200 ml (½ pt or 1 US cup) water
4 bay leaves
3 cloves garlic
10 cloves
2 tbs salt
olive oil to cover

Clean the mushrooms thoroughly, discarding any that are not firm. In a saucepan large enough to take the mushrooms, bring to the boil the vinegar, water and wine. Add the bay leaves, cloves, salt and mushrooms. Bring back to boiling and simmer for 6–8 minutes; the mushrooms tend to float so you have to push them down with a spoon while they are cooking. They will lose water as they cook and reduce in volume, becoming lighter to touch. Drain and without touching the mushrooms with your hands, put them to cool and dry on a clean cloth, stem side down so that no liquid can be trapped.

Sterilize a preserving jar and pour a little olive oil in the bottom. Using a spoon, put in a layer of mushrooms, 1 bay leaf and half a clove of garlic, cover with oil and proceed in this way up the jar, pressing the mushrooms into spaces making sure you have no air trapped. The oil must cover the final layer of mushrooms. They will keep for a long period – unless, of course, you are tempted to eat them straight off!

GIARDINIERA
Pickled Vegetables

Pickles have an important role to play in the Italian meal. They both tease the appetite and stimulate the gastric juices into greater activity. In a mixed hors d'œuvre or antipasto misto, there is nearly always something slightly vinegary. Garden pickles (giardiniera) are particularly popular as nearly all the vegetables to be found in the garden can be used. They can be kept in jars for long periods to be used a little at a time, dressed with some olive oil. These pickles can be bought ready prepared in good Italian delicatessens, but as they are extremely easy to prepare, I think you should try to make them yourself.

Makes a 3.3 litre (5 pt) preserving jar

about 2 kg (4½ lb) prepared vegetables:
2 turnips weighing 250 g (½ lb)
4 large carrots weighing 450 g (1 lb)
1 red bell pepper weighing 250 g (½ lb)
1 celeriac weighing 500 g (1 lb)
250 g (½ lb) broccoli or cauliflower florets
4 celery stalks weighing 150 g (6 oz)
100 g (4 oz) green French beans
50 g (2 oz) mange tout
150 g (6 oz) small white onions
about 1.2 litres (a good 2 pt) white wine vinegar
2–3 small sprays bay leaves
2 tsp whole black peppercorns
3–4 large cloves garlic

Wash and peel the turnips, carrots and celeriac. Wash and cut into quarters the red pepper, removing all the seeds. Top and tail the beans and mange tout. Separate the cauliflower and broccoli florets and wash them. Peel the onions.

Cut all the vegetables into 1 cm (½ inch) thick slices, using a special crinkle-edged cutter. Bring a large saucepan of water to the boil, add a little salt and put in the celeriac, carrots, red pepper and turnips first. Allow them to boil for 10 minutes then add the remainder of the vegetables. All the vegetables should be cooked al dente, not soft. Drain and lay them out to dry on a clean cloth. Meanwhile wash and thoroughly dry your preserving jar or jars. Slice the garlic and wash the bay leaves. When the vegetables are completely dry, pour a little of the vinegar into the bottom of the jar, lay a spray of bay leaves and then start to fill up with your vegetables, using a spoon as it is important not to touch the vegetables after they have been cooked. As you fill the jar, place the peppercorns, slices of garlic and bay leaves among the vegetables. Fill up with the vinegar as you progress, making sure you have no air trapped between. The vinegar should completely cover all the vegetables. Seal the jar and keep for at least 3 months before using.

INVOLTINI DI MELANZANE
Aubergine (Eggplant) Rolls

My idea of aubergine rolls is a variation on the use of the vegetable in dishes alla parmigiana or al funghetto.

Serves 4

1 large aubergine (eggplant) weighing about 350 g (¾ lb)
olive oil for frying
1 tbs parsley
1 tbs pine nuts
1 tbs capers
1 clove garlic

Clean the aubergine and slice it lengthwise to a little less than 1 cm (about ⅓ inch) thick, sprinkle with salt and set aside for 10 minutes. Pat them dry. Preheat the oven to 190°C (375°F or gas mark 5). Heat the oil and fry the pieces on each side until golden in colour. Remove and leave to drain on kitchen paper. Coarsely chop together the parsley, pine nuts, capers and the garlic. Spread this mixture on the aubergine slices, roll each slice up and fasten with a toothpick. Place the rolled slices in a small baking dish and bake in a moderate oven for 25 minutes. Serve in a clean dish.

INSALATA DI PEPERONI ARROSTITI
Roast Pepper Salad

This recipe is an example of the way in which the flavour of the fleshy red and yellow bell peppers can change completely according to whether they are fried or roasted: the removal of the skin alters the taste of the peppers totally.

This is without a doubt one of my favourite recipes. It can be eaten either by itself, with some good wholesome bread, or as an accompaniment to meat dishes – especially pork.

Serves 6

4 fleshy yellow and red bell peppers
3 tbs olive oil
1 tbs coarsely chopped parsley
2 cloves garlic, coarsely chopped
salt

Roast the peppers over a charcoal grill (broiler), turning them frequently until black and blistered. Leave them to cool and then peel off the skin, which should come away quite easily if the peppers are well roasted. Remove the stalk and the seeds. Cut lengthwise into narrow strips and place in a dish, adding the coarsely chopped garlic. Dress with oil, parsley and salt. This dish can be eaten hot or cold, but improves with standing, and is excellent eaten the next day.

INSALATA CAPRICCIOSA
Raw Vegetable Salad

'Capricious' is quite an apt term for describing this salad, which can be used in many ways: in sandwiches, or as part of many antipasto dishes. It is particularly popular as a starter in Piedmont.

Serves 4

8 small pickled artichokes (carciofini) in oil
100 g (4 oz) celeriac
100 g (4 oz) carrots
2 tbs mayonnaise (see page 32)
juice of half a lemon
salt and freshly ground black pepper

The preparation is very simple. Simply peel the celeriac and the carrots and cut into matchsticks. Mix in the drained artichokes, cut into small strips, and the mayonnaise mixed with the extra lemon juice, and season with salt and pepper.

Overleaf: Home-made preserves. From left to right: aubergines (eggplant) in oil, stuffed dried tomatoes in oil (top), mushrooms (*Boletus badius*) in oil, pickled artichokes (front), giardiniera or pickled vegetables (back), cep (*Boletus edulis*) in oil, yellow and red peppers in vinegar, mushrooms in oil

MELANZANE SOTT'OLIO
Aubergines (Eggplants) in Oil

Aubergines (eggplants) are an excellent vegetable, especially popular in the south of Italy. Indeed, most of the Italian recipes I know that use aubergines come from either Sicily, Calabria or Campania. This recipe, for example, comes from the Puglia region, where the aubergines are left out in the sun to take away their bitter juice before being boiled for a short time in vinegar, then preserved in oil with oregano, garlic and chili. The preserved aubergines are then eaten in winter along with home-made salami and cheese. Through immigration, southern produce is now available in northern markets, much to the satisfaction of local people there.

Aubergines made in this way are extremely spicy and make an excellent antipasto. Choose long thin ones to make slices that are not too large in diameter.

Makes a 1 litre (1 pt) preserving jar

1.25 kg (3 lb) aubergines (eggplants)
1.5 litres (2½ pt) white wine vinegar
750 ml (1¼ pt) water
50 g (2 oz) coarse salt
2 cloves garlic, sliced
1 tbs dried oregano
1 chili pepper
about 500 ml (1 pt) olive oil

Wash and slice the aubergines across into slices 1 cm (½ inch) thick. Arrange in layers on a chopping board, putting coarse salt on each layer. (This process eliminates the bitter taste and removes excess water, so it is important to position the board where the liquid can run off. To speed up the dehydration process, place a weight on top of the aubergines.) Leave for at least an hour. Bring the vinegar and water to the boil in a large saucepan. Add the sliced aubergines, bring back to the boil and cook, holding them beneath the liquid, for a couple of minutes. Drain and lay out to dry on a clean cloth. Sterilize your preserving jar. Pour a little oil in the bottom of the jar and with a spoon make a layer of aubergines, sprinkle with oregano, a little crushed chili and some slices of garlic, pour over more oil and continue up the jar with layers of aubergine until full. Cover with oil, pressing the aubergines to expel any air bubbles. Store for at least a month before eating.

PEPERONI GIALLI CON BAGNA CAUDA
Yellow Peppers with Bagna Cauda

Even though Piedmont has no sea coast, anchovies play an important part in local gastronomy. Indeed, there is a valley in the province of Cuneo where the villagers occupy themselves exclusively with the conservation of this fish in salt. Of the many recipes using anchovies, this is certainly one of my favourites: the distinctive flavour of the bagna cauda is juxtaposed with the sweet taste of the roasted peppers. This dish is also excellent served cold.

Serves 4

2 fleshy yellow bell peppers
For the bagna cauda:
8 cloves garlic
150 ml (¼ pt or ⅔ US cup) milk
a nut of butter
20 anchovy fillets in oil

Clean the peppers, remove the stalks and seeds, and cut them into quarters. Put the cloves of garlic in a pan with the milk and cook gently until soft for about 35 minutes. Meanwhile, preheat the oven to 220°C (425°F or gas mark 7). Throw away most of the milk, add the nut of butter and the anchovies and let the mixture slowly dissolve over a low heat until a paste is produced. Pass it through a sieve. Place the pepper pieces on a greased dish and put them in the hot oven for 15 minutes. Remove from the oven and turn the heat down to 190°C (375°F or gas mark 5). Fill each piece of pepper with some of the paste and put back into the oven for a further 15 minutes, until the peppers go brown at the edges.

POLPETTINE DI SPINACI
Spinach Fritters

This is a very simple dish and is ideal either as an antipasto or as a party food. Serve hot or cold.

Serves 4 (plus a taster for the cook!)

500 g (1 lb) fresh spinach
2 eggs
4 tbs freshly grated Parmesan cheese
¼ nutmeg, grated
30 g (good 1 oz or ⅓ US cup) dry bread crumbs
salt and freshly ground black pepper
oil for frying

Clean, cook and drain the spinach. After it has cooled down, squeeze it well to remove all excess water and chop coarsely. Beat the eggs and add to them the grated Parmesan, the nutmeg, bread crumbs, salt and pepper. Incorporate this mixture into the spinach. Put about 1 cm (½ inch) of oil into a pan and heat until it is very hot. Shape the spinach mixture with a spoon and your hands into little golf balls and fry in the oil for about 4 minutes on each side until golden-brown.

POMODORI SECCHI SOTT'OLIO
Stuffed Dried Tomatoes in Oil

Even though dried tomatoes are rarely to be found outside Italy, I am including this delicious recipe just in case you happen to come across some. Dried tomatoes are an excellent food in themselves, if a bit tough; in this preparation they are rendered slightly more tender. Tomatoes prepared in this way will keep for a long time and can be consumed when the occasion arises. They are ready when you can no longer resist the temptation to taste them.

Ingredients for a 1 litre (2 pt) preserving jar

500 g (1 lb) dried tomatoes
500 ml (1 pt) vinegar
1 litre (2 pt) water
olive oil to cover – about 350 ml (a generous ½ pt or 1¼ US cups)
1 tsp oregano
1 clove garlic, chopped (optional)
40 g (1½ oz) anchovy fillets

Put the tomatoes to soak in a china or glass dish in a solution of the vinegar and water which should just cover them. After 1 hour turn the tomatoes over in the dish and continue to soak for a further hour. Drain and lay them out to dry on a clean cloth. Then put the tomatoes in a large bowl and pour over them at least 1 cup of olive oil (the surplus oil can be used later), turning the tomatoes over so that each half is coated. Season with the oregano and with chopped garlic if you wish. Cut the anchovies into pieces about 1 cm (½ inch) long. Take two halves of tomato and place a piece of anchovy inside one half, cover with the second half and squeeze together. Arrange the tomatoes thus prepared in layers in your glass jar, pressing them together and pouring a little oil over each

layer as you proceed up the jar. Push a long knife down the side of the jar to release any air trapped between the tomatoes. The oil should cover the contents of the jar.

ZUCCHINI ALLA SCAPECE
Fried Courgette (Zucchini) Salad

This is a typically Neapolitan method of dressing not only cooked greens and other vegetables but also anchovies. Aubergines (eggplants) make an equally tasty alternative to the courgettes suggested here. The origin of this dish is not quite certain, but is probably derived from the Spanish or Provençal escabeche, which means to dress with a marinade of oil, vinegar and spices. It is an excellent appetite-teaser.

Serves 6

1 kg (2 lb) courgettes (zucchini)
salt
oil for frying
a bunch of fresh mint
2 tbs olive oil
1 tbs wine vinegar
1 clove garlic, sliced coarsely

Slice the courgettes 5 mm (¼ inch) thick and fry them, a few at a time, in hot oil in a pan until they are a good brown colour on both sides. Remove them from the pan, place them in a dish and sprinkle with salt. Tear the mint leaves off the stem and scatter them whole among the courgettes. Add the oil and vinegar and then the pieces of garlic, and mix well together. Leave to marinate for at least a couple of hours before serving to allow the flavours to develop fully.

IL PRIMO

────────── THE FIRST COURSE ──────────

Il primo is the first 'real' course in the Italian meal. Traditionally, it was the 'filler', and on rare occasions the whole meal would be pared down to this one course. Often it is a plate of pasta or a creamy risotto. Or it might be a light broth with cappelletti or a minestrone. In various parts of the north polenta may be served.

There are some wonderful soups in the Italian repertoire. Each coastal region has its own distinctive fish soup, and there is an infinite variety of vegetable soups. Rice may be added in the north, pasta in the south and beans in central Italy; in Liguria the soup might be predominantly green and give off the heady fragrance of pesto, while around Naples it will be based on tomatoes, onions and garlic.

The glorious pasta dishes Italy is so famous for range from the simplest – spaghetti tossed in garlic and olive oil or in a lightly cooked tomato sauce – to complicated baked lasagnes and timbales and stuffed pasta like tortelloni and ravioli. Then there are gnocchi, a type of pasta dumpling made from a potato or maize flour paste. Interestingly, it has become popular in restaurants in Italy to serve small assaggini, or titbits of pasta – consisting of three or four different kinds of pasta, each with separate complementary sauces.

Risotto is a northern speciality. It is made with Arborio or Vialone rice – grown in the fields of Piedmont, Lombardy and the Veneto – which is slowly cooked in butter and a small amount of liquid, and sometimes flavoured with saffron. Simple vegetable risottos are made with asparagus or ceps, while the Venetians like to add clams and mussels. For a special occasion, the risotto may be decorated with slivers of white truffles, as is the custom in Piedmont.

Another dish from the north is polenta. It is a type of porridge made from maize flour and can be fried or baked, eaten with simple sauces, and used instead of bread to accompany meat and poultry. So it is really impossible to classify simply as a first course, although it is often eaten as one.

I have also included pizza recipes in this section, although they too defy strict classification, usually being served by themselves, rather than as part of a meal. Any of these dishes, in fact, makes an excellent lunch or light supper, accompanied by a salad and a bottle of wine, and followed by a good cheese and fresh fruit.

BRODO DI CARNE O DI GALLINA
Beef or Chicken Stock

The single most important factor when making these stocks, which form the basis of most Italian minestre or thick soups, risottos and other dishes, is to ensure that the meat used is of good quality. Beef stock should be made from the meat of a mature animal, and a bone with marrow can be added if you want to thicken the broth, for example when making consommés. If the full flavour of the beef is to be savoured in the stock, it is advisable to mince (grind) the meat first. Choose a piece of silverside, brisket or topside if you are going to use the meat for a dish on its own, such as boiled beef salad. For the chicken stock you should choose a bird which is neither too old (when it will be too tough) nor too young (when it will be devoid of any flavour). The cooked chicken can itself be used in the recipe for Pollo in gelatina.

Makes about 3 litres (5½ pt) stock

1 kg (2 lb) stewing beef and some bones, or 1 chicken weighing around 2 kg (4 lb), or half and half according to your taste
a couple of carrots, cut in pieces
1 onion
some celery stalks, roughly chopped
several bay leaves
a few peppercorns
4 litres (7 pt) water
salt

Immerse the meat in a large saucepan full of lightly salted water and bring to the boil. Skim off the froth and add the vegetables and herbs. Bring back to the boil and allow to simmer for 2 or 3 hours, depending on the meat. Strain. The best way of removing the fat is to allow the stock to cool so that the fat solidifies and can be lifted off.

BRODO DI PESCE
Fish Stock

Fish stock is comparable to the previous recipe in that it forms the basis of a number of soups and seafood risottos, is simple to make and is excellent value for money. If left to cool down, fish stock tends to set into a jelly.

More or less any part of a fresh fish can prove useful in the making of a stock. It's a good idea to establish a rapport with your local fishmonger, who will be able to supply you with the heads of larger fish, which are normally not sold.

Makes about 2 litres (4 pt) stock

1–2 kg (2–4 lb) mixed fish pieces (head etc)
2–3 celery stalks, roughly chopped
2 carrots, cut in pieces
a bunch of parsley
1 onion
2 cloves garlic
a couple of fennel seeds
salt and freshly ground black pepper
4 litres (7 pt) water

Clean and gut the fish. Place in a saucepan with the lightly salted water, bring to the boil and skim away the froth. Add all the vegetables and herbs, and leave to simmer for an hour. Strain the liquid through a sieve, allow to cool and keep in the refrigerator until required.

BRODO DI VEGETALI
Vegetable Broth

Vegetable broth is a delicious alternative to meat-based stocks: it can be not only very flavoursome but also nutritious. For the tastiest stock, choose vegetables with a distinctive flavour, such as celery, parsnips and so on. This is not so much a recipe, with a list of specific quantities, as a general principle: the amount depends on how much stock you require, but the following amount makes 4 average servings.

Makes about 1 litre (2 pt) broth

1.5 kg (3 lb) vegetables: carrots, celeriac, celery, onions, parsnips
1 clove garlic, chopped
parsley and any other herbs you have to hand
1.5 litres (3 pt) water
salt and freshly ground black pepper
2 tbs cream (optional)

Prepare and roughly chop the vegetables and put into a pan with the herbs, seasonings and water. (You can also make use of the vitamin-rich water in which you have previously cooked spinach, for example: so don't throw it away if you are likely to be making vegetable broth.) Simmer for 20 minutes or so, until the vegetables are tender.

Vegetable stock is light and refreshing simply strained and served by itself. To make it into a more substantial soup, blend the cooked vegetables and mix them into the broth with a little cream. Check for seasoning before serving.

BRODO DI CACCIAGIONE
Game Stock

In my opinion it would be a pity to buy really good game merely in order to create a stock. I far prefer to cook and eat the game as a meat and then afterwards use the leftovers (there is usually more than sufficient meat left on the bones) to make a stock. More or less any kind of leftovers will serve the purpose – pheasant, partridge, quails and even duck, goose and turkey. As the flavour of a game stock is subtly exotic, it can be used with great success in consommés, sauces or even as a gravy for roasts. Indeed, such is the versatility of a game stock that I would heartily recommend that you never throw anything which is in the least edible away when you are preparing a game dish!

Makes about 1.5 litres (3 pt) of stock

whatever game leftovers you have, equivalent to 2 pheasant carcasses or 3–4 small birds
1.5–2 litres (3–4 pt) of water
1 carrot, cut in pieces
1 leek, roughly chopped
1 parsnip, cut in pieces
1 small onion
1 clove garlic
1 bay leaf
plus any varied selection of vegetables you happen to have

A good stock is made by putting the aforementioned leftovers into a saucepan with the water and the vegetables. Bring to the boil, skim and cook for about 2 hours. After this time the stock should be sieved, cooled and kept in the refrigerator to be used a little at a time when the need arises.

CONSOMMÉ CON UOVA
Consommé with Egg Yolk

The one slight drawback about this consommé is that it can never be served piping hot as the egg yolk should merely float in the broth and not be coagulated as in stracciatella.

This egg yolk consommé is a delicious soup which can be served up at almost any time of the day, and in any way you like – even as a nourishing drink. If you are giving a summer party with quite a few courses, this dish will allow you to bridge one course with another.

This consommé can be based on a beef, chicken or vegetable stock depending on the courses that you are planning to precede and to follow it. A fishy stock, however, is not recommended.

Serves 4

1 litre (2 pt) stock
4 egg yolks
freshly ground black pepper
2 tbs finely chopped chives
croûtons and freshly grated Parmesan cheese

Heat the stock until reasonably warm, pour into four cups. Into each cup put a whole egg yolk, which the guests can then stir into the broth. As a final decoration add some of the chopped chives and serve with bread croûtons and a sprinkling of Parmesan.

BRODO DI POLLO CON CAPPELLETTI
Cappelletti in Chicken Broth

This is a slightly richer version of the traditional pastina in brodo or fine spaghetti in broth which can be found on the menu of most Italian restaurants and which can be made with a great variety of fine pasta such as stelline, tubettini, biavette, etc. The cappelletti owe their name to their resemblance to hats and can be hand-made if you happen to possess a great deal of patience. If this is not the case, I would heartily recommend that you buy them from a good Italian delicatessen, naturally paying attention to the 'sell-by' date. The best cappelletti to buy are probably those sold in a hermetically sealed pack and of recent manufacture. This type of pasta is a speciality of Bologna and of the Emilia Romagna region. However, they are also popular in most other areas of Italy. The Piedmontese and

Lombards, however, seem to prefer raviolini, which are similar to the cappelletti in taste but not in shape.

Serves 4

1 litre (2 pt) chicken or beef stock
120 g (4 oz) dried cappelletti or raviolini, or 200 g (7 oz) fresh cappelletti
30 g (1 oz or ¼ US cup) freshly grated Parmesan cheese

Bring the stock to the boil and add the cappelletti or raviolini. Bring back to the boil and simmer until the pasta is cooked: this should take about 15 minutes for dried and about 10 minutes for fresh pasta. Serve in a warm plate with the addition of a little Parmesan cheese grated on top.

CREMA DI FUNGHI PORCINI
Wild Mushroom Soup

Simply handling the main ingredients for this soup – wild mushrooms – fills me with ecstasy and reminds me of autumnal walks in beautiful woods in search of them. This soup can be made in two ways, both of which are delicious. In the Neal Street Restaurant I serve the version made with fresh ceps, and it has become one of the most popular items on the menu in the autumn. (During the rest of the year I make it with ceps I have frozen.) It is a very simple dish to prepare and will satisfy the guest with the most demanding palate. The alternative version is even simpler and (unless you have gathered your own ceps) cheaper. You could even make an exception and, for once, use a bouillon cube for convenience.

Serves 4

500 g (1 lb) fresh ceps, or alternatively 500 g (1 lb) field mushrooms plus 25 g (1 oz) dried ceps
1 medium onion, finely chopped
4 tbs olive oil
1 litre (2 pt) beef stock
4 tbs double (heavy) cream
salt and freshly ground black pepper
For the croûtons:
a nut of butter
2 slices white bread

If you are using fresh ceps, clean them and cut them into pieces. Cook the finely chopped onion

in the oil for 3–4 minutes, then add the ceps and sauté them for 6–7 minutes. Add the stock, bring to the boil and simmer for 20 minutes. (If you are not using fresh ceps, soak the dried ones in lukewarm water for 10 minutes. Meanwhile, fry the field mushrooms together with the onions and then add the soaked ceps with their water and the stock. Simmer for about half an hour.) To finish either method, take the pan from the heat and blend the contents. Then return the soup to the pan, add the cream, salt and pepper and heat slowly. Remove from the heat before it boils, and serve hot. To make croûtons, merely cut the bread into little cubes and fry in butter so that they become crisp and golden.

CREMA DI GAMBERONI
Cream of Prawn (Shrimp) Soup

This is an exquisite soup with a subtle taste and is ideal for elegant dinner parties. It is very simple to prepare. I would recommend using fresh prawns (shrimp), preferably the large sort, which are particularly juicy. You can, however, also make this soup with frozen prawns, which will give it a slightly different taste.

Serves 4

3 tbs olive oil
2–3 spring onions (scallions), finely chopped
500 g (1 lb) fresh giant prawns (jumbo shrimp) with shells
500 ml (1 pt) water
salt and freshly ground black pepper
1 sachet powdered saffron
5 tbs double (heavy) cream

Heat the olive oil in a large saucepan, add the finely chopped onions and fry well but do not brown. Add the water and bring to the boil. Throw in the prawns and let them simmer for about 15 minutes. Then add the saffron and the salt and pepper to taste. Strain the stock and then shell the prawns, taking care to extract all the juices by squeezing the head with your fingers before discarding it. Put the flesh into a little of the stock and liquidize until smooth. Add this liquid to the remainder of the stock and reheat. Remove from the flame and gently stir in the cream. Serve in warm plates.

ZUPPA DI PESCE
Fish Soup

This recipe of mine is merely a version of one of the hundreds of fish soups that can be found in all Italian coastal towns. It is a dish that can be tasty even if you have only a couple of kinds of fish to choose from. Monkfish, prawns (shrimp) and even mussels are ideal for this soup as they have a good flavour and do not disintegrate when cooked. For an even tastier soup you may well wish to include some heads of the larger fish, as I suggested in the recipe for fish broth. If you increase the proportions of fish, this soup can even become a main course.

Serves 4

4 tbs olive oil
1 shallot or onion, chopped
1 carrot, chopped
1 celery stalk, chopped
half a glass of dry white wine
8 prawns (shrimp)
20 mussels
250 g (½ lb) monkfish cut into pieces, or substitute scallops for the monkfish
1.5 litres (3 pt) fish stock
4 slices of buttered toast
1 clove garlic
salt and freshly ground black pepper

Put the oil in a large pan and fry the shallot together with the carrot and the celery until the onion becomes golden and soft. Pour in the wine, bring to the boil, and allow it to evaporate for 1 minute. Add the fish and the stock and simmer for 20 minutes. Remove the heads and shells from the prawns and shell the mussels, and return their flesh to the soup. Lightly rub the clove of garlic over the toast and place one slice in the bottom of each soup bowl. Pour in the soup and serve straight away.

ZUPPA DI CARDO CON POLPETTINE
Cardoon Soup with Dumplings

This cardoon is a member of the artichoke family and is a speciality of the Piedmont region, where it is mainly eaten in Bagna cauda. It is a very versatile vegetable with a slightly bitter taste. The centre near the root of the cardoon tends to be particularly bitter, so cut this out before cooking.

Last summer when I was exploring the

Cardoons

province of Alessandria I came across a whole field of cardoons which were being specially treated to blanch them. This is done by tying them and half-burying them underground up until the first frost. Normally, only the inside of the plant is eaten, this being the most tender. Here is the recipe that my mother used to prepare with this vegetable.

Serves 4

1.5 litres (3 pt) meat broth
1 cardoon weighing about 350 g (¾ lb)
200 g (7 oz) minced (ground) beef
1 tbs finely chopped parsley
4–5 grates of fresh nutmeg
1 tbs freshly grated Parmesan cheese
1 egg
1 tbs dry bread crumbs
salt and freshly ground black pepper

Wash the cardoon and chop it into pieces about 2 cm (1 inch) thick, then put them to cook in the meat broth until they are tender – about 20 minutes. Meanwhile, into a bowl put the meat, parsley, nutmeg, Parmesan cheese and bread crumbs and add the beaten egg and the salt and pepper. Knead this mixture thoroughly so as to obtain a smooth paste. Shape this with your hands into little dumplings and put them to simmer in the hot broth for about 10 minutes. Serve hot with a light sprinkling of Parmesan cheese if you so wish.

ZUPPA DI ERBE STRACCIATELLA
Herb and Egg Soup

This is a soup for springtime – its refreshing taste is particularly suited to this season. It is extremely simple to prepare, especially if you ignore the clamours of the purists and use bouillon cubes.

Serves 4

1.5 litres (3 pt) beef or chicken stock, or water plus 2 bouillon cubes
a nut of butter
2 tbs mint, chopped
3 tbs basil, chopped
1 tbs coriander, chopped
2 tbs parsley, chopped
2 whole eggs, plus 1 yolk
salt and freshly ground black pepper
freshly grated Parmesan cheese for serving

Put the stock or water on to boil. Add the butter and all the herbs (all fresh and finely chopped) and cook for 2 minutes. Beat the eggs together with the salt and pepper and pour the mixture slowly into the boiling broth, mixing with a whisk so that the egg does not coagulate into one lump. The soup thus obtained is very flavoursome and should have quite a thick consistency. When serving, add Parmesan cheese to taste.

ZUPPA DI ASPARAGI
Cream of Asparagus Soup

Ideally this soup should be made with the wild asparagus that grows along the sunny roads of southern Italy in the springtime. However, instead you can successfully use the larger tender, dark green asparagus cultivated in Piedmont, California and, of course, Britain.

Serves 6

1 kg (2 lb) asparagus
1.5 litres (3 pt) water
1 small onion, finely chopped
50 g (2 oz) butter
50 g (2 oz) white flour
salt and freshly ground black pepper

Cut away the tougher, woodier section of the asparagus stalks. Peel and chop the rest into pieces about 5 cm (2 inches) long, keeping the tips on one side. Put the water on to boil with some salt, then immerse the pieces of asparagus stalk and cook for 10 minutes. Add the tips and cook for a further 10 minutes, then remove them before they disintegrate and put aside.

Heat the butter in a pan, add the finely chopped onion and cook until it becomes soft. Add the flour and cook slowly for 2–3 minutes, stirring from time to time so that it does not stick. Then, stir in a little at a time the hot asparagus water until you have incorporated all the water and asparagus pieces. Finally add salt and pepper to taste and serve with the asparagus tips added to the individual servings.

CREMA DI TOPINAMBUR
Jerusalem Artichoke Soup

Apart from being one of the most important ingredients of the classic Bagna cauda, Jerusalem artichokes can also be served as a vegetable. With a delicate taste similar to that of the globe artichoke (but of quite a different texture), Jerusalem artichokes are ideal for making a creamy soup.

Serves 4

1 small onion, finely chopped
3 tbs olive oil
500 g (1 lb) Jerusalem artichokes
250 g (½ lb) potatoes, cut into small cubes
1 litre (2 pt) chicken stock
salt and freshly ground black pepper
1 tbs chopped parsley
For the croûtons:
a nut of butter
2 slices of white bread

Fry the onion in the oil until soft. Add the peeled artichokes and the potato cubes and finally the stock. Simmer until all the ingredients are fully cooked, for approximately 30 minutes, then blend everything together, add salt and pepper, sprinkle with parsley and serve hot with croûtons.

This is a very delicate soup. To make it creamier, increase the proportions of vegetables to liquid. Set aside some of the broth before you blend the soup, and then add it gradually to the purée in the blender until the consistency is according to your taste.

Right: Herb and egg soup

CREMA DI PISELLI
Pea Soup

This is a wonderful winter soup which is popular not only in the north of Italy but also in northern European countries. It is a very adaptable dish which can be made into a main course with the simple addition of some kind of salted meat. Like most simple and genuine foods, this soup is full of flavour and nourishment.

Serves 4

300 g (10 oz) split green peas
350 g (¾ lb) floury potatoes
50 g (2 oz) smoked bacon, chopped
3 tbs olive oil
a pinch of oregano
salt and freshly ground black pepper
1.5 litres (3 pt) water

Soak the peas in cold water for at least 12 hours. Peel the potatoes and chop them into small cubes. Fry the chopped bacon in the oil in a large saucepan, add the potatoes and lightly fry these as well. Add the water and the drained peas (don't use the water from the peas in the cooking). Bring to the boil and continue to simmer until the peas and the potatoes are disintegrating and almost overdone (skim off any fat that rises to the surface). This should take about 2½ hours. Half-way through the cooking, add a pinch of oregano and salt and pepper. The resulting soup should naturally cook to quite a thick, creamy consistency.

MINESTRONE

This soup is so well known throughout the world that it is certainly not necessary for me to give a translation. The name derives from minestra, meaning a soup. (In many parts of Italy minestra means green.) Normally this is prepared with whatever leftover vegetables are to be found in the kitchen, and so to list the precise ingredients needed for a minestrone would be nonsensical, even dictatorial! Almost all the different regions in Italy have their own typical minestrone, which will then be suffixed 'alla milanese', 'alla genovese', 'alla piemontese', etc.

Perhaps the most practical hint for you to follow (and which will immediately transform even the dullest of vegetables) is that the fine flavour of Parma ham is essential to the success of this dish. You can ask for bits and pieces of prosciutto from your Italian grocer or delicatessen, for example, the skin, the pieces cut out from around the bone and the tail-end piece.

Serves 4

1.5 litres (3 pt) water
a total of 1.5 kg (3 lb) vegetables, made up of any or all of the following: carrots, celery, courgettes (zucchini), cauliflower, potatoes, fresh peas, beetroot (beet), garlic, leeks, Brussels sprouts, parsnips, marrows (squash)
1 small onion
8 tbs olive oil
400 g (14 oz) can borlotti beans (if you can find fresh ones, so much the better)
some fresh basil leaves, or 1 tsp dried basil
a good 250 g (½ lb) prosciutto scraps
2 small tomatoes, skinned
4 tbs freshly grated Parmesan cheese

Heat the oil in a large saucepan. First fry the chopped onion, then add the prosciutto pieces and the water, letting this simmer for an hour. Meanwhile, clean the vegetables and chop into cubes. Discard the prosciutto pieces and add the other vegetables of your choice, as well as the drained beans. Add the skinned tomatoes after a further 20 minutes. Cook for at least a further 30 minutes, after which time you should taste to see that all the vegetables are cooked, particularly the carrots. Then add the basil and serve piping hot. Minestrone is also a delicacy when eaten cold. Freshly grated Parmesan should be served separately.

ZUPPA DI CICORIA E FAGIOLI
Dandelion and Bean Soup

The ingredients for this soup are quite difficult to come by if you live in a town, but extremely easy to obtain in the country. Indeed, cicoria or dandelion leaves can be found almost anywhere outside the city, especially by the roadside. It is preferable to pick them in the springtime when they are still young and tender.

Serves 6

600 g (1¼ lb) dandelion leaves
1 onion, finely chopped
100 g (4 oz) smoked bacon, cut into matchsticks
3 tbs virgin olive oil

1 clove garlic, sliced
750 ml (1 ½ pt) chicken stock
two 400 g (14 oz) cans cannellini beans
2–3 small red dried chili peppers
salt
6 slices of wholemeal bread, toasted

Thoroughly wash the dandelion leaves and cut them up coarsely. Fry the chopped onion and the bacon in the oil, adding the sliced garlic towards the end. When the onion has become soft and the bacon is coloured add a little of the stock, then the dandelion leaves and the drained cannellini beans. Cook for a few minutes. Crumble the chili peppers and add them to the soup together with the rest of the stock and salt if required. Place the lid on the saucepan and simmer gently until the dandelion is cooked – approximately 20 minutes. In the meantime prepare some well-browned toast, put a piece in the bottom of each soup bowl and pour the soup on top.

ZUPPA DI FAGIANO AL PORTO
Pheasant Soup with Port

This is a soup that has an intense, gamy flavour and is particularly appropriate during the autumn hunting season when a variety of game is on the market. Whenever I serve roast pheasant, I always take care to keep the leftovers and the cooking juices, which form the basis of an exceptional soup. You will make your guests feel like royalty if this soup is followed by 'The partridge and the pear', and accompanied by a vintage wine.

Serves 4

For the stock:
scraps and leftovers of pheasant or other game
2 tbs olive oil
1 medium-sized onion, chopped
1 carrot, cut in pieces
2 celery stalks, chopped
about 1 litre (2 pt) water
a nut of butter and a little flour
1 glass of port
2 tbs double (heavy) cream
salt and freshly ground black pepper
white truffle (optional)
For the croûtons:
a nut of butter
2 slices of white bread

Fry the chopped onion gently until golden brown. Add to this the chopped carrot and celery and the scraps of meat and bone. Pour in enough water to cover all these ingredients, and leave to simmer for about 1 ½ hours. Pass the stock through a sieve. Melt the butter and mix into it the flour, the cream and the port. Add this to the stock and reheat gently. Salt and pepper to taste and serve with either some croûtons or, if you are able, a couple of slices of white truffle.

ZUPPA DI CAVOLO ALLA CANAVESANA
Savoy Cabbage Soup

The Canavese region is situated near Ivrea in the northern tip of Piedmont and is particularly renowned for its excellent cuisine. You will find here restaurants of international fame serving all kinds of antipasti and wonderful soups and minestre. This recipe comes from my sister-in-law, Rosalba, and resembles the famous Tuscan ribollita. This soup is a meal in itself.

Serves 4

750 g (1 ½ lb) Savoy cabbage, shredded
4 tbs olive oil
2 cloves garlic, cut into slices
1 litre (2 pt) chicken stock
10 anchovy fillets
6 slices of bread
100 g (4 oz or ½ US cup) butter
60 g (2 oz or ½ US cup) freshly grated Parmesan cheese
200 g (7 oz) fontina cheese, sliced thin
salt and freshly ground black pepper

Preheat oven to 200°C (400°F or gas mark 6). Meanwhile, fry the garlic gently but don't let it colour. Add the cabbage, three-quarters of the stock and a good pinch of salt. Cook for about 20 minutes, until the cabbage is tender, stirring from time to time. Fry the bread until golden-brown in some butter (each slice will absorb quite a lot of butter). Place half of the slices of fried bread in an ovenproof dish, cover with a layer of cabbage, half the anchovies and some thin slices of fontina cheese. Intersperse each layer with some Parmesan cheese. Pour some stock over this and repeat the layers of bread, cabbage, anchovies and cheese, making sure there is enough stock to keep the mixture moist. Finish with a layer of fontina and Parmesan. Place the dish in the hot oven for 25 minutes.

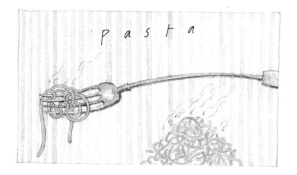

PASTA ALL'UOVO
Basic Pasta Dough

Italian cooks use a great deal of imagination combining pasta with local produce, ending up in many cases with really superlative dishes. For the most part these dishes have been created with hand-made pasta, and some people still consider that this more than repays the considerable time and energy spent in its making. My mother turned this laborious task into a social event: a number of her friends would sit gossiping round the large table while she rolled out her fusilli.

In recent years a multitude of pasta-making machines has appeared on the market. I have tried out nearly all the different types and have come to the conclusion that unless you wish to make enormous quantities of pasta, the greatest help is given by the simplest of hand-driven machines which allow you to produce dough of different thicknesses and to cut the pasta into strands of different sizes. Here, however, I'll describe the process of making pasta by hand.

The ideal proportions are one large egg to every 100 g (4 oz or 1 US cup) of flour, but variations in temperature and humidity as well as in the ingredients themselves may produce slightly different textures, and you may need to vary the quantity of flour slightly: the thing to

aim for is a dough which has been kneaded until it is perfectly smooth, and elastic yet firm.

Makes 450 g (1 lb) pasta dough

300 g (10 oz or 2½ US cups) plain (all-purpose) flour
3 large, very fresh eggs
generous pinch of salt

Pile the flour in a volcano-shaped mound on a spacious work surface – ideally of marble. Break the eggs into the centre and add some salt. Stir the eggs into the flour, with a fork at first and then with your hands, until it forms a coarse paste: add a little more flour if the mixture is too moist.

At this stage you may bring a pasta-making machine into play. Otherwise, it's a good idea at this point to clean your hands and the work surface before you start kneading the dough. Lightly flour the surface and your hands, and knead the dough with the heel of your hand, pushing it away from you and folding it back towards you, one hand at a time. Flour the surface and your hands from time to time while you work. After about 10–15 minutes the dough should be smooth and elastic.

Allow the dough to rest for 15–30 minutes before rolling it out. Once again, dust the surface and the rolling pin with flour. Roll the dough gently, working away from you, and rotating the dough by a quarter-turn so that it remains circular.

The thickness to aim for should be 2 mm (³/₁₆ inch) for ravioli and cappelletti and 4 mm (³/₈ inch) for lasagne and cannelloni. If you are making stuffed pasta such as ravioli, don't allow the sheet of dough to dry, but proceed to incorporate the filling as instructed in the appropriate recipes. If you are simply making lasagne or cutting strips of noodles, place a clean towel on the work surface and leave the pasta on

The first stages of pasta making

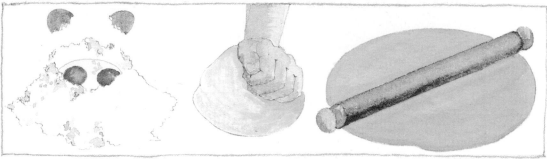

it to dry for about half an hour, letting different sections of it hang over the edge in turn. Then fold the sheet of pasta into a loose roll on the work surface and cut it into ribbons of the desired width. Open out the rolls of noodles gently and allow them to dry for a further 10 minutes or so before cooking.

Cook pasta in a large saucepan, preferably with a rounded base. Use plenty of boiling water: the general rule is 1 litre (2 pt) water and 1 tsp salt to every 100 g (4 oz) pasta. When you put the pasta into the pot, give it a quick stir to prevent it from sticking together. (It is only with lasagne, which must be immersed one sheet at a time, that it is necessary to add a few drops of oil to the water.) Cooking time varies according to the kind of pasta, its thickness and whether it is stuffed, but home-made noodles and ribbons will take about 3–5 minutes. Stir the pasta while it is cooking, preferably with a long wooden fork. Always test the pasta when you think it should be almost done: it is ready when it is al dente, and slightly resistant. A little before it reaches that stage, take the saucepan off the heat, add a glass of cold water, and leave for a couple of seconds. Then drain the pasta and return immediately to the saucepan or a preheated dish, mixing it with a little sauce and perhaps some grated cheese. Serve it immediately.

Coloured Pasta

Pasta can be bought in different colours. Often the colouring is a gimmick, for visual effect, with the exception of green pasta based on spinach: check the packet to make sure that the colouring is not artificial.

Here are some suggestions for making your own coloured pasta by adjusting the proportions in the basic recipe to incorporate a colouring ingredient. The resulting dough should have exactly the same consistency and texture, but you may find that these adulterated doughs are slightly more tricky to knead and harder to roll out into thin sheets. You may sometimes have to add a little extra flour to stiffen the dough.

Green Pasta

350 g (12 oz or 3 US cups) flour
3 eggs
80 g (3 oz) cooked spinach
salt

The spinach should be cooked in a little water,

drained very thoroughly and finely puréed. You may need a little extra flour to stiffen the dough. Here the colouring makes a subtle contribution to the flavour.

Purple Pasta

400 g (14 oz or 3½ US cups) flour
2 eggs
6 tbs beetroot juice
salt

Use a juicer or a food processor to obtain the juice, which will colour the dough a deep mauve.

Red or Pink Pasta

400 g (14 oz or 3½ US cups) flour
3 eggs
2 tbs tomato purée
salt

The tomato paste introduces a slightly acid flavour into the pasta.

Brown Pasta

380 g (13 oz or 3¼ US cups) flour
4 eggs
2 tbs bitter chocolate powder
salt

The quantity of flour is reduced and unsweetened cocoa powder substituted. This kind of pasta is often served in Italy together with game sauce.

Black Pasta

400 g (14 oz or 3½ US cups) flour
2 medium eggs
100 ml (¼ pt or ½ US cup) dilute cuttlefish ink

You will need the ink from one large or two small cuttlefish to colour the black pasta for four servings. The ink sac, which is a silverish tube shape about 10 cm (4 inches) long and 2 cm (¾ inch) in diameter, is found at the extreme bottom of the body. Be careful to withdraw it intact. Mix the thick black substance, the ink, with water to make 100 ml of liquid. Take care not to make this dough too soft.

MARILLE CON SUGO STRACCIATELLA
Marille with Tomato, Basil and Egg Sauce

One of the sauces best suited to this new type of pasta designed by Giugiaro and produced only by the firm Voiello, is the stracciatella sauce, which I presented on television during the course of a series on healthy cooking. This version is slightly richer, as butter is used instead of oil. It is very simple to cook and each mouthful of this pasta (which, by the way, greatly increases its volume when boiled) is a delicacy. If you are unable to find marille, rigatoni could be substituted – but it's not nearly as excellent.

Serves 4

400 g (14 oz) Voiello marille
For the sauce:
1 large onion, finely sliced
45 g (1½ oz or 3 tbs) butter
2 tbs olive oil
1 large can peeled plum tomatoes
2 fresh eggs, beaten
60 g (2 oz or ½ US cup) freshly grated Parmesan cheese
8–10 fresh basil leaves
salt and freshly ground black pepper

Put the pasta water on to boil: this type of pasta takes 15–18 minutes to cook. As soon as the water is boiling, add salt and the marille.

In the meantime, prepare the sauce. Put the canned tomatoes and their juice through a mouli, or blend them to obtain a thin purée. Heat the oil and butter together in a saucepan and fry the sliced onion until it becomes transparent. Add the tomato purée to the onions and cook for 15 minutes on a medium heat, reducing the liquid to a thin sauce. Lower the heat and, stirring continuously with a wooden spoon, add the 2 beaten eggs – you should gradually see the sauce thicken and acquire a creamy texture. Don't let it get too hot or the eggs will curdle. At this stage, mix in half of the grated Parmesan and four basil leaves, each torn into three or four bits. Season with salt and freshly ground black pepper.

Drain the pasta when it is al dente and mix in half of the sauce. Serve in preheated pasta bowls and top each serving with some of the remaining sauce and a whole basil leaf. Offer the rest of the Parmesan at the table.

MACCHERONI CON LE SARDE E ACCIUGHE
Macaroni with Sardines and Anchovies

Another typical Sicilian dish is pasta with sardines. Yet once more we see local produce such as sardines and anchovies, which abound on the southern Italian coast, used in a recipe to maximum effect. The incorporation of raisins suggests that this recipe has Arabic origins. Cultivated fennel has been substituted for the wild fennel used in the Sicilian version. Remember, however, to keep the green tips of the fennel to use as decoration.

Serves 4

350 g (¾ lb) fresh fennel
60 g (2 oz) seedless raisins
45 g (1½ oz) blanched and split almonds
1 small onion, thinly sliced
3 tbs olive oil
4 anchovy fillets (preferably salted), washed and cut into 1 cm (½ inch) pieces
1 small sachet of powdered saffron, or a pinch of saffron threads
salt and freshly ground black pepper
4 fresh sardines
flour for dusting
oil for frying
350 g (¾ lb) pasta (gomiti or sedanoni)

Cut the fennel into quarters, removing the hard stem at the base and keeping the green tips for decoration. Drop the pieces of fennel into a pan of lightly salted boiling water and simmer for 15–20 minutes or until the fennel is cooked, then drain and roughly chop it – but be sure to keep the water, as the pasta will be cooked in it at a later stage. In the meantime, soak the raisins in a little warm water. Dry-roast the almonds in a thick pan over a medium flame, shaking it gently until they have turned a golden colour. Slice the onion finely and fry it in the olive oil. When the onion has turned in colour, add the pieces of anchovy and stir until they are wholly dissolved in the oil. Finally, add the almonds, raisins, saffron and the cooked fennel, and fry these together for a couple of minutes.

Clean and fillet the sardines, toss in flour and salt and fry them, taking care to preserve them intact. Cook the pasta in the fennel water for 10 minutes or so until al dente, drain and mix with the sauce. Decorate each dish with a sardine and some chopped green tufts of fennel.

A selection of pasta shapes

TAGLIATELLE CON RADICCHIO ALLA LINO
Tagliatelle with Radicchio and Cream

This recipe is simplicity itself to prepare. I came across it in the restaurant Da Lino situated in Soligheto, near Treviso. As a dish it is a typical example of the putting to good use of a local product – in this case radicchio. The result is truly delicious, particularly if you have the time to make your own tagliatelle. I recommend that you drink a local Prosecco wine from Conegliano (in the province of Treviso) with this dish. The custom here is to serve this sparkling wine from a glass decanter without ceremony.

If you are in this part of Italy, try and visit the Da Lino restaurant as there are some other excellent dishes which are worth tasting.

Serves 4

450 g (1 lb) tagliatelle, preferably home-made
225 g (8 oz) radicchio, roughly chopped
2 small onions, finely chopped
115 g (4 oz) smoked bacon or ham, finely chopped
half a glass of white wine
200 ml (½ pt or 1 US cup) cream
100 g (4 oz or ½ US cup) butter
60 g (2 oz or ½ US cup) freshly grated Parmesan cheese
salt and freshly ground black pepper

Melt the butter and fry the chopped onion and the bacon or ham over a low flame for 10 minutes. Add the chopped radicchio and fry for another 5 minutes on a low heat. Add the white wine and raise the heat. When the wine has evaporated, add the cream and stir until the cream has thickened, but be careful not to boil it. Season with salt (very little if the bacon is salty) and pepper and keep warm.

Meanwhile, cook the tagliatelle until it is al dente (home-made tagliatelle should take 3–4 minutes at most), and add it to the pan with the radicchio mixture, tossing. Add the Parmesan cheese and serve piping hot.

TAGLIATELLE CON CARCIOFI
Tagliatelle with Artichokes

It is a typically Sienese habit to bring together artichokes and pasta. I came across this combination of tagliatelle and artichokes in a small trattoria in Siena where I was once eating. The taste was so distinctive and remained so impressed on my memory that I have no trouble at all reconstructing it here. For this dish you will need particularly small artichokes.

Serves 4 as a main course

4 fresh and tender small artichokes
juice of half a lemon
2 large ripe tomatoes or 4 small ones
4–6 spring onions (scallions), chopped
3 tbs virgin olive oil
2 tbs white wine
salt and freshly ground black pepper
2 tbs chopped parsley
450 g (1 lb) home-made tagliatelle, or 400 g (14 oz) dried tagliatelle
60 g (2 oz or ½ US cup) freshly grated Parmesan cheese

Clean and trim the artichokes retaining only the bottom and the most tender leaves (see page 39). Cut into slices and put in a bowl of water with lemon juice to prevent oxidization.

Peel the tomatoes and cut into chunks. Fry the chopped spring onions in the olive oil and almost immediately add the artichokes and tomatoes; cook over a moderate flame for 10–15 minutes or until the artichokes are tender. Then add the wine and simmer for another 5 minutes, season with salt, pepper and the parsley.

Cook the tagliatelle as usual, drain and mix in half the sauce. Serve in warm plates with the remainder of the sauce and with grated Parmesan cheese sprinkled on top.

TAGLIATELLE CON TARTUFI
Tagliatelle with White Truffles

One of the most popular and sought-after dishes in Alba is simply the combination of freshly made tagliatelle with the sophisticated rich white truffle only to be found from October through to the end of January, in the district of Piedmont. I hope you have a good friend who will give you a present of a truffle.

For this dish choose only the best Parmesan.

Serves 4

450 g (1 lb) home-made tagliatelle
100 g (4 oz or ½ US cup) unsalted butter
60 g (2 oz or ½ US cup) freshly grated Parmesan cheese from a newly opened parmigiano reggiano
1 small white truffle
salt and freshly ground black pepper

Cook the tagliatelle al dente. Toss in the butter and mix in the freshly grated Parmesan cheese. Season with salt and pepper. Present the tagliatelle to your guests served on separate plates. Shave the precious truffle with a 'mandolino' directly on to each serving.

AGNOLOTTI, BURRO E SALVIA
Agnolotti with Butter and Sage

Most of the work that is involved in this recipe consists of making the agnolotti, and so I have combined them with a very simple sauce of butter and sage. For the filling, which can be very varied, the ideal ingredient is scraps of roast meat: when finely chopped and mixed with the other ingredients, these will give an excellent flavour. Serve 10 agnolotti per person if their size is 4 cm (1½ inches) or so; serve a few more if they are smaller.

Agnolotti is the name they have in Piedmont for ravioli.

Serves 4

450 g (1 lb) fresh pasta dough (see basic recipe)
For the filling:
50 g (2 oz) roast turkey or pork
50 g (2 oz) sliced mortadella
250 g (8 oz) Swiss chard or spinach
1 tbs finely chopped parsley
4 grates of nutmeg
salt and freshly ground black pepper
For the sauce:
60 g (2 oz or 4 tbs) unsalted butter
10 fresh sage leaves
60 g (2 oz or ½ US cup) freshly grated Parmesan cheese

Make the pasta dough and keep it covered until you are ready to roll it out in sheets.

To make the filling, cook Swiss chard (with its white stalks removed) or spinach in lightly salted water, drain well, squeezing out all the water, and chop. Meanwhile, chop the meat and

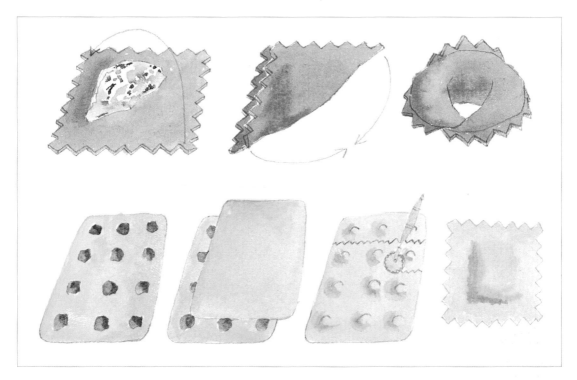

Making tortelloni (top) and ravioli or agnolotti (bottom)

mortadella and mix together with the cooked Swiss chard or spinach, parsley, salt, nutmeg and black pepper. Thoroughly stir or blend the mixture in order to obtain a smooth paste. Make the agnolotti as illustrated. Cook them in plenty of salted water for about 7 or 8 minutes. Meanwhile, melt the butter in a large pan, add the whole sage leaves and fry briefly. Drain the agnolotti and add to the melted butter. Lightly toss with a wooden spoon to make sure that the sage leaves and butter are well distributed. Sprinkle with some beautiful freshly grated Parmesan cheese and serve.

TORTELLONI DI MAGRO
Meatless Tortelloni

The word 'magro' means that the filling is based on vegetables and cheese and does not contain any meat. It is a very light and tasty dish which I wouldn't hesitate to recommend to all vegetarians. Accompany this dish with a fresh wild salad, and you will have a lovely summer meal. If, however, you add a meat sauce, you can make a more substantial main-course dish.

The essential ingredients are ricotta, which is a very low-fat cheese, and herbs, which can be varied according to their availability. I have made this dish with such herbs as mint, basil, coriander, chives, parsley, and either a little Swiss chard or its substitute, spinach.

Serves 4

450 g (1 lb) pasta dough (see basic recipe)
For the filling:
250 g (8 oz) Swiss chard or spinach leaves
150 g (5 oz or ⅔ US cup) fresh ricotta
1 tbs chopped mint, or other herbs
4 tbs freshly grated Parmesan cheese
salt and freshly ground black pepper
For serving:
60 g (2 oz or 4 tbs) butter
60 g (2 oz or ½ US cup) freshly grated Parmesan cheese

Clean and cook the chard or spinach leaves, drain well and squeeze out excess water, then finely chop. Make the filling by mixing together the chopped chard or spinach, the crumbled ricotta, the herbs, Parmesan cheese and salt and pepper. Prepare the pasta as in the basic recipe and roll it out as thinly as possible. Make the tortelloni as illustrated. Boil this pasta as usual and add to it a little melted butter and serve with extra Parmesan cheese at the table.

CAPPELLACCI AL SUGO DI PORCINI
Cappellacci with Mushroom Sauce

Once you are practised at making home-made pasta it will not be too much of a problem to make this dish which, like the two previous recipes, requires a little patience and a fair amount of ambition. The result will make you a truly popular person with your guests. These cappellacci can even be made the day before, but they must be stored overnight in the refrigerator wrapped in a clean cloth to prevent them from sticking together.

If you are unable to find fresh ceps, excellent results may be obtained by using common field mushrooms and 25 g (1 oz) of dried ceps.

Serves 6–8 (about 5 cappellacci each)

450 g (1 lb) fresh pasta (see basic recipe)
1 beaten egg for sealing the cappellacci
For the filling:
150 g (5 oz) fresh Italian sausage, or finely minced (ground) fresh pork
50 g (2 oz) roasted hazelnuts, finely chopped
4 tbs freshly grated Parmesan cheese
2 tbs chopped parsley
2 tbs chopped chives
5 grates of nutmeg
1 tbs olive oil
3–4 tbs double (heavy) cream
For the sauce:
250 g (½ lb) fresh ceps, or 250 g (½ lb) field mushrooms plus 25 g (1 oz) dried ceps soaked for 10 minutes in warm water
60 g (2 oz or 4 tbs) butter
1 clove garlic
half a glass of dry white wine
salt and freshly ground black pepper
1 tbs chopped parsley
60 g (2 oz or ½ US cup) freshly grated Parmesan cheese

Make the pasta according to the basic recipe, and set it aside while you make the filling. Lightly fry the sausage meat or pork for a few minutes in the olive oil, then set aside to cool. In a bowl mix together all the other ingredients for the filling and add the cooled meat.

Roll out the pasta dough as thin as possible and cut into circles of 8–9 cm (up to 3½ inches) in diameter. Cut only 2–3 circles at a time and always leave the pasta sheet covered with a cloth to prevent it from drying. Place a level teaspoon of the filling on each circle and fold over, sealing the edge with a little beaten egg. Then roll the semicircle of sealed pasta into a sausage and bend it round to join the ends together, pressing the seal down on the work surface with your thumb.

For the sauce, thoroughly clean the mushrooms, then cut them into slices and fry in butter. After they have cooked for a little while, add the finely chopped garlic and continue to cook for a couple of minutes more. Add the white wine, salt and pepper and let the liquid evaporate over a high flame for a minute or two. Then add the parsley. In the meantime, cook the pasta for about 8 minutes, drain and mix it into the sauce, sprinkling with the Parmesan cheese and serve immediately.

PAPPARDELLE AL SUGO DI ARROSTO
Pappardelle with Roast Beef Sauce

Pappardelle is a typical Tuscan dish which is usually served with a sauce based on hare meat. I find, however, the roast beef sauce even more succulent. The sauce is made simply by heating up the dish in which you have previously roasted some beef and dissolving the delicious pan juices in some wine.

Serves 4

fresh pappardelle made from 450 g (1 lb) pasta dough (see basic recipe) or 400 g (14 oz) dried pappardelle
60 g (2 oz or 4 tbs) butter
a glass of white wine
200 ml (½ pt or 1 US cup) roast beef juices (use stock to augment the meat juices if necessary)
salt and freshly ground black pepper
60 g (2 oz or ½ US cup) freshly grated Parmesan cheese

To make the sauce, scoop away most of the congealed fat from the pan in which you cooked the beef. Heat the dish over a low flame and use a spoon to scrape away and dislodge the tasty residue in the bottom of the pan. As the meat juices begin to bubble, stir in some white wine to deglaze the pan. Add a nut of butter and some salt and pepper if necessary. Meanwhile, cook the bought or home-made pappardelle al dente, drain and immediately mix with the rest of the butter, the freshly grated Parmesan cheese and the seasoned meat juices. Serve in heated pasta bowls as an exceptional first course.

PASTA E FAGIOLI
Pasta with Beans

This is one of the rare pasta dishes that enjoys equal popularity in all the different Italian regions. Apparently the best version of this dish is to be found in Naples, where scraps of pasta from the ends of different packets are mixed with spaghetti, which is crushed into spoon-sized pieces prior to cooking.

The best flavour is obtained by using fresh borlotti beans, which are admittedly slightly hard to come by in markets abroad. In Italy they are commonly found in the shops and markets around the month of August and are recognizable by their green and reddish colour. If you are unable to find the fresh variety you can also use the borlotti beans that are found in cans. Another excellent substitute are white cannellini beans (well favoured by the Neapolitans) which are smaller than the borlotti ones but very tasty.

Whenever I go for the first time to a new Italian restaurant I usually order pasta e fagioli in order to get an idea of the cook's skill. Indeed, because it is a dish that is easy to prepare, many cooks do not give it much of their attention and end up by completely spoiling one of the more famous rustic pasta meals.

Serves 6

1 kg (2 lb) fresh borlotti beans (with their skins); or 250 g (½ lb) dried borlotti or cannellini beans; or 2 medium cans of unsalted borlotti beans
2 celery stalks, finely chopped
4 tbs virgin olive oil
2 cloves garlic
100 g (4 oz) prosciutto trimmings, chopped into small cubes
2 medium potatoes, cut into cubes
3 ripe tomatoes, skinned and chopped, or a medium can of peeled plum tomatoes, chopped in the can
1 red chili pepper, chopped
100 g (4 oz) tubettini or mixed pasta
10 fresh basil leaves
1 litre (2 pt) stock
salt and freshly ground black pepper

If you are using dried beans leave them to soak in water the night before you use them. Then boil them in some unsalted water for 2–3 hours until they are tender. If you are using fresh beans boil these for 30–40 minutes until they are cooked. Of course, if you are preparing the dish with canned beans, there is no need to precook these, and they can be drained and added directly to the sauce.

Fry the chopped celery and the chopped prosciutto in a large saucepan in the olive oil over a medium flame. After a few minutes, add the chopped potatoes and chili, stirring to prevent the prosciutto from browning. After about 10 minutes add the finely chopped garlic and cook it for a couple of minutes before adding the tomatoes. Wait a further 10 minutes before adding two-thirds of the drained beans, but keep the remainder of these aside to be reduced to a mash and added to thicken the sauce. Pour in the broth or the water and bring to the boil. Now add the pasta and after 10 minutes, add the basil leaves and the mashed beans. Season with salt and pepper.

When serving you may find that pouring a trickle of olive oil over the dish greatly enhances the flavour. You can also place a basil leaf on top as a decoration.

SPAGHETTI CON BOTTARGA
Spaghetti with Bottarga

Bottarga is a typically Sardinian and Sicilian speciality. It merely consists of mullet roe – eggs that have been dried and salted, resulting in something like a dry caviar! As it is rather difficult to come by abroad, I always try to buy up a quantity when I am in Italy, as it keeps for some time. These dried eggs are simply grated over the cooked pasta, and give it a very distinctive flavour.

Serves 4

400 g (14 oz) thick spaghetti
50 g (2 oz or 3 tbs) butter
50 g (2 oz) bottarga
1 small dry red chili pepper (or 2 if you like), finely chopped
salt and freshly ground black pepper

Cook the large spaghetti for about 15 minutes or until it is al dente, melt some butter over it and sprinkle with some dried chili pepper. Serve on preheated dishes and grate the bottarga over the pasta. Season with black pepper and salt – taking into account, of course, that the bottarga will itself be very salty.

It is essential that you grate the bottarga over the spaghetti only seconds before serving.

GNOCCHETTI SARDI CON BROCCOLI
Sardinian Gnocchi with Broccoli

Another recipe that I have created is based upon
the combination of Sardinian gnocchetti, made
by the firm De Cecco, and greens. It has the
advantage of being absurdly easy to prepare. If,
for any reason, you cannot obtain calabrese or
broccoli, you can substitute cauliflower, though
the former is preferable for the distinct taste and
colouring it gives to the sauce.

Serves 4

500 g (1 lb) broccoli tips (cooked weight)
60 g (2 oz) smoked bacon, finely chopped
4 tbs olive oil
3 cloves garlic, sliced
200 ml (½ pt or 1 US cup) milk
400 g (14 oz) Sardinian gnocchetti
a little hot water from cooking the pasta
60 g (2 oz or ½ US cup) freshly grated Parmesan cheese
salt and freshly ground black pepper

Clean the broccoli tips, then boil them in some
lightly salted water until they are soft (about
12–15 minutes). Drain them, chop finely and then
put them to one side. Take quite a large pan and
start to fry the chopped bacon in the olive oil.
Once it begins to brown, add the slices of garlic,
which should not be allowed to colour. Next add
the chopped broccoli and the milk and cook for
10–15 minutes over a high flame, stirring every
now and again. At the end of this time the
broccoli should be reduced to a creamy texture.

Cook the gnocchetti for 12–15 minutes until
they are al dente, drain (reserving a little of the
water), then pour into the pan with the broccoli
mixture, adding the Parmesan, salt and pepper.
Add a spoonful or two of cooking water so that
the mixture is creamy rather than stiff. Stir well
over a moderate flame for a few minutes or so,
and serve in warm dishes.

Marille with tomato, basil and egg sauce (top left)
Sardinian gnocchi with broccoli (top right)
Bucatini with bacon, eggs and cream (bottom)

RAVIOLI DI PESCE
Fish Ravioli

Although ravioli can be made with almost any kind of fish, the best results are generally obtained with delicately flavoured firm-fleshed fish. Likewise, the accompanying sauce should be neither too rich nor too thick. One of my favourite recipes, given here, is based on a filling made with smoked salmon and large prawns (jumbo shrimp). Ravioli made in such a way needs only a simple sauce, such as saffron cream with chopped chives.

Serves 4

450 g (1 lb) pasta dough (see basic recipe)
For the filling:
100 g (4 oz) smoked salmon
100 g (4 oz) peeled giant prawns (shrimp)
1 tsp chopped chives
4 tbs freshly grated Parmesan cheese
1 tbs very finely chopped parsley
salt and freshly ground black pepper
For the sauce:
45 g (1½ oz or 3 tbs) butter
1 tbs white flour
1 sachet powdered saffron or a pinch of saffron strands
200 ml (½ pt or 1 US cup) water in which the prawns were poached
salt and freshly ground black pepper
For decoration:
1 tsp chopped chives

Cook the whole prawns in a little water, which you should keep for the sauce. When cooked, peel the prawns and blend them together with the other filling ingredients for about 10 seconds, or until they are only roughly puréed.

In the meantime, prepare the pasta dough and roll it out into thin sheets of equal size. Place on the pasta sheets at intervals of about 5 cm (2 inches) about half a teaspoonful of filling for each ravioli. Cover this with a second layer of dough and proceed to cut out the ravioli shapes. For the sauce, start to melt the butter in a pan over a low flame. Add to this the flour and the saffron and cook for a minute. Reheat the broth and gradually mix it into the flour mixture with a whisk until you obtain a creamy sauce. Season with salt and pepper.

Cook and drain the ravioli, cover with the sauce, and at the last moment sprinkle finely chopped chives over it.

Fresh pasta

SPAGHETTI ALLA CHITARRA
'Guitar' Spaghetti

As the name of this dish suggests, this type of square-section pasta is made with an instrument similar to a guitar with wires strung across it which cut the dough when pressed with a rolling pin. This is a speciality of the Abruzzo region where the sauces accompanying the spaghetti are usually based on either pancetta, tomatoes, pecorino cheese or Parmesan cheese. Unless you have in your possession a 'guitar' for making spaghetti, the only other alternative is to buy ready-made spaghetti.

Serves 4

350 g (¾ lb) square 'guitar' spaghetti, or 450 g (1 lb) pasta dough (see basic recipe)
For the sauce:
100 g (4 oz) smoked pancetta or bacon, sliced thinly
4 tbs olive oil
1 large sprig of fresh rosemary
1 large can of peeled tomatoes
salt and freshly ground black pepper
60 g (2 oz or ½ US cup) grated pecorino cheese, or Parmesan cheese

If you happen to possess the instrument for making 'guitar' spaghetti, take special care to knead the dough extremely thoroughly (alternatively, buy ready-prepared spaghetti).

For the sauce, fry the bacon (sliced into small pieces) in the oil until it is golden-brown. Add first the rosemary, which you should take out before serving, then the peeled and finely chopped tomatoes, and simmer for 15–20 minutes. Add pepper, but test before adding any salt, as the pancetta is often sufficiently salty. Cook the pasta until it is al dente, mix together with the tomato sauce and half of the grated pecorino cheese. Serve with the rest of the grated pecorino.

SPAGHETTINI CON FRUTTI DI MARE
Seafood Spaghettini

In every coastal town in Italy and in most restaurants you can find on the menu spaghetti with clams, mussels or other types of seafood. These seafood pastas are basics of Italian gastronomy but will vary enormously from region to region. These dishes are extremely easy to prepare – the most important point to remember is that the fish should be very fresh, as the main flavour of the dish comes from the water that the clams or mussels produce in cooking. It is the taste of this water that reminds me of balmy summer evenings at the seaside.

Serves 4

2 kg (4 lb) mixed fresh shellfish such as clams, mussels, etc
4 tbs olive oil
2 cloves garlic, thinly sliced
1 dried hot red chili pepper
half a glass of white wine
2 tbs chopped parsley
400 g (14 oz) spaghettini
salt and a generous quantity of freshly ground black pepper

Clean the shellfish under running water with a scrubbing brush. Then put them all into a saucepan containing about half a wineglass of water and heat over a high flame. Cover the pan with a lid and shake vigorously a few times until all the shells have opened. Remove from the heat and leave to cool. Then take the fish from their shells and filter the remaining liquid.

Heat the olive oil in a large heavy pan, add the thinly sliced garlic and fry for about a minute, taking care that the garlic does not become brown. Crumble the chili into the garlic and add the white wine, letting it evaporate a little. Pour in the shelled fish and their liquid and finally add the chopped parsley.

Cook the spaghettini according to the instructions on the packet in plenty of salted water. When it is al dente, drain and mix in a little of the sauce. Serve in preheated dishes with the remainder of the sauce and the freshly ground pepper.

FUSILLI CON RICOTTA E MOZZARELLA
Fusilli with Ricotta and Mozzarella

Even though the best kind of fusilli is the home-made variety, this recipe can be successful using the spiral type which is to be found in almost any store. As liquid is readily absorbed by this pasta, it is best to make a larger quantity of sauce than normal for this dish. Ideally, you should use ripe freshly picked tomatoes, but if this proves impossible the canned variety preserved with basil will do. This is a delicious dish to serve to your vegetarian friends.

Serves 4

750 g (1½ lb) ripe 'sauce' tomatoes, or a large can of peeled tomatoes, chopped in the can
1 small onion
3 tbs olive oil
some fresh basil leaves
350–400 g (12–14 oz) fusilli
1 mozzarella, cut into small cubes
150 g (5 oz or ⅔ US cup) ricotta
salt and freshly ground black pepper
30 g (good 1 oz or 6 tbs) freshly grated Parmesan cheese

Immerse the tomatoes for a minute or so in boiling water so that the skin comes away easily and then roughly chop them. Slice the onion and lightly fry it in the olive oil until it becomes golden. Add the tomatoes and cook for 15 minutes, stirring from time to time. At the final stage add the basil leaves and seasoning.

Preheat the oven to 200°C (400°F or gas mark 6). Cook the pasta until it is al dente, drain it, and mix it with half of the tomato sauce. Put half of this seasoned pasta into a flat ovenproof dish (the earthenware dishes sold for lasagna are best), cover with a layer of crumbled ricotta (use only half), and then dot with half of the mozzarella cubes. Pour over this the remaining pasta mixture, and top this layer with the rest of the ricotta and then the mozzarella. Finally spoon over the remainder of the tomato sauce, and sprinkle Parmesan cheese over the top. Bake in the medium-hot oven for 25–30 minutes.

TRENETTE COL PESTO
Trenette with Pesto Sauce

The famous Pesto alla genovese is without doubt one of the classic sauce recipes of Italian cooking. Its true home, however, is in Liguria, where the ingredients needed can be obtained all the year round. There are many different variations of this sauce, which is always accompanied by the large flat spaghetti called trenette, or else by home-made pasta shapes called trofie.

In summer when basil is in season and abundant, it's worth not only making pesto freshly for this dish according to the accompanying recipe, but making a quantity large enough to freeze. Out of season, however, when you can come by only a couple of fresh basil leaves, I suggest you 'improve' a jar of bought pesto by freshening it up in the following way.

Serves 4

400 g (14 oz) trenette
For the 'improved' pesto sauce:
4 tbs virgin olive oil
120 g (4 oz) jar of bought pesto
2 tbs chopped fresh basil
½ clove garlic, finely chopped
20 g (¾ oz or 1½ tbs) butter
4 tbs freshly grated Parmesan cheese

Cook the trenette in boiling salted water until al dente (about 10 minutes). Meanwhile, make the sauce. Gently heat the olive oil in a small saucepan, add the pesto sauce from the jar, the chopped fresh basil, the garlic and the butter. Stir briefly, and then add half a ladleful of pasta cooking water. Drain the trenette and mix with half the sauce and the grated Parmesan, then put the remainder of the sauce on top. Mix well and serve immediately.

If you are lucky enough to be using freshly made pesto, gently warm 200 g (7 oz) pesto over a low heat, but do not boil. Dilute the sauce with 2 or 3 spoonfuls of the pasta cooking water, drain the trenette and proceed as above.

PESTO ALLA GENOVESE
Pesto Sauce

This recipe requires a fair amount of fresh basil, if you cannot find enough, supplement one fistful with fresh flat-leaved Italian parsley. This alternative makes an excellent, albeit different, pesto. In most countries, it is possible to make a lot of pesto when basil is plentiful and not at an exorbitant price. To preserve it, you should take the quantities in this recipe and multiply them by four. This will give you about 16 or so individual portions. These are best divided into small jars.

You may also preserve pesto by freezing. Fill the squares of an ice tray with pesto and place in the freezer. When frozen, remove the squares from the ice tray and store in a plastic bag in the freezer. The advantage of this is that you can take out individual cubes without having to defrost the others.

The simplest way to make this sauce is to put all the ingredients in an electric mixer and blend very briefly until you have a rough textured sauce. You can also pound the ingredients in a pestle and mortar. The resulting pesto will have a completely different texture to the machine-made one. (However, I prefer to chop all the ingredients using a very sharp large knife: this method seems to me to retain the flavours better.)

Makes 200 g (7 oz) of pesto

1 clove garlic
2 fistfuls fresh basil leaves
25 (1 oz) pine nuts
4 tbs grated pecorino picante
4 tbs grated Parmesan cheese
100 ml (¼ pt or ½ US cup) olive oil
salt

Chop the basil leaves roughly and slice the garlic. In your pestle, grind the garlic to a paste, add the basil leaves and pound until they begin to break up. Add the pine nuts and as you pound them they will begin to amalgamate with the basil. At this point, slowly start to dribble in the olive oil; when the sauce has become liquid, add the pecorino and Parmesan cheese, stir in well and season with salt. How much salt depends on the type of pecorino cheese you have used. Some varieties can be very salty.

ORECCHIETTE BARESI AL RAGÙ
Orecchiette with Ragout

This recipe is a speciality of Bari in the Puglia region. Orecchiette are a type of pasta known in other areas as cecatielli, and are generally hand-made. Their conical form resembles little hats more than the ears to which the name refers. For commercially produced orecchiette you can turn to the De Cecco firm.

The ragout served with this pasta needs to be left to simmer for about 2 hours so the sauce is condensed considerably. In southern Italy the custom is to eat the sauce with the pasta as a first course and then serve the meat as a main course. The best meat to use for this is a good piece of pork together with a chunk of lamb, preferably on the bone. My mother used to make the ragout with little dumplings prepared with 1 kg (2 lb) minced meat, 2 tablespoons chopped parsley, 1 clove of garlic, the crumbs from 3 bread rolls and 60 g (2 oz) of grated Parmesan. These 'dumplings' were first slightly grilled on all sides before being put into the sauce. It was a simple, economical but delicious dish.

Serves 4

500 g (1 lb) pork with bone
500 g (1 lb) lamb with bone
4 tbs olive oil
1 large onion
1 large glass of red wine
1 kg (2 lb) ripe 'sauce' tomatoes (if you use fresh tomatoes they must be very ripe and juicy) or 1 large and one medium can of peeled tomatoes
salt and freshly ground black pepper
400 g (14 oz) orecchiette
60 g (2 oz or ½ US cup) grated Parmesan cheese

Lightly fry the meat in the oil so that it turns a golden colour. Add the onion and continue to fry over a high flame until this too becomes light brown. Add the glass of wine and allow it to bubble, which will accentuate the flavour of the meat juices. Now add the tomatoes and cut them roughly with a knife in the pan. Stir to combine with the meat. Continue to cook the sauce over a very low flame for at least 2 hours, taking care to stir it every now and again so that nothing sticks to the bottom of the pan. Finally, season with salt and pepper. The sauce will have extra flavour if cooked in a terracotta pot. If you find that it becomes too thick, you may add a drop of water. Because this is a sauce that requires a lengthy cooking time, it may be prepared the day before and then reheated when the dish is to be served.

Boil the orecchiette until they are al dente. Remove the meat from the sauce, mix the sauce with the pasta and the grated Parmesan cheese, then stir together for a moment or the low heat.

The meat, as I have already suggested, can be served as a second course together with peas or boiled new potatoes.

BUCATINI ALLA CARBONARA
Bucatini with Bacon, Eggs and Cream

Some people say the name carbonara is derived from the Carbonari, those revolutionaries who before 1861 worked to unify Italy. Somebody else says carbonara derives from coal. Wherever it comes from, whoever cooked it for the first time had a brilliant idea: the use of uncooked yolks of eggs as a sauce. In the recipe use Barilla's spaghetti no. 7 (fairly thick) or bucatini, spaghetti with a hole through it.

Serves 4

400 g (14 oz) bucatini
200 g (7 oz) pancetta affumicata (in one piece)
3 tbs olive oil
2 egg yolks (preferably free-range eggs)
2 whole eggs
4 tbs double (heavy) cream
60 g (2 oz or ½ US cup) freshly grated Parmesan cheese
salt and freshly ground black pepper

Remove the skin and little bones from the piece of pancetta. Cut into 1 cm (½ inch) strips. Put a large saucepan of water on to boil. Beat the egg yolks with the eggs, add the cream, a pinch of salt (this depends on how salty the pancetta is) and the grated Parmesan.

Heat the olive oil in a pan and fry the pieces of pancetta, turning them over until they become golden and slightly crisp.

Put the bucatini into boiling salted water; it will take about 8–10 minutes to cook, then drain it. Use the water you drain from the pasta to heat your serving bowl. Mix the drained bucatini with the pancetta and the hot oil from the pan. Put into your heated serving bowl and mix together with the egg, cream and Parmesan mixture. Season and serve immediately with additional Parmesan at the table.

FETTUCCINE NERE CON PEOCI
Black Fettuccine with Mussels, Garlic and Parsley

Peoci are those beautiful Adriatic mussels, very
sweet in taste, that you can find only in Venice.
Also in Venice the deep black ink of the very
small tender seppia or cuttlefish is the basis for
many delicious recipes. I use the ink to create
one of the most sophisticated and elegant pasta
dishes you can imagine. You must try this recipe
which is not only beautiful but delicate in
flavour and will certainly give you plenty of
admiration from your guests.

Serves 4

400 g (14 oz) home-made black fettuccine (see basic recipe for black pasta on page 59)
1.5 kg (3 lb) fresh mussels in their shells
4 tbs olive oil
1 clove garlic
half a glass of white wine
2 tbs chopped parsley
salt and freshly ground black pepper
50 ml (2 fl oz or ¼ US cup) water

Scrub the mussels clean. In a saucepan with a lid
put the mussels, 2 tablespoons of the olive oil
and a little water. Over a strong flame steam the
mussels open. The moment they are all open put
the pan aside to cool a little. When cool remove
the mussels from their shells and strain the liquid
remaining in the saucepan.

Put the pasta water on to boil. In a separate
pan heat the remainder of the olive oil, fry the
garlic for a minute, add the wine and the liquid
from the mussels, evaporate a little just to reduce
the sauce and then add the mussels and remove
from the heat. Cook the fresh fettuccine al dente
– it will take less than 1 minute – add the
drained pasta to the mussels in the pan, stir
together for a minute to fully incorporate the
flavour of the sauce. Scatter the parsley over it
and serve immediately.

TAGLIOLINI PRIMAVERA
Spring Tagliolini

Why I persist in calling this dish 'spring' tagliolini
is a mystery even to me, as most of the herbs
involved are to be found throughout the
summer months. You may, however, make this
recipe as soon as you find sufficient quantities of
the fresh herbs which are the basis of the sauce.

The ideal pasta to be used in this dish would be
home-made tagliolini, but once more
compromise is permitted, and commercially
bought 'paglia e fieno' can prove satisfactory.

Serves 4

400 g (14 oz) paglia e fieno, or 450 g (1 lb) fresh pasta dough (see basic recipe)
2 tbs chopped fresh mint
2 tbs chopped fresh coriander
2 tbs chopped fresh parsley
1 tbs chopped fresh dill
1 tbs chopped sage
2 tbs chopped fresh basil
30 g (good 1 oz or 6 tbs) pine nuts, chopped
2 tbs olive oil
100 g (4 oz or ½ US cup) butter
1 clove garlic, finely chopped
30 g (good 1 oz or 6 tbs) freshly grated Parmesan cheese
salt and freshly ground black pepper

Make the pasta dough according to the basic
recipe. Roll it out and cut it into tagliolini – the
thinnest of pasta ribbons. Make a paste by
chopping together on a board all the herbs
(include any others that you might have, such as
thyme or marjoram) and the nuts, and mixing in
the oil. In a pan melt the butter and add the
chopped garlic, which should just be allowed to
soften.

Boil the pasta in salted water; the dried variety
will take 5 minutes, the home-made sort 3
minutes. Drain, retaining a little of the cooking
water. At this point, mix the garlic and butter in
with the herb paste and the Parmesan cheese,
season with salt and pepper, and add a drop of
the hot pasta water to make the sauce a more
creamy consistency.

Thoroughly mix the paste into the pasta, taste
for seasoning, and serve on warm plates.

ZITI AL FORNO CON MELANZANE E RICOTTA
Timbale of Pasta with Aubergine (Eggplant) and Ricotta

This dish which slightly resembles the Greek
moussaka is typical of extreme southern regions
of Italy such as Sicily and Calabria. It is set apart
from other pasta dishes as it is substantial
enough to be served as a main course
accompanied merely by a salad. Any large type

of pasta may be used and you can even mix different varieties. However, in this recipe I use ziti, which make the timbale slightly softer.

Serves 6–8

400 g (14 oz) ziti
500 g (1 lb) aubergine (eggplant), thinly sliced
300 ml (15 fl oz or 1⅔ US cups) oil for frying
flour for dusting
For the layers:
300 g (10 oz or 1⅔ US cups) ricotta cheese
80 g (3 oz or ⅔ US cup) grated Parmesan cheese
100 g (4 oz) thin slices of Neapolitan salami
For the tomato sauce:
4 tbs olive oil
1 clove garlic
1 large can plum tomatoes (chopped in the can)
10 fresh basil leaves
salt
For the béchamel:
1.2 litres (a good 2 pt) milk
80 g (3 oz or 5–6 tbs) butter
65 g (2½ oz or 8 tbs) plain white flour
4 grates of nutmeg
salt and freshly ground black pepper

Slice the aubergines, salt them and leave for 30 minutes in a colander to sweat out their bitter juices. In the meantime, make the tomato sauce and the béchamel.

For the tomato sauce, heat the olive oil and fry the garlic only for a minute or two, then add the chopped tomatoes and cook together, reducing the tomatoes to a sauce. Cook for 15 minutes. Season with the basil leaves at the end so that their full flavour is not impaired, and add salt and pepper.

To make the béchamel, heat the milk in a small saucepan to hot but not boiling. Melt the butter in a separate saucepan and stir in the flour. Cook, stirring all the time, over a moderate heat for at least 5 minutes. Don't let the butter and flour brown. Then slowly add the hot milk little by little, continue to stir until you have incorporated all the milk. Turn the flame down low and simmer for a further 5–10 minutes. Season with the grated nutmeg, salt and pepper.

Put on a large saucepan of water to cook the pasta and preheat the oven to 200°C (400°F or gas mark 6). Wipe the aubergine slices dry and dust with flour. Heat some of the oil for frying the aubergine and when hot fry the slices 3 or 4 at a time. When golden, put aside to drain on kitchen paper. It takes time to fry all the aubergines and you will have to add further oil to the pan from time to time.

Put the ziti to boil in the salted water and cook until al dente. Drain and mix with a little pasta water to prevent sticking.

Take a large baking tin or dish. Spread 3 or 4 spoonfuls of the tomato sauce over the bottom, arrange a layer of the pasta on top and then make a layer of half the aubergine slices followed by the salami. Crumble half the ricotta cheese over the salami, sprinkle this with grated Parmesan and then generously pour over some béchamel sauce. Start again with a layer of tomato sauce followed by the pasta, etc. Fill up the dish with a second layer. The final layer should be tomato sauce dribbled over the béchamel and then scattered with a crust of Parmesan. Place the dish in the oven and bake for 20 minutes.

CRESPOLINE ALLA FIORENTINA
Crespoline with Ricotta and Spinach

Nobody can explain why when spinach and ricotta are brought together it is called 'alla fiorentina'. Indeed, crespoline (or crespelle) alla fiorentina figures on the menu in many Italian restaurants. This is an excellent dish to serve to any vegetarian. Here I use pancakes to roll round the filling, though giant pasta shells or hand-made pasta made in the shape of cannelloni can also be used as containers.

Serves 4

For 8 pancakes 10 cm (4 inches) in diameter:
1 egg
60 g (2½ oz or ½ US cup plus 1 tbs) flour
60 ml (2 fl oz or ¼ US cup) milk
oil for frying
For the filling:
400 g (14 oz) fresh spinach
280 g (9 oz or 1½ US cups) ricotta
salt and freshly ground black pepper
6 grates of nutmeg
For the tomato sauce:
5 tbs olive oil
half a small onion, chopped
1 large can peeled plum tomatoes
salt and freshly ground black pepper
8 fresh basil leaves
150 ml (5 fl oz or ¼ pt) béchamel sauce (see left)
40 g (scant 1½ oz or 8 tbs) freshly grated Parmesan cheese

Make the pancake batter by beating the egg with a whisk and gradually adding the flour, salt and finally the milk until you obtain a liquid batter. Put aside to stand for half an hour.

For the filling, clean and cook the spinach. Squeeze out excess water, then finely chop the spinach and add it to the ricotta, mixing in at the same time the salt, pepper and nutmeg.

To make the sauce, chop the onion and fry it gently in the oil for a few minutes. Add the tomatoes (which you have roughly chopped up in the tin using a long knife), and salt and pepper. Cook for 15 minutes and then add the basil just before the end, when the sauce has thickened. Heat a little oil in a pancake pan and fry 8 very thin pancakes. Meanwhile, preheat the oven to hot (220°C, 425°F or gas mark 7). Make the crespoline by putting a spoonful or two of filling into each pancake and then rolling it up, resulting in something resembling a cannelloni.

Now line a large shallow baking dish with half the tomato sauce, cover this with half the béchamel, place the crespoline in the dish, cover them with a further layer of béchamel and finally the remainder of the tomato sauce. Sprinkle with the Parmesan and place in a hot oven for 15–20 minutes.

FESTONI DEL GHIOTTONE
Gourmet Lasagna

This dish reminds me above all of those interminable Christmas meals where succulent course follows succulent course. As it requires quite a lot of preparation work, I would recommend that you only attempt to make it on important occasions. Because festoni is such a rich and substantial dish, you may wish to make it a main course, accompanied only by salad.

Serves 8 as a main course

For the meatballs:

300 g (10 oz) minced (ground) meat
1 clove garlic, finely chopped
1 tbs chopped parsley
30 g (good 1 oz or 6 tbs) freshly grated Parmesan cheese
2 medium eggs
40 g (1½ oz or 1 US cup) fresh bread crumbs, soaked in a little milk and then squeezed dry
salt and freshly ground black pepper
oil for frying

For the sauce:

4 tbs olive oil
1 medium onion, chopped
100 g (4 oz) chicken livers, washed, dried and chopped
2 large cans of peeled tomatoes
5 basil leaves
salt and freshly ground black pepper

For the layers:

500 g (1 lb) festoni
100 g (4 oz) spicy Neapolitan salami, sliced
300 g (10 oz) fontina cheese, sliced
80 g (3 oz or ⅔ US cup) freshly grated Parmesan cheese
4 medium eggs, beaten

Preheat the oven to 200°C (400°F or gas mark 6).

Make a paste by mixing the minced meat, the finely chopped garlic, parsley, Parmesan cheese, eggs and the soaked bread crumbs. When you have thoroughly stirred this mixture and added some salt and pepper start shaping from it little walnut-sized meat balls which you then fry in oil until they are of a golden colour.

Prepare the sauce by frying in fresh oil the chopped onion; when it is only half-cooked, add the chopped chicken liver. When these ingredients are cooked (after about 3 minutes) you can add the chopped tomatoes and continue to simmer for about half an hour over a low heat. Towards the end of this time, add the fresh basil leaves, the salt and the pepper.

Cook the pasta for 5–7 minutes or until it is al dente, drain, then add some of the sauce so that it is all coated. Take a deep baking tin and start making the timbale by spreading a layer of sauce over the bottom on to which you arrange some of the cooked festoni. Next on top of the pasta place some of the sliced salami, some meat balls and some slices of fontina cheese. Cover these with another 3 or 4 spoonfuls of sauce and a sprinkling of Parmesan cheese. Repeat this procedure until you have used up all the ingredients. When you have reached the final layer of fontina, pour on the well-beaten eggs, which will bind the pasta together. Over this pour the last of the sauce and the Parmesan cheese.

Put the tin in the oven for 25 minutes. When ready, leave the dish for 5 minutes before dividing into portions with a knife and serving hot. You will find the washing up involved in this recipe quite considerable but it is more than justified by the end result.

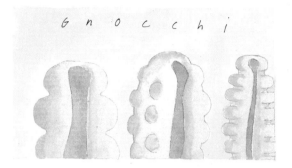

GNOCCHI
Basic Gnocchi Recipe

This is a variation on the normal pasta recipe containing the extra ingredient of potatoes: choose good-quality floury ones. It is an Italian speciality par excellence and can be made in a variety of ways. In Italy the region of Piedmont is considered the capital of gnocchi.

Serves 4–6

900 g (2 lb) floury potatoes
200 g (7 oz or 2¼ US cups) flour
salt and freshly ground black pepper
butter and freshly grated Parmesan cheese for serving

Peel the potatoes and boil them in a little water in a closed saucepan until they are completely cooked. Drain away the remaining water and thoroughly mash the potatoes while they are still warm – take particular care to leave no lumps. Then start to knead the mash on a working surface adding flour from time to time so that you obtain a soft but elastic dough. Next, take a piece of the dough, sprinkle with some flour and roll it with your hands into a sausage-like shape with a diameter of 2 cm (¾ inch).

Slice the cylinder of dough into little squares 3 cm (1¼ inches) long and repeat this operation until all the dough is transformed into chunks.

Then take a large, preferably wooden fork, hold it in your left hand prongs down and with your thumb squeeze the chunks of dough against the prongs, letting the gnocchi roll off on to a clean cloth. Repeat with all the chunks. They should curl up like ribbed shells as they roll off the fork.

Cook the gnocchi in abundant salted boiling water. When they are ready you will see them float to the surface and should be scooped out and placed directly in a preheated dish. Sprinkle with a little freshly grated Parmesan cheese and pieces of butter.

Other sauces that go exceedingly well with gnocchi are a simple tomato sauce made with fresh basil or the Piedmontese sauce alla bava.

STRANGOLAPRIEVITI
Priest-choker

The strange name given to this dish is based on the commonly known fact that a good priest likes good food. Indeed, one such Neapolitan priest liked his food so much that he was suffocated by eating too much all at once!

However, do not be put off by this lugubrious story – especially as the sauce involved is simplicity itself to prepare.

Serves 6

gnocchi made with 900 g (2 lb) potatoes and 200 g (7 oz or 2¼ US cups) flour (see basic recipe)
For the sauce:
3 tbs olive oil
1 large can peeled tomatoes
10 basil leaves
salt and freshly ground black pepper
60 g (2 oz or ½ US cup) freshly grated Parmesan cheese

Make the sauce by pouring the tomatoes, which you can roughly chop in the can with a long knife, into the heated olive oil. Simmer for 15 minutes, stirring from time to time, until the sauce has begun to thicken, then add the basil leaves, salt and pepper.

Now cook the gnocchi as described in the previous recipe, add the cheese and the sauce and mix thoroughly into the gnocchi. Serve hot – and be careful not to choke.

Fresh gnocchi

GNOCCHI DI SPINACI E GORGONZOLA
Spinach and Gorgonzola Gnocchi

The essence of gnocchi is their lightness.
However, I remember once inviting to supper a
friend of mine who was going to start up a
restaurant and wanted some advice on how to
compose a menu. I naturally wanted to impress
her, and served up these spinach gnocchi.
Imagine my embarrassment when the gnocchi I
had prepared turned out as hard as lead, and
made a sound like a report as they went down
the throat into the stomach! To avoid a similar
experience, make sure the spinach is well
drained, and use the right proportions of
ingredients for the desired lightness of texture.

Serves 4

750 g (1½ lb) floury potatoes (peeled weight)
200 g (7 oz) spinach
200 g (7 oz or 2¼ US cups) flour
salt and freshly ground black pepper
For the sauce:
60 g (2 oz or 4 tbs) butter
100 ml (5 fl oz or ½ US cup) milk
100 g (4 oz) gorgonzola cheese
60 g (good 2 oz or ½ US cup) freshly grated
Parmesan cheese

Cut the gorgonzola cheese into cubes and soak in
the milk for half an hour while you make the
gnocchi. Cook the potatoes and pass them
through a food mill. Wash the spinach
thoroughly and cook it in very little water.
Drain, squeeze out all excess water, then chop
finely. Add the spinach to the potatoes and the
flour and mix well together, then make gnocchi
as in the basic recipe.

Prepare the sauce by melting the butter in a
saucepan, then add the gorgonzola and milk,

and stir until the ingredients have become
amalgamated. When the gnocchi are cooked,
add them to the sauce, add the freshly grated
Parmesan cheese, mix well and serve hot.

GNOCCHI ALLA BAVA
Gnocchi with Fontina Cheese

This is one of the most typical of Piedmontese
dishes. The term alla bava refers to the cheese
which comes away in strands when served on
top of the piping hot gnocchi. Many good
restaurants and some small inns invariably
include this dish on their menu.

Serves 6

gnocchi made with 900 g (2 lb) potatoes and
200 g (7 oz or 2¼ US cups) flour (see basic recipe)
175 g (6 oz) fontina cheese from the Val d'Aosta,
cut into small pieces
30 g (good 1 oz or 2 tbs) butter
80 g (3 oz or ⅔ US cup) freshly grated Parmesan
cheese
salt and freshly ground black pepper

Preheat the oven to 220°C (425°F or gas mark 7).
Cook the gnocchi as described in the basic
recipe. Butter a baking dish and cover with a
layer of gnocchi, sprinkle this layer with fontina
cheese cut into small pieces, a little of the
Parmesan, salt and pepper and finally cover the
surface with little bits of butter. Repeat these
layers until you have used up all the ingredients.
The top should be liberally sprinkled with
Parmesan.
Put the dish into a very hot oven for 15
minutes and serve with a generous quantity of
Parmesan cheese and a sprinkling of freshly
ground black pepper.

GNOCCHI ALLA ROMANA
Semolina Gnocchi

This speciality from the Lazio region does not bear much resemblance to ordinary gnocchi as the pasta is made differently, using semolina flour cooked in milk. Care must be taken to think out the menu if you are serving this dish, because although it is delicious it is also extremely filling.

Serves 4

1 litre (1¾ pt or 4½ US cups) milk
½ tsp salt
4 grates of nutmeg
450 g (1 lb or 2½ US cups) coarse semolina flour
2 whole eggs plus 1 yolk
60 g (2 oz or 4 tbs) butter
30 g (1 oz or 6 tbs) freshly grated Parmesan cheese

Heat the milk together with a pinch of salt and some nutmeg. When it begins to boil add the semolina flour little by little stirring all the time with a whisk so that lumps don't begin to form. Once all the semolina is so incorporated, leave the mixture to simmer for about 20 minutes over a low heat, stirring from time to time. Next take the pan from the stove, leave it a moment or so to cool down, then thoroughly stir in the beaten eggs. Pour the mixture out on to a working surface (this should preferably be marble but if it is wood take care to slightly dampen the surface beforehand).

Using some kind of spatula, evenly spread the warm mixture to a thickness of 2 cm (¾ inch). Let it cool down. In the meantime, grease a baking tin with some butter. Preheat the oven to 220°C (425°F or gas mark 7).

Using a glass or a pastry cutter with a 5 cm (2 inch) diameter, cut out discs from the pasta and then place them in the tin, one overlapping the other. Dot the gnocchi with little pieces of butter and place in a very hot oven until the tips of the gnocchi begin to brown – about 15 minutes.

Take the dish out of the oven, sprinkle with some freshly grated Parmesan cheese and serve immediately.

Right: Semolina gnocchi

RISOTTO
Basic Risotto Method

Choose Arborio or Vialone rice, which will cook to the right consistency for a good risotto. Use a heavy saucepan with a rounded bottom to prevent the rice from sticking in the corners. It should be big enough to contain the rice, plus the liquid (broth or stock and wine) that will be slowly added to it, increasing the volume by as much as three times. The spoon for stirring must be a wooden one. The heat must be moderate and constant. The stock that is to be added to the rice must be kept simmering to avoid interruption of the cooking process; keep this pan next to the risotto pan.

Carefully coat the rice in the initial butter or oil before adding any liquid and turn the rice in the pan with a wooden spoon. You start to add the boiling stock when the rice is well and truly impregnated with butter and starts to stick to the bottom of the pan. Add only as much hot stock at a time as the rice calls for – that is, not too wet and drowning the rice, but enough to see the grains gradually absorbing the liquid as they cook – about a ladleful at a time. Continue to stir and add the stock until the rice appears to be cooked (after 20–25 minutes).

At this stage remove the pan from the heat and, without stirring, let the rice absorb the last liquid. The risotto should have a creamy consistency, but still be firm to bite. Just before serving add (with the exception of seafood and champagne risottos) a knob of butter and the freshly grated Parmesan cheese and stir well into the rice. This last operation is called mantecare, possibly from the Spanish manteca which means butter. Taste finally for the right seasoning and serve straight away. It is important to time the cooking so that this little work of art can be enjoyed and fully appreciated the moment the cheese has melted and the risotto is ready.

RISOTTO NERO
Black Risotto

This is a typically Venetian dish and is not always popular with everybody because of its slightly funereal appearance. It does, however, have an exceptional taste and is invariably to be found on the menu of all the renowned restaurants in Venice. This is another of my favourite dishes, which inevitably causes a stir when served. Use small cuttlefish, as the bigger ones are tougher.

Serves 4

500 g (1 lb) cuttlefish, to make 300 g (10 oz) when cleaned
1 small onion, chopped
2 tbs olive oil and 30 g (1 oz or 2 tbs) butter for frying
half a glass of white wine
350 g (12 oz or 1¾ US cups) Arborio rice
1.5 litres (3 pt) fish stock
a generous nut of butter
salt and freshly ground black pepper

Clean the cuttlefish: first pull off the head with the tentacles, then pull out the rest of the contents of the body, which is bag-shaped. Take out the backbone and remove the outside skin from the bag, which should end up white. Among the contents of the body, find the small sac containing the ink, and put it to one side, taking care that it does not split. (You will recognize it by its exterior colouring, which is a bluish-silver.) Discard the mouth, which is shaped like a small ball and situated in the middle of the tentacles, and the eyes, which are on the top of the head. Wash well and then slice the tentacles and body into 1 cm (½ inch) pieces.

Over a moderate flame heat the oil and butter for frying. Add the chopped onion and cook gently until it becomes transparent. Then add the cut-up cuttlefish and continue to fry for at least another 10 minutes, until the cuttlefish has coloured. Add the wine to the pan and without increasing the heat cook for another 5 minutes. Now pour in the rice, allow it to absorb the flavour for a couple of minutes, then gradually add the simmering fish broth as in the basic risotto method.

When the rice is nearly ready, add the ink from the cuttlefish sac to the last ladle of stock and stir into the rice. Finish cooking and remove from the fire, add the remaining nut of butter, salt and pepper to taste, and serve hot.

RISOTTO ALLO CHAMPAGNE
Champagne Risotto

Even though it is not at all necessary to use real champagne in this recipe, a certain degree of snobbism on my part has dictated that the recipe be called champagne risotto. In fact, a dry sparkling wine from Conegliano, to my mind, yields just as good results as if you had used a vintage Krug.

Serves 4

300 g (10 oz) fresh or frozen whole prawns (shrimp) – peeled weight – or 150 g (5 oz) scallops and 150 g (5 oz) peeled prawns
60 g (2 oz or 4 tbs) unsalted butter
5 tbs olive oil
1 small onion, chopped
2 cloves garlic, finely chopped
350 g (12 oz or 1¾ US cups) Arborio rice
1.5 litres (3 pt) fish broth (you can use the water in which the prawns were cooked and add 2 bouillon cubes)
2 glasses champagne or sparkling wine
1 tbs canned green peppercorns
salt
1 tbs chopped parsley

Boil the prawns for about 5 minutes in lightly salted water, drain, keeping the liquid, remove the shells and cut the flesh into small pieces.

Fry the onion in the oil and half the butter until it turns transparent. Add the finely chopped garlic and the prawns, tossing for a couple of minutes so all the flavours are absorbed. Then add the rice. Follow the basic method for cooking risotto, slowly adding the boiling broth and stirring continually with a wooden spoon. Towards the end of the cooking time, start pouring in the wine, instead of the last two ladlefuls of broth. Since the wine is cold, you will need to increase the heat so that the cooking process is not interrupted. Next, add the green pepper and the salt and just before serving add the rest of the butter and the parsley.

Serve piping hot, without cheese.

RISOTTO CON PORCINI
Mushroom Risotto

This dish is popular throughout northern Italy, especially in Piedmont. Together with truffle risotto, it is my favourite dish. (I know: 'Yet another!' you say to yourself, only this time it is true, for it combines both an excellent flavour and my favourite hobby of picking and eating wild mushrooms.) Faced with the perennial problem of finding fresh ceps in generous quantities, you can use ordinary mushrooms plus a few dried porcini for extra taste. But this risotto is also eminently suitable for those wild mushrooms that you have gathered in season and then frozen.

Serves 4

300–350 g (about 12 oz) firm small fresh ceps, or fresh button mushrooms plus 25 g (1 oz) dried ceps
1 small onion, finely chopped
2 tbs olive oil
30 g (1 oz or 2 tbs) butter
350 g (12 oz) Arborio rice
1.5 litres (3 pt) chicken stock, or water plus 2 bouillon cubes
salt and freshly ground black pepper
a further nut of butter
60 g (2 oz or ½ US cup) freshly grated Parmesan cheese

Gently clean the ceps or other mushrooms, using a sharp knife and a brush (avoid washing them whenever possible). If you are using dried ceps, put them to soak in a small bowl of water for 15 minutes. Meanwhile, slice the fresh ceps or mushrooms. Finely chop the onion and fry in the oil and butter. When the onion begins to colour, add the sliced ceps and continue to fry over a moderate flame for a couple of minutes. If using the dried ceps, chop them into small pieces and add to the mushrooms, keeping the water they soaked in to add to the risotto later with the stock. Add the rice and proceed according to the basic risotto method.

When the rice is al dente, remove from the heat, season, and stir in the nut of butter and the Parmesan cheese. Serve hot, if you like decorating each portion with a slice of mushroom.

RISOTTO CON ASPARAGI
Asparagus Risotto

Other vegetable risotto dishes can be prepared along the lines of this asparagus recipe. Instead of the asparagus, use any other vegetable that when slightly overcooked dissolves, leaving a creamy substance ideal for a risotto: broccoli, spinach, artichokes, marrow (squash), courgettes (zucchini), cauliflower. With some you can follow the principle of holding back a few choice pieces and decorating the cooked dish with broccoli florets or with rings of courgette, just as here asparagus tips are used. To enhance the flavour of the rice, recycle the water in which you cook the vegetables.

These risottos are perfect for vegetarians.

Serves 6

500 g (1 lb) fresh green asparagus (weighed cleaned and trimmed)
1.5 litres (3 pt) water (for cooking asparagus and for risotto)
2 bouillon cubes (you can buy vegetarian ones)
1 small onion, thinly sliced
60 g (2 oz or 4 tbs) butter
350 g (12 oz) Arborio rice
60 g (2 oz or ½ US cup) freshly grated Reggiano Parmesan cheese
salt and freshly ground black pepper

Wash and peel the asparagus and cut away 3 cm (1 good inch) or so of the hard white stalk at the bottom (use this and the skin to add flavour to the cooking water). Cut off about 5 cm (2 inches) of the tips and set them aside (as they are tender they will need less cooking) and keep them intact for decoration. Boil the asparagus stalks with the skins and scraps in 1.5 litres (3 pt) water to which you have added the stock cubes. When they are half-cooked add the tips. When fully cooked strain the stock and keep it simmering. Separate out the asparagus tips and stalks. Set the tips aside for decoration, but chop the stalks finely.

Fry the onion in half the butter, then add the chopped asparagus and toss it for a couple of minutes. Now add the rice and proceed as for the basic risotto method, adding the broth until the rice is al dente and creamy but not too solid with asparagus sauce. Remove from the heat and wait for a minute or two, then stir in the remaining butter and the freshly grated Parmesan cheese. Serve in bowls and decorate with asparagus tips.

RISOTTO ALLA MARINARA
Seafood Risotto

This delicious flavoursome dish is characteristic of nearly all coastal Italian regions. Even though different types of fish and shellfish are used in different areas, the common denominator may be considered to be their absolute freshness. The most common ingredients are clams, mussels, sea-dates, sea-truffles and even sea-urchins, and almost any shellfish found in the local market is added. Beware of using the frozen equivalents as they far from achieve the same effect. In this recipe, I particularly recommend that only olive oil be used.

Serves 4

500 g (1 lb) clams in their shells
500 g (1 lb) mussels in their shells
100 g (4 oz) prawns (shrimp) – peeled weight
200 g (7 oz) squid – cleaned weight
1 small onion, chopped
6 tbs olive oil
2 cloves garlic, chopped
half a glass of white wine
350 g (12 oz or 1¾ US cups) Arborio rice
1 tbs chopped parsley
1.5 litres (3 pt) water
salt and freshly ground black pepper

Clean all the shellfish with a scrubbing brush under running water. Put them in a saucepan with half a glass of water, and boil with the lid on until all the shells open (it helps if you shake the pan gently). Take the meat from the shells, set it aside and strain the cooking liquid. Clean the squid following the instructions given in the recipe for calamari fritti (page 113) and boil it together with the prawns in 1.5 litres (3 pt) of lightly salted water for 10 minutes.

Remove the squid and the prawns. Filter their cooking liquid and add it to the broth. Peel the prawns and cut the squid into pieces.

Fry the chopped onion in the oil over a moderate flame, adding the chopped garlic later. Pour in the wine and let it evaporate over an increased flame for about one minute. Next, add the rice and all the other shellfish (including the chopped squid) to the sauce, reduce the heat and proceed to cook the rice according to the basic risotto method, adding every now and again some of the broth. Once the rice is fully cooked, add the parsley, salt and pepper and serve straight away.

Seafood risotto (top) and asparagus risotto (bottom)

RISOTTO ALLA MILANESE CON LUGANEGA
Saffron Risotto with Sausage

Any rice dish that is described as 'milanese' usually contains some saffron. Saffron rice is in itself a very delicate dish; the addition of luganega turns it into something rather more substantial, which can even be served up as a main course. Luganega is fresh pork sausage that is sold by length (its name derives from the Greek 'lukanika'). This typically Lombardian or Milanese product was usually made in the winter months when the household pig was killed. Nowadays, however, this sausage can be found all the year round. It is recognizable by the fact that it is made in a very long intestine of about 3 cm (about 1¼ inches) in diameter. I suggest you substitute fresh pork if you can't obtain luganeghe.

Serves 4

300 g (10 oz) luganega pork sausage, or fresh minced (ground) pork meat
optional: salt, freshly ground black pepper and 4 grates of nutmeg to season fresh pork
1 small onion, chopped
60 g (2 oz or 4 tbs) butter
2 tbs olive oil
half a glass of dry white wine
350 g (12 oz or 1¾ US cups) Arborio rice
1.5 litres (3 pt) beef broth, or water plus 2 bouillon cubes
2 sachets powdered saffron, or 2 pinches saffron strands
100 g (4 oz or 1 US cup) grated Parmesan cheese

Remove the sausage skin and break the meat into pieces, or, if you are using fresh pork, season it with pepper, salt and nutmeg.

Fry the finely chopped onion in half the butter and the oil, added the sausage meat or the seasoned minced pork. After the onion has turned golden and the meat has browned, add the wine which you should let evaporate for a couple of minutes before pouring in the rice. You start to add the stock when the rice has absorbed all the butter and oil and when it begins to stick to the pan. Proceed now as for other risotto dishes, adding the salt, pepper and saffron as you progress.

When the rice is nearly cooked, incorporate the rest of the butter and half of the cheese. Serve on dishes with more grated cheese on top.

RISOTTO ALLE ERBE
Herb Risotto

This is a deliciously refreshing dish which is particularly suitable for meals in late spring when many varieties of herbs can be found and when, if the weather permits, meals may be eaten outside. It is not necessary to restrict yourself to the herbs mentioned here, but as in the recipe for tagliolini primavera, you may use whichever fresh herbs you please. However, don't attempt this dish using dried herbs.

Serves 4

1 small onion, chopped
60 g (2 oz or 4 tbs) butter
350 g (12 oz or 1¾ US cups) Arborio rice
1.5 litres (3 pt) chicken stock
at least 8 tbs finely chopped fresh herbs chosen from: mint, coriander, rosemary, sage, parsley, dill (use sparingly), basil, oregano, tarragon, thyme
10 walnut halves
1 clove garlic
60 g (2 oz or ½ US cup) freshly grated Parmesan cheese
salt and freshly ground black pepper

Lightly fry the chopped onion in half the butter over a moderate flame. Add the rice and proceed according to the basic risotto method, adding stock as needed. Meanwhile, chop the herbs and the walnuts with a knife and squeeze or crush the garlic. When the rice is half-cooked, add the chopped herbs, walnuts and garlic. When the rice is cooked, add the Parmesan and the rest of the butter. Add salt and pepper to taste and serve straight away.

RISOTTO AL BAROLO CON TARTUFI
Risotto with Barolo and Truffles

This dish can safely be nominated the most prestigious of all risottos. I have already suggested some uses for this 'jewel' of the fungus world in my pasta recipes, but this highly expensive and sought-after 'mushroom' also has many other virtues about which I will discourse in greater depth in a future book. However, in the meantime, I will permit myself to say that the white truffle from Alba is the most delicately flavoured food to be found in nature.

Owing to the fact that it is impossible to

cultivate the truffle and that it is sought after by many, its price is correspondingly exceedingly high. To set off this luxurious food I have incorporated it with one of the most princely Piedmontese wines – Barolo, which gives extra flavour and colour to the dish.

Serves 4

60 g (2 oz or 4 tbs) butter
1 small onion, finely chopped
2 glasses of Barolo wine
350 g (12 oz or 1¾ US cups) Arborio rice
1.5 litres (3 pt) clear meat or chicken broth, or water plus 2 bouillon cubes
salt and freshly ground black pepper
60 g (2 oz or ½ US cup) freshly grated Reggiano Parmesan cheese
white truffle, about 40 g (1½ oz), thinly sliced

Lightly fry the finely chopped onion in half of the butter. When this is fully cooked, add the two glasses of Barolo wine, and let it evaporate a little. Then add the rice and proceed as for other risottos, pouring in some broth gradually as the rice absorbs the liquid. When the rice is fully cooked, add salt, pepper and the remaining butter with the cheese. Mix well and serve on hot dishes. Decorate with slices of truffle.

POLENTA CONCIA ALLA NINA
Nina's Polenta

I have dedicated this polenta dish to Nina Burgai, who is the hospitable owner of a small hotel situated in the mountains of Chanpoluc in the Val d'Aosta. To visit her you first have to climb 2,000 metres, either on foot or with the help of the 'ovovia'. On arriving you soon discover that her hotel is more aptly described as a social club: indeed, when meeting her again after an absence, she will treat you to a powerful embrace followed closely by a double 'genepy', a liqueur made from mountain gentian. This is served not in the small bar but in the kitchen. Here, over the wood-fuelled stove, two large

Nina in her wonderful mountain environment in the Aosta valley

saucepans simmer, one containing polenta and the other a cabbage soup, giving the room a snug feel of isolation from the wintery weather outside. Even in summer, when the air is perfumed by the smell of pine trees, the odours produced in this kitchen provoke an incurable appetite. Not a hundred yards from this kitchen, the two main ingredients of this dish are produced: the first is the delicately flavoured alpine butter, the second is the fontina cheese made from the milk of Nina's cows. The other two ingredients, polenta and Parmesan cheese, are manufactured in the plains. Nina served this polenta with a chicken stew. Hare stew or, indeed, any other kind of stew would do just as well – although I am often tempted to eat it by itself.

Serves 4

1.5 litres (3 pt) salted water
300 g (10 oz or 1¾ US cups) polenta flour, or 1 packet (370 g, 13 oz or 2¼ US cups) Valsugana polenta
100 g (4 oz or ½ US cup) butter
100 g (4 oz or 1 US cup) freshly grated Parmesan cheese
100 g (4 oz) fontina cheese, cut into chunks

Bring the salted water to the boil. Then, very carefully add the flour, stirring constantly with a wooden spoon so that no lumps appear. You must continue to stir the polenta until you see that it starts to come away from the side of the saucepan. (This will take only 5 minutes if you are using Valsugana polenta, 30 minutes if you are using polenta flour.) When this happens, add the butter, the grated Parmesan cheese and the chunks of fontina, stirring all the time until you see that all the ingredients have melted and are thoroughly mixed with the polenta. Serve directly on to heated plates with your own choice of stew.

Polenta

PASTICCIO DI POLENTA
Timbale of Polenta

This polenta can be made in the same way as in the previous recipe, leaving out, however, the fontina and Parmesan cheeses. Only butter should be stirred into the cooked polenta: here the cheeses are added in layers to the dish before it is baked. You can prepare the polenta the day before.

Serves 4–6

1.5 litres (3 pt) salted water
300 g (10 oz or 1¾ US cups) polenta flour, or 1 packet (370 g, 13 oz or 2¼ US cups) Valsugana polenta
For the sauce:
1 small onion, chopped
2 tbs olive oil
1 large can peeled plum tomatoes, well chopped
a few fresh basil leaves, if available
salt and freshly ground black pepper
For the layers:
60 g (good 2 oz or 4 tbs) butter
200 g (7 oz) fontina cheese, cut into chunks
100 g (4 oz) gorgonzola cheese
100 g (4 oz or 1 US cup) freshly grated Parmesan cheese

Prepare a stiff polenta mixture, cooking the mixture slightly longer than in the previous recipe: 10 minutes for Valsugana polenta, 35 minutes for polenta flour. The polenta must begin to leave the sides of the pan. When cooked, spread it out on a board or surface with a spatula to a thickness of about 2.5 cm (1 inch). When it is cool, cut the polenta into 5 cm (2 inch) squares.

Preheat the oven to very hot: 230°C (450°F or gas mark 8). Fry the chopped onion in the olive oil until golden-brown. Add the well-chopped tomatoes and cook, stirring from time to time, for about 10 minutes. Season the sauce with salt and pepper and with fresh basil leaves if available.

To assemble the pie, oil a baking dish, spread a layer of tomato sauce and cover with the polenta squares. Then sprinkle over this little pieces of fontina and crumbs of gorgonzola, a couple of spoonfuls of the tomato sauce and some grated Parmesan. Repeat the layers until the dish is full, finishing with tomato sauce and Parmesan. Place in the hot oven for 20 minutes, and serve straight away.

Polenta with wild mushrooms

POLENTA CON FUNGHI
Polenta with Wild Mushrooms

This recipe reminds me of outings into the mountains made in my youth, invariably finishing up in some trattoria or other, where polenta with mushrooms would always be on the menu, especially in the autumn. The memory of this polenta which would be prepared in a large copper pot over a wood fire makes my mouth water even today. For the ceps which are usually quite hard to come by, you may substitute ordinary field mushrooms combined with a few dried ceps to give flavour.

Serves 4

For the sauce:

1 small onion, chopped
3 tbs olive oil
30 g (1 oz or 2 tbs) butter
350 g (12 oz) fresh ceps, or field mushrooms plus 25g (scant 1 oz) dried ceps
1 small can peeled plum tomatoes
6 fresh basil leaves
salt and freshly ground black pepper

For the polenta:

1.5 litres (3 pt) salted water
300 g (10 oz or 1¾ US cups) yellow polenta flour, or 1 packet (370 g, 13 oz or 2¼ US cups) Valsugana polenta
30 g (1 oz or 2 tbs) butter
60 g (2 oz or ½ US cup) freshly grated Parmesan cheese

Clean and slice the mushrooms and soak dried ceps for 10 minutes in lukewarm water. Prepare the sauce by frying the chopped onion in the oil and butter, followed by the sliced mushrooms. Cook these two ingredients together over a high flame for 10 minutes, then add the liquidized tomatoes and continue cooking for another 20 minutes so that the water from the tomatoes evaporates. When everything is fully cooked, add the salt and pepper and basil leaves.

Cook the polenta as in the previous recipes, and when it is ready, add the butter and half the Parmesan cheese. Serve in shallow bowls, pouring some sauce into the middle of each and sprinkling the remaining Parmesan cheese over the top.

CROSTONI DI POLENTA
Polenta Crusts

At home in my childhood, in the larder, there was always a polenta turned out ready for making into crusts. A wonderful alternative to potatoes. I do know some restaurants in Italy who use a hot iron with a criss-cross design like the shape of a grill to make an impression on the fried polenta crust just before serving.

Serves 8

1 370 g (13 oz or 2¼ US cups) packet of Star polenta (the precooked variety)

1.5 litres (3 pt) water

salt

60 g (2 oz or 4 tbs) butter

For grilling:

2 tbs olive oil

For frying:

a nut of butter

Bring the water to the boil, add the salt and slowly pour in the polenta, stirring all the time with a wooden spoon. Stir continually as the polenta cooks: it will only take 5 minutes. The polenta is cooked when it begins to come away from the sides of the saucepan: now add the butter.

The easiest way to cut the polenta into slices is to take a deep rectangular dish. Rinse it with water and then pour the cooked polenta in and leave to set. When set, turn the polenta out on a board and cut into 2 cm (¾ inch) thick slices.

To grill, brush each slice with olive oil and put under the grill until it browns a little and forms a crust.

To fry, melt a nut of butter in a thick-bottomed pan and when hot, fry the slices of polenta on both sides until crisp and brown.

PIZZA DI POLENTA
Polenta Cake

Polenta cake or pie is made in a completely different way from ordinary polenta, and we need a pan, preferably made of cast iron, in which to cook it. My granny used to use a shallow terracotta dish called a 'tiano', and the result was delicious. Once when I felt lonely and in need of a cheerful meal, I cooked this dish and ate every bit of the cake myself, ending up feeling slightly sick but considerably happier.

Serves 4

350 g (12 oz or 2 US cups) polenta (not the precooked type)

300 ml (11 fl oz or 1⅓ US cups) water

salt

2–3 tbs olive oil

Preheat the oven to 230°C (450°F or gas mark 8). Boil the water. Put the polenta into a mixing bowl. Pour in the boiling water, add the salt and mix together. Using 1 tablespoon oil, grease a small oval cast-iron casserole dish. Pour in the polenta, smooth it down and dribble a second tablespoon of oil over the top. Place in the hot oven and bake for 30 minutes. You may dribble a little extra oil on top half-way through baking. The top should be a lovely crisp golden-brown. Serve with meat and game – and, of course, with Cime di rape (rape tops).

PIZZA
Basic Pizza Dough

There are so many different combinations of ingredients that it is hard for me to give a global definition of pizza. If pressed, however, I would say that it is a species of flat bread which (as its cooking time is very short) can be topped by anything that takes your fancy. The only rule is not to add too many juicy tomatoes or other liquids, otherwise you will find that the pizza becomes soggy.

The basic dough used in all pizzas and many tarts is similar to a simple bread dough, so you could save yourself a lot of time and effort by persuading your local baker to sell you some dough directly. Having said that, a pizza is the easiest thing in the world to prepare, if you take a little care with the ingredients and the making.

Ideally, use plain white (all-purpose) flour, though wholemeal flour can be used as a substitute. I usually use fresh compressed yeast, which has the advantage of freezing well, but you may find it more convenient to use dried yeast granules or powdered yeast: check the packet for the equivalent quantities. Olive oil (of any kind) is a must, and when tomatoes are called for in the topping, they should be as ripe as possible, for which reason I recommend the canned San Marzano variety. Wild oregano is best as it has a more intense flavour, and the mozzarella used should be the best that you can lay your hands on.

Apart from the ingredients, the most important element in the making of a tasty pizza is naturally the oven. It is probably useless for me to insist that this should be a wood-fired brick oven; since these are few and far between, you will have to make do with your gas or electric oven.

Makes 4 pizzas 27 cm (11 inches) in diameter

600 g (1¼ lb or 5 US cups) plain white (all-purpose) flour
45 g (1½ oz) compressed yeast (or the equivalent quantity of dried yeast powder or granules: see maker's instructions)
a pinch of salt
300 ml (16 fl oz or 2 US cups) warm water
2 tbs olive oil

Dissolve the yeast in the warm water to which you have added the salt and olive oil. Pour the flour into a mound on a clean working surface and make a hole in the centre of it. Add the yeast mixture drop by drop into the centre of the flour, mixing with your hands until all the liquid is absorbed, forming large lumps. Knead the dough with your hands until it has a smooth texture, then roll it into a ball. A good pizza depends on the quality of the dough used.

Next, sprinkle some flour into a large tin or dish and place the dough in it, spreading a little oil over the top to prevent a crust from forming. Cover the bowl with a dry linen cloth and leave to rise for 1 hour in a warm place – not less than 20°C (68°F). (It was at this stage that my grandmother used to 'bless' the dough by making the sign of the cross in order that it should turn out well.) After this time the dough should have increased in volume by three times.

Now begins the preparation of the pizza proper. Preheat the oven to 230°C (450°F or gas mark 8). Rub the four 27 cm (11 inch) pizza pans with olive oil. Flour the working surface. Divide

your dough into four and roll each into a ball. (It is better not to use a rolling pin but to ease the dough by gently pressing out the dough with the plump part of your hand, the heel of your thumb and with your fingers.) Starting from the middle, smooth the dough out to a thickness of about 6 mm (¼ inch). I suggest you make the edges slightly thicker to prevent the topping from running away, and this method of rolling leaves the characteristic round edge which should go crisp in the oven.

Place each pizza on an oiled pizza pan, spread the topping on the pizza and bake in the hot oven for anything from 8 to 15 minutes, depending on the ingredients: see times specified for each individual recipe.

PIZZA ALLA NAPOLETANA
Neapolitan Pizza

This classic pizza is both one of the simplest to prepare and the most tasty. In Naples it is customary to eat pizza in one's hands.

Makes 4 27 cm (11 inch) pizzas

dough made with 600 g (1¼ lb) flour (see basic recipe)
For the sauce:
2 tbs olive oil
1 clove garlic, chopped
12 ripe plum tomatoes, skinned and halved, or 1 large can plum tomatoes, chopped in the can
For the topping:
2 tsp dried oregano
4 tbs olive oil
salt and freshly ground black pepper

Prepare the dough as described in the basic recipe. Make the tomato sauce while the dough is rising. Preheat the oven to 230°C (450°F or gas mark 8).

Heat the oil in a pan and fry the garlic for just a few seconds and then add the tomatoes (if using canned tomatoes you may have to strain out some of the extra liquid). Simmer the sauce, stirring from time to time, for 15 minutes. Season with salt and pepper.

Grease each pizza pan or flat pie pan with a brush dipped in oil. Divide the dough into four and roll each into balls. Work the balls with your hands on a floured surface until it becomes flat and circular. Now place the dough in the pan and smooth it out so that it fits perfectly and is of a uniform thickness. Spread on each circle of dough 2 spoonfuls of the tomato sauce. Sprinkle this with the oregano. Pour a trickle of olive oil over the top and place in a very hot oven for about 10–15 minutes, until you see the edges become a golden-brown colour.

PIZZA MARGHERITA

Another classic pizza as simple to prepare as the previous recipe with the addition of mozzarella cheese.

Makes 4 pizzas

dough made with 600 g (1¼ lb) flour (see basic recipe)
For the sauce:
2 tbs olive oil
2 cloves garlic, chopped fine
12 ripe plum tomatoes, skinned and halved, or 1 large can plum tomatoes, chopped in the can
salt and freshly ground black pepper
For the topping:
200 g (7 oz) mozzarella cheese
12 fresh basil leaves
4 tbs olive oil

Make the basic dough and leave it to rise. Then follow the instructions for the previous recipe, Pizza napoletana, until you come to the final topping.

Chop the mozzarella into small cubes, and scatter them over the dough which you have spread with the tomato sauce. Add the basil leaves, dribble all over with the olive oil and season with salt and pepper. Bake as before in the very hot oven for 10–15 minutes.

PIZZA FRITTA
Fried Pizza

This is a simple pizza that my mother often used to make in order to feed the six ravenous mouths of myself and my brothers.

You will probably need slightly more dedication to make this pizza. It has to be eaten as soon as it is cooked, in order to savour in full its crusty texture. This is such a tasty dish that you will unfortunately be kept working as your guests ask for second helpings. Don't worry if the dough seems to be swimming around in the oil while it is frying, as it will hardly absorb any at all. This is an incredibly delicious dish.

I will never forget the time I was at a television audition and was making pizza fritta. The smells from the cooking were so alluring that by the end all the technicians and other staff had gathered round to taste the pizzas that I was turning out.

Makes 8 small pizzas

dough made with 600 g (1¼ lb) flour (see basic recipe)
For the topping:
2 cloves garlic, sliced
6 tbs olive oil
1 large can peeled tomatoes, finely chopped
5 or 6 fresh basil leaves
salt
150 g (5 oz or 1½ US cups) freshly grated Parmesan cheese
frying oil (1 cm or ½ inch deep in a pan)

Make the basic dough as described in the basic recipe and divide it into 8 balls. Fry the sliced garlic in the olive oil until it turns a light golden-brown. Then immediately add the tomatoes, the basil and the salt, and cook together for 10 minutes.

Heat the frying oil to boiling point. Flatten out the dough balls until they are about 2 cm (1 inch) thick and then fry them (taking good care not to burn yourself when you turn them) until they become a dark golden-brown and are fully cooked inside.

Extract the pizzas from the pan with a fork and put them on a plate, after having shaken off any excess oil. Place a couple of spoonfuls of the sauce on top and sprinkle with a generous amount of grated Parmesan before serving immediately.

CALZONE IMBOTTITO
Stuffed Pizza

Because the calzone is a kind of 'inside-out' pizza, it is able to keep intact all the flavours contained in the filling. This is a slightly heavier recipe than the other pizzas. It can also be made with a variety of different ingredients such as salami, cheese or vegetables.

Served with a salad this pizza can be transformed into an excellent main course. If you wish to make a more substantial dish all you need to do is to increase the quantity of filling.

The calzone that my mother used to cook was based on fontina cheese, ham, sausages and eggs. The more classic calzone, however, contains mozzarella.

Makes 4 calzone

dough made with 600 g (1¼ lb) flour (see basic recipe)
For the filling:
100 g (4 oz) mozzarella
200 g (7 oz or 1 scant US cup) ricotta
100 g (4 oz) cooked ham
2 tbs freshly grated Parmesan cheese
2 eggs, beaten
4 fresh basil leaves
salt and freshly ground black pepper
a little milk for glazing

Make the dough as described in the basic recipe. Prepare the filling by cutting the mozzarella and the ham into strips. Beat the eggs (keeping a little aside for sealing the dough envelopes) and add the Parmesan cheese, the chopped basil, a pinch of salt and 2 or 3 grinds of black pepper. Mix this in with the ricotta, mozzarella and ham so as to form a reasonably soft paste. Preheat the oven to 220°C (425°F or gas mark 7).

Divide the dough into 4 balls. Flatten these one at a time so as to form a pizza 1 cm (½ inch) thick. Next place them on a dry cloth and put a quarter of the filling on half of each pizza. Cover the filling by folding the pizza in half and seal it by wetting the edge with a little beaten egg and pressing a fork on the join. Brush the dough over with a little milk – the calzone will become a golden-brown when cooked. Place the calzone on a well-oiled baking tray and place in the oven for around 15 minutes.

FOCACCIA AL ROSMARINO
Pizza Bread with Rosemary

To breakfast off a delicious piece of freshly baked focaccia will immediately lift you out of even the foulest of moods when you have got out of bed on the wrong side. Professional bakers (who make bread in their shops) in Genoa and throughout Italy also usually sell delicious focaccia. The most common variety that is produced is merely topped by some oil and salt and it comes in large rectangular shapes which are then cut into slices. It can also be made, however, in the shape of a pizza. The focaccia should be slightly thicker than a normal pizza as it is very similar to bread in consistency and like bread it can accompany all sorts of food or else chopped into pieces it can be consumed with aperitifs.

Serves 8–10

For the dough:
1 kg (2 lb or 8 US cups) flour
75 g (3 oz) fresh yeast, or the equivalent amount of dried or powdered yeast
4 tbs olive oil
600 ml (20 fl oz or 3 US cups) water
2 tsp brown sugar
For the topping:
3 tbs fresh rosemary leaves
coarse salt and freshly ground black pepper
4 tbs olive oil for the top and the baking tray

Prepare the dough as described in the basic recipe and roll it out until it is either a rectangle or a circle 2 cm (1 inch) thick: this amount of dough makes one big rectangular pizza about 35 × 50 cm (14 × 20 inches). Place it on an oiled baking tray. Preheat the oven to 230°C (450°F or gas mark 8).

Prick the dough all over with a fork then dribble with olive oil, scatter the rosemary leaves, generously grind fresh pepper and finally sprinkle salt over the whole surface. Bake in the very hot oven for 20 minutes: the top should be golden, but the rosemary must not brown.

PIZZA MARINARA
Pizza with Anchovies, Tomatoes and Garlic

The combination of garlic, oregano, basil and anchovies with the addition of tomatoes has always been synonymous with Italian food. When eating this classic pizza, you certainly will recall some good things on holiday in Italy. This classic is equally good hot or cold.

Makes 4 pizzas

dough made with 600 g (1¼ lb) flour (see basic recipe)
24 anchovy fillets
1 tbs oregano
4 cloves garlic, finely chopped
8 fresh basil leaves
8 tbs olive oil
freshly ground black pepper
For the tomato sauce:
1 medium can chopped Italian tomatoes
2 tbs olive oil
1 clove garlic, sliced
salt and freshly ground black pepper
4 fresh basil leaves

Make the pizza dough as in the basic recipe and leave to rise for 1 hour. Preheat the oven to 230°C (450°F or gas mark 8).

In the meantime, make the tomato sauce. Fry the sliced garlic in hot olive oil, add the chopped tomatoes almost immediately and leave to simmer for 15 minutes. Season with salt, pepper and 4 fresh basil leaves torn into pieces.

Press out the dough to make 4 pizzas and lay them in oiled pizza pans. Spread each pizza with tomato sauce, place 6 anchovies on each pizza, scatter the chopped garlic over the surface and then the oregano. Tear the basil leaves into small strips and place them amongst the anchovies. Dribble the olive oil over the whole surface and season with freshly ground pepper – no salt, as the anchovies provide sufficient. Bake the pizza in a hot oven for 10 minutes. Serve hot or cold.

PIZZA CON PANCETTA AFFUMICATA
Pizza with Italian Smoked Cooked Bacon

If you imagine that pizza is nothing more than freshly baked bread, the topping can be as varied as you wish. In this case a bacon and cheese bread. The wonderful smoked pancetta, which is obtainable from most Italian delicatessens, combined with the smoked mozzarella and the contrasting element of those little preserved green peppers is a balance of tastes making something very appetizing indeed.

Makes 4 pizzas

dough made with 600 g (1¼ lb) flour (see basic recipe)
280 g (10 oz) pancetta affumicata (buy it in one piece)
350 g (12 oz) smoked mozzarella
12 small green preserved peppers
salt and freshly ground black pepper
4 tbs olive oil

Make the dough as in the basic recipe and leave to rise for 1 hour. Preheat the oven to 230°C (450°F or gas mark 8).

Press the dough out into your oiled pizza pans. Cut the pancetta into small pieces 5 mm × 2 cm (¼ × ¾ inch). Slice the smoked mozzarella. Cut the small green peppers into 2 or 3 pieces. Scatter the pancetta pieces on to each pizza, dot with the slices of mozzarella cheese. Place the bits of green pepper in between the slices of cheese. Generously grind over black pepper, sprinkle with salt. Finally dribble over olive oil and bake in the hot oven for 8–10 minutes. The cheese should melt and the pancetta become slightly golden. Serve hot.

Right: Pizza with pesto and pine nuts (top)
Pizza with Italian smoked cooked bacon (left)
Pizza with anchovies, tomatoes and garlic (right)
Pizza with garlic, oil and green peppercorns (bottom)

PIZZA AL SALMONE AFFUMICATO
Smoked Salmon and Spinach Pizza

Buckingham Palace seems to be the setting
where some of my best thinking is done. I pass it
in my car every morning en route to the Neal
Street Restaurant. It is while I am stuck in the
early morning traffic here that my mind moves
into a higher gear and conjures up new food
combinations and recipes. The idea for this dish
came to me in just this way.

Serves 4

dough made with 600 g (1¼ lb) flour (see basic recipe)
about 150 ml (¼ pt or ⅔ US cup) olive oil
80 g (3 oz or ⅔ US cup) freshly grated Parmesan cheese
100 g (4 oz) smoked salmon, cut into strips
300 g (10 oz) cooked spinach or Swiss chard
½ nutmeg, grated
salt and freshly ground black pepper

Prepare the dough as described in the basic
recipe and put aside to rise for an hour. Preheat
the oven to 230°C (450°F or gas mark 8).

Divide the dough into four and press it out
into the oiled pizza pans. First dribble about a
teaspoon of oil over each pizza. Then sprinkle a
quarter of the Parmesan cheese over each. Make
sure that all the water has been squeezed out of
the cooked spinach or Swiss chard, and cover the
pizza dough with the leaves, spreading them out
as thinly as possible. Lay the strips of smoked
salmon in a pattern of rays or a lattice over the
spinach. Sprinkle with plenty of grated nutmeg
and ground black pepper. Use very little salt, as
the smoked salmon will already be salty. Dribble
over each pizza about 2 tbs olive oil. Place in the
hot oven and bake for about 10 minutes. Serve
immediately – it's delicious.

PIZZA AI QUATTRO FORMAGGI
Pizza with Four Cheeses

This is a very substantial pizza to be enjoyed as a
main course.

Makes 4 pizzas

dough made with 600 g (1¼ lb) flour (see basic recipe)
4 large spring onions (scallions), or 4 small thin leeks, sliced
4 tbs olive oil for frying
200 g (7 oz or scant 1 US cup) ricotta cheese
200 g (7 oz) gorgonzola cheese
200 g (7 oz) fontina cheese
4 tbs freshly grated Parmesan cheese
1 tbs dried oregano
salt
4 tbs olive oil for the top

Make the pizza dough as in the basic recipe and
leave to rise for 1 hour. Preheat the oven to
230°C (450°F or gas mark 8).

Slice the leeks or spring onions. Heat the olive
oil and fry them gently for 5 minutes: they
should become soft and lightly golden. Cut the
gorgonzola and fontina into 1 cm (½ inch)
cubes, crumble the ricotta cheese and grate the
Parmesan. Press out your pizzas and place in
your oiled pizza pans. Spread each with the leek
or spring onions and the oil they cooked in.
Crumble the ricotta cheese over the leeks or
spring onions. Sprinkle with the pieces of
gorgonzola and fontina cheese, then scatter a
layer of grated Parmesan and finally dribble olive
oil over the top. Bake in the very hot oven for
10–15 minutes.

PIZZA ALLE VONGOLE E COZZE
Seafood Pizza

The seafood best suitable to top this pizza are
molluscs, like mussels and clams. The
combination of these with tomatoes, garlic and
parsley gives you the full flavour of the
Mediterranean.

Makes 4 pizzas

dough made with 600 g (1¼ lb) flour (see basic recipe)
56 whole clams
48 whole mussels
4 cloves garlic, chopped
8 tbs olive oil
salt and freshly ground black pepper
For the tomato sauce:
2 tbs olive oil
1 clove garlic, chopped
1 medium can of chopped tomatoes
4 tbs chopped parsley

Make the dough as described in the basic recipe
and leave to rise for 1 hour. Preheat the oven to
230°C (450°F or gas mark 8).

94

To make the tomato sauce, which should be a little thinner than the previous ones, heat the olive oil and when hot fry the garlic for a minute or less, then add the tomatoes: keep back a few of the pieces, but use all the juices from the can. Simmer gently for 15 minutes, add salt and pepper at the end. Put aside while you cook the mussels and clams. Thoroughly scrub the mussels and rinse them with the clams. Put them in a large saucepan with a lid, add a wineglass of water and steam open. Shake the pan from time to time to make sure all the shells have opened. Put aside; when cool, remove the mussels and clams from their shells.

Press out the pizzas and place in oiled pizza pans. Spread each pizza with a layer of the thin tomato sauce. Divide the mussels and clams equally and place on the sauce. Sprinkle with the chopped garlic and parsley and a few pieces of tomato, and finally dribble over the olive oil. Bake in a hot oven for 10 minutes. The aroma from baking will astonish you!

PIZZA AL PESTO
Pizza with Pesto and Pine Nuts

An amusing pizza which cut in small pieces could be served as a snack. Good hot or cold.

Makes 4 pizzas

dough made with 600 g (1¼ lb) flour (see basic recipe)
4 tbs pesto paste from a jar
4 tbs olive oil to mix with the pesto
8 fresh basil leaves
2 cloves garlic, chopped
8 tbs freshly grated Parmesan cheese
4 tbs pine nuts
freshly ground black pepper
4 tbs olive oil for the top of the pizza

Prepare the dough as described in the basic recipe and leave to rise for 1 hour. Preheat the oven to 230°C (450°F or gas mark 8).

Mix the pesto paste with 4 tablespoons of olive oil and the chopped garlic.

Press out your pizza dough and place it on your four oiled pizza pans and spread each one with a layer of the pesto mixture. Tear the basil leaves into 4 and scatter them with the pine nuts on to the pesto. Cover with the grated Parmesan, sprinkle with pepper and dribble each pizza with some olive oil. Put in the hot oven to bake. This

may take between 8 and 10 minutes. Serve immediately.

PIZZA AL TONNO E CAPPERI
Tuna Fish Pizza with Whole Capers

This pizza should be made with very thin pizza bread and baked to become crispy. More likely to be served with drinks at parties as a snack than served as a meal.

Makes 4 pizzas

dough made with 600 g (1¼ lb) flour (see basic recipe)
6 tbs olive oil
2 large onions, or 4 medium-sized ones
280 g (10 oz) canned tuna fish, drained of its oil
4 tsp fresh thyme
4 tbs whole capers
salt and freshly ground black pepper

Make the dough as described in the basic recipe and leave to rise for 1 hour. Preheat the oven to 230°C (450°F or gas mark 8). Press out the pizza dough into four large pizzas as thin as you can without tearing them. Place in oiled pizza pans.

Heat the olive oil in a pan and fry the sliced onions until they become soft and golden. Spread the onions over the pizzas with the oil they were cooked in. Break up the tuna fish and scatter it over the onions. Season the tuna fish with the roughly chopped thyme and evenly place the capers on top. Season with freshly ground black pepper and a little salt (depending on how salty the capers are). Bake in the very hot oven for 10 minutes until crisp. Cut into slices and serve.

Pasta shop in Turin

PIZZA CON MOZZARELLA AFFUMICATA
Pizza with Smoked Mozzarella

Smoked mozzarella combines the pleasant melting properties with the interesting smoked taste. This pizza is a variation of the well-known pizza theme of tomato, mozzarella and basil.

Makes 4 pizzas

dough made with 600 g (1¼ lb) flour (see basic recipe)
For the tomato sauce:
1 medium can chopped tomatoes
1 clove garlic, chopped roughly
2 tbs olive oil
12 fresh basil leaves
salt and freshly ground black pepper
350 g (12 oz) smoked mozzarella

Prepare the dough as described in the basic recipe and put aside to rise for 1 hour. Preheat the oven to 230°C (450°F or gas mark 8).

Meanwhile, make the tomato sauce. Heat the oil in a saucepan, add the garlic and almost immediately the chopped tomatoes. Simmer together for 15 minutes and season with salt and pepper. Then add the fresh basil leaves, torn into pieces.

Divide the dough into four and press out into your oiled pizza pans. Spread each pizza with tomato sauce. Cut the mozzarella into slices and evenly scatter them on top of the tomato sauce. Grind some black pepper over each pizza and place a basil leaf or two among the slices of mozzarella. Put in the hot oven and bake for 10 minutes. Serve immediately.

PIZZA CON AGLIO, OLIO E PEPE VERDE
Pizza with Garlic, Oil and Green Peppercorns

Like the pizza 'al tonno e capperi', this pizza is more an interesting bread than a meal. Wonderful to cut into pieces and serve with drinks or to accompany other dishes as a savoury bread. It is equally delicious hot or cold.

Makes 6 pizzas

dough made with 600 g (1¼ lb) flour (see basic recipe)
10 tbs olive oil for the top
6 cloves garlic, roughly chopped
6 tbs green peppercorns
salt

Prepare the dough as described in the basic recipe, and leave to rise for 1 hour. Preheat the oven to 230°C (450°F or gas mark 8).

Oil your pizza pans then press or roll out six circular pizzas as thick as possible. Chop the garlic roughly. Scatter first the garlic and then the green peppercorns over each pizza, dribble over the olive oil (try to cover the whole surface of the pizza) and sprinkle with salt. Bake in a very hot oven for 8 minutes until golden and crispy. Cut into slices to serve.

CALZONCINI FRITTI
Little Fried Calzone

These pizzas are wonderful for parties and picnics as all the goodies are enclosed. Children love them. They are equally delicious hot or cold. If you make them to eat as a main course, serve them with tomato sauce.

Makes 24 calzoncini

dough made with 600 g (1¼ lb) flour (see basic recipe)
400 g (12 oz or 2 US cups) ricotta cheese
5 eggs (1 egg for sealing)
200 g (7 oz) smoked bacon
1 tbs olive oil
4 tbs chopped parsley
6 grates of nutmeg
salt and freshly ground black pepper
60 g (2 oz or ¼ US cup) freshly grated Parmesan cheese
oil for frying

Make the dough as described in the basic recipe and leave to rise for 1 hour. Beat the ricotta cheese.

Cut the bacon into matchsticks and fry them in 1 tablespoon of olive oil for a few minutes until golden and slightly crisp. Beat the ricotta together with four eggs, add the fried bacon, Parmesan and parsley. Stir well to incorporate the mixture, season with salt, freshly ground pepper and the grated nutmeg. Divide the dough into 24 equal pieces. Flour your work surface and roll each piece into little balls and then press out into little circular pizzas measuring 10 cm (4 inches) in diameter. Place a tablespoon of ricotta mixture on one half of the pizza and fold over to form a half-moon. Seal the join with beaten egg. When you have made all your little calzoncini, heat 1 cm (½ inch) of olive oil in your pan. When the oil is hot, place the calzoncini in the oil to fry two or three at a time, according to the size of your pan. The oil should not smoke, but be hot enough to turn the calzoncini gently golden as they cook. They will take about 3 minutes on each side. Drain on kitchen paper and serve warm or cold.

PIZZA CON PORCINI
Pizza with Mushrooms

I make this pizza in the autumn, using freshly gathered wild mushrooms with their obviously wonderful flavour. Cultivated field mushrooms cooked in the same way offer a good alternative.

Makes 4 pizzas

dough made with 600 g (1¼ lb) flour (see basic recipe)
400 g (14 oz) fresh ceps or field mushrooms
4 tbs olive oil
1 clove garlic, chopped
1 tbs fresh thyme
8 fresh basil leaves
4 tbs freshly grated Parmesan cheese
salt and freshly ground black pepper

Make the dough as described in the basic recipe and leave to rise for 1 hour. Preheat the oven to 230°C (450°F or gas mark 8).

Clean the mushrooms, preferably with a brush and small knife, rather than washing them. Slice the mushrooms, including the stalks. Heat the oil in a pan and when it is hot, stir-fry the mushrooms for 2 minutes, keeping the flame up high. Add the chopped garlic halfway through frying. Remove from the heat and add the torn basil leaves.

Press out the pizzas and place in oiled pizza pans. Spread the mushrooms with their oil over each pizza, sprinkle with the fresh thyme, salt and pepper. Cover each pizza with a layer of freshly grated Parmesan and finally dribble a little oil over. Bake in the very hot oven for 10 minutes and serve hot.

PIZZA CON CARCIOFINI
Artichoke Pizza

This pizza is to be served as a complete meal. The richness of mortadella sausage combined with the pickled artichoke hearts makes an interesting piquant contrast.

Makes 4 pizzas

dough made with 600 g (1¼ lb) flour (see basic recipe)
20 preserved artichoke hearts
225 g (8 oz) mortadella, sliced
4 tbs olive oil
salt and freshly ground black pepper

Make the dough as in the basic recipe and leave to rise for 1 hour. Preheat the oven to 230°C (450°F or gas mark 8).

Press out 4 pizzas and lay them in oiled pizza pans. Cut the mortadella into thin strips and lay them on the pizzas. Cut the artichokes in 4–5 pieces and place them on top of the mortadella, season the pizzas with salt and freshly ground black pepper, dribble with olive oil and bake in the hot oven for 10 minutes or longer. The topping for this pizza is thick, so the dough may take 2 minutes longer than usual to cook.

IL SECONDO

——————THE MAIN COURSE——————

There will be a decent interval after il primo is finished before il secondo is served. This is usually meat, poultry or fish accompanied by one or two lightly cooked vegetables or a small salad. There might be several thin slices of meat, sometimes two different types of meat with their juices deglazed from the pan, or a piece of roast chicken cooked with potatoes, a small grilled fish or a dish of marinated fish on skewers. The vegetables will be chosen from those in season and to complement the main dish.

If you are staying in Italy near the sea, it is well worthwhile getting up very early to visit the local fish market. It will be bustling with life, full of beautifully shaped, colourful fish side by side with ugly, even repellent ones, baskets of shellfish, and noisy vendors haggling with the customers, who are invariably very knowledgeable and very demanding. They will be buying the fish to be eaten later in the day, possibly having been grilled or roasted, or made into a stew or soup. Fish from the Mediterranean is famous for its intense flavour. I love it when it is simply dressed without rich or fatty sauces. A freshly caught lobster, boiled and served with oil and lemon juice, is absolutely delicious.

Italian poultry can be excellent, even though some brands of chicken taste of fish, being battery raised and fed on fish meal, but you can still buy free-range chickens and turkeys. They are often roasted and grilled, and the way of cooking poultry breasts is one that is uniquely Italian. There is a great variety of game to choose from – anything that can be shot is shot, including pigeons, partridges, guinea fowl, quail, deer, pheasants and hare – I must confess to having enjoyed a sparrow once, although I never repeated the experience, preferring to see the birds bathing in a puddle than trussed on a table. There have been a number of restrictive laws passed against hunting recently, but you still see large groups of men with guns and hunting dogs out at the beginning of every season – sometimes making their way home via the local game seller. There are many interesting recipes for cooking game. The most traditional are roasting and grilling, and there are plenty of hearty stews as well.

Italy has never been a great nation of meat eaters and relatively few animals are bred for food. The meat that is

produced, however, is usually of very good quality. One famous example is the beef grown in the Val di Chiana; it is sold as huge, tender T-bone steaks, which are known as fiorentina and are grilled over wood or charcoal fires. Then there is the veal from the Valley of Piedmont, a pinkish meat of exceptional flavour. You would never find a good mixed stew in the region that did not include this meat, and it is a favourite for escalopes and roasts. Lamb is produced mainly in southern Italy and has a remarkably delicate flavour. It is excellent grilled, roasted and made into stews. I like to cook it with vegetables such as artichokes and chicory. Starting with salami and ham, there is an infinite number of recipes using different pork products – the Italians consider every single part of the pig edible. And there are distinctive regional tastes in pork meat: in Naples, for example, you hear street sellers calling 'O musso', which is boiled pig's nose served with lemon; in the north the pig shin is considered a luxury, while in Tuscany the local roast is the famous arista al forno.

I have very fond memories of one particular pig. In the last years of the war, when I was eight, the Germans laid down a regulation outlawing the possession of more than one pig. We owned two. So during the night, my father and some local butchers slaughtered and butchered one of them – in perfect silence! The meat tasted even better than usual in those times of food shortages.

Quail with grappa raisins and polenta crusts

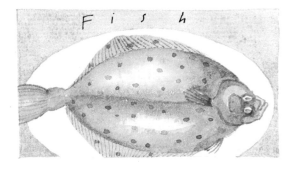

ANGUILLA ALLA GRIGLIA
Grilled (Broiled) Eel

The eel is a curious but tasty creature which can sometimes be found in fresh water, sometimes in the sea. It is not an overly popular fish, perhaps because of its resemblance to a snake, but once you manage to overcome any initial prejudice, you might well find yourself becoming very enthusiastic.

For this recipe you will need very fresh medium-sized eel. Ideally, cook it over charcoal, where any excess fat in the fish can drip away. The direct heat slightly scorches the skin, giving the fish a particularly delicious flavour.

The region in Italy where eel is prepared according to a thousand or more recipes is the area around Venice where the lagoons and 'valli' abound in this fish.

Serves 6

about 1 kg (2 lb) fresh eel
salt and freshly ground black pepper
2 tbs olive oil
flour for dusting
lemon slices for serving

Cut the eels into 10 cm (4 inch) lengths and remove the backbone. You will need a small, very sharp pointed knife. Mind your fingers, as it is a very fiddly job – especially when the eels are still wriggling! Alternatively, ask your fishmonger to bone the eels for you. Sprinkle the pieces of eel with salt and pepper, dip them in the flour so they are dusted all over, and then brush lightly with olive oil.

Place on a charcoal grill (broiler) and cook on both sides until they are slightly charred in appearance: eel cooks very quickly. Serve immediately with slices of lemon.

LUCCIO AL FORNO
Pike with Fennel

It is more than just that an evil predator fish such as the pike should finish his days in the oven. Although there are other ways of cooking this fish I believe baking to be most suitable for its dry but delicate flesh. The best method is to wrap the fish up in some aluminium foil together with herbs and vegetables. An excellent dish for dinner parties – if pike is hard to find, hake is equally delicious cooked this way.

Serves 4

1 whole pike, weighing 2 kg or more (about 4 lb), cleaned
2 fennel bulbs
2 lemons
4 tbs butter
1 small bunch chives, chopped
3 or 4 fresh sage leaves
1 tbs chopped parsley, plus 3 or 4 sprigs parsley
salt and freshly ground black pepper
1 large sheet aluminium foil

Preheat the oven to 190°C (375°F or gas mark 5). Slice the fennel vertically so that each slice remains intact. Blanch the slices in boiling salted water for 2 or 3 minutes only. Remove and drain.

Gut and wash the fish; if you find any eggs, throw them away as they are not edible. Season the fish inside and out with salt and pepper. Lay out a sheet of aluminium foil large enough to wrap up the fish. Cut the lemons into thin slices. On the foil prepare a bed of blanched fennel, sprinkle with half the chopped parsley and then cover with a layer of lemon slices. Scatter a few chopped chives over the lemon and dot with some pieces of butter. Stuff the fish with a piece of butter, the sprigs of parsley, the sage leaves and a few more chives and place it on the bed of fennel. Cover the fish with the remainder of the lemon slices, dot these with pieces of butter and sprinkle with salt and pepper.

Wrap up the fish, sealing it carefully so that no juice can escape. Place in the moderately hot oven and bake for about 30 minutes. Remove from the oven and leave wrapped for 5–10 minutes before opening. Present the fish to your guests on its bed of fennel before removing the bones. Serve with the fennel.

CARPA BLU
'Blue' Carp

When you are choosing your carp make sure that it comes from either a lake or a river, but not from a pond: you will find the flesh of the latter much less digestible. In my view the slight taste of mud in carp makes this fish all the more interesting. Its flesh is usually quite dense but oily – when you are purchasing the fish, try and choose the ones with the least fat.

You may be wondering about the name of this recipe: preparing the fish with vinegar before cooking makes the skin turn a bluish colour. Trout may equally well be prepared in this way.

Serves 6

1 carp weighing 2 kg (4 lb), which will give you about 900 g (2 lb or so) of cleaned fish
1 wine glass of wine vinegar
1 small onion
1 large sprig parsley
1 bay leaf
6 young carrots
salt and freshly ground black pepper
6 peeled potatoes

Gut the fish and cut the head and tail off. Scrape away any tough scales and cut off the fins, but don't wipe away the surface 'sliminess', as it is this that gives the blue effect. Now cut the fish in half lengthwise along the back, and then cut each half in two lengthwise. Thoroughly wash the 4 pieces of carp and immerse them in the wine vinegar for about 10–15 minutes.

In the meantime, prepare a court bouillon with the onion, parsley, bay leaf, carrots, salt and pepper in a large saucepan half-filled with water. Bring the court bouillon to the boil, add the vinegar in which the carp pieces have been soaking, and when it returns to the boil put in the pieces of fish. Reduce the flame and very lightly simmer the fish for 15 minutes. Boil the potatoes separately and serve the fish accompanied by the carrots and potatoes. A celeriac purée, for example Pure di carote e sedano rapa, is an excellent accompaniment to this dish.

CARPA IMPANATA E FRITTA
Carp in Bread Crumbs

When I was living in Vienna I used frequently to visit a restaurant near the Danube which specialized in cooking carp that was caught locally. The secret of the success of this restaurant lay almost entirely in the superb flavouring and texture of the bread crumbs with which the carp was covered.

Serves 4

4 pieces of carp weighing a total of about 800–900 g (1¾ lb) when cleaned
1 clove garlic, crushed
2 tsp olive oil
2 eggs, beaten
2 tbs chopped parsley
salt and freshly ground black pepper
flour for dusting
100 g (about 4 oz or 1 US cup) dry bread crumbs
oil for frying
1 lemon for garnish

Gut the carp under running water, remove the large hard scales and then cut the flesh from the bones so that you have 2 large fillets, one off each side of the fish. Cut each fillet into two. Crush or squeeze the garlic and add the juice to the olive oil. (Alternatively, use olive oil in which you have soaked for at least a few days some peeled cloves of garlic.) Beat the eggs and add the garlic oil, the parsley, salt and pepper. Dust the carp pieces in flour, dip them in the egg mixture and then cover them in bread crumbs.

Heat about 1 cm (½ inch) oil in a large pan until hot, but not smoking; fry the pieces of carp gently until the bread crumbs are golden and the fish is cooked. Depending on the thickness of your pieces of carp, they should be cooked after 15 minutes of frying. Serve garnished with pieces of lemon and accompanied by a basil, tomato and onion salad.

TINCHE IN CARPIONE
Marinated Tench

'In carpione' means that the fish is fried and then put in a cooked marinade consisting of water, oil, vinegar and herbs. This is a typical summer dish which is usually eaten cold. Tench is one of my favourite fish. This is a typical recipe from the Piedmont region, where many varieties of freshwater fish are consumed, but sardines are also delicious served this way.

Serves 4

1 kg (2 lb) tench
flour for dusting
corn oil for frying
For the marinade:
2 medium onions, sliced
3 cloves garlic, sliced
8 tbs olive oil
1 tbs white sugar
2 wine glasses of wine vinegar
1 glass of white wine
4 bay leaves
1 sprig fresh rosemary
1 tbs whole peppercorns
salt

Clean, scale and wash the fish and thoroughly dry them with a cloth. Roll the fish in flour so that they are dusted on all sides.

Heat the frying oil in a large frying pan – the oil should be about 1 cm (½ inch) deep. Fry the fish over a medium flame until they are crisp and golden on each side. Remove them from the pan and leave on kitchen paper to drain of oil. Meanwhile, in a pan heat up the olive oil and fry the sliced onions. When they become transparent, add the slices of garlic, cook together, stirring to prevent the garlic from browning, for 3 or 4 minutes, then add the sugar, vinegar, wine, bay leaves, rosemary, salt and peppercorns. Bring to the boil and remove from the stove.

Lay the fried fish side by side in a shallow earthenware dish. Pour the hot marinade over them and leave for at least 24 hours before serving.

TROTA ALLO ZENZERO
Trout with Ginger

Ginger is a root which has a particularly strong flavour, especially when it is fresh. Although it is most used in Eastern cooking, Italians also favour it in their more exotic dishes.

Serves 4

4 trout weighing 250 g (½ lb) each or 2 trout weighing 500 g (1 lb) each
salt
4 tbs milk
flour for dusting
75 g (3 oz or 5 tbs) butter
a walnut-sized piece of fresh ginger root, cut into matchsticks
1 bunch spring onions (scallions), chopped
the juice of a lemon
freshly ground black pepper

Gut and clean the trout under running cold water, and dry each one carefully with a cloth. Salt inside and outside and then moisten the fish with milk. Roll them in the flour so that they are lightly dusted.

Heat the butter in a large heavy pan and when it fizzes add the trout and fry gently over a medium flame until golden on both sides. The fish should be cooked in 15 minutes. Remove them from the pan and keep warm in a serving dish. Cut the ginger into matchsticks and chop the spring onions. Fry the ginger in the butter in same pan, increasing the heat, and almost immediately add the spring onion and the lemon juice. Stir all together just for a minute, season with salt and pepper, then pour this sauce over the trout. Serve immediately

TORTIERA DI ACCIUGHE
Baked Anchovies with Oregano

This is a typical dish from Naples where it is called either Tortiera or 'anchovies au gratin'.

You will need some fresh anchovies (alternatively, if these are hard to come by, small sardines will do). I have tried using frozen anchovies with quite a good result. In the chapter on antipasti I have already described several ways of preparing anchovies: this is another simple yet tasty recipe.

Serves 4

800 g (1¾ lb) fresh anchovies
3 tbs olive oil
1 clove garlic, finely chopped
1 tsp oregano
the juice of a lemon
2 tbs dry bread crumbs
salt

Preheat the oven to 200°C (400°F or gas mark 6).

Clean and fillet the anchovies. To do this, cut off the head and tail, open the fish along the stomach and gently pull out the backbone with your thumb and finger. You will thus obtain two fillets joined together by the skin of the back. Grease a flat baking tray with a little of the olive oil. Lay in it the anchovies skin side down, as close as possible to one another, but not overlapping. Scatter the chopped garlic and the oregano over the anchovies, sprinkle with the lemon juice, then cover with a light layer of bread crumbs. Trickle over the bread crumbs the remainder of the olive oil, season with salt and then place the tray in the oven for 7–8 minutes. Once the bread crumbs are golden-coloured and crisp, the fish will be ready. Serve immediately with a mixed salad and some good bread.

Fresh anchovies

DENTICE AL FORNO
Baked Sea Bream

Bream can perhaps be considered as one of the fish that is most appreciated by the Italians. Its flesh is white, delicate and very tasty. The bream that one can buy is usually quite big, for which reason it is best to bake the fish whole in the oven. Smaller bream are more suitable for this dish. Other fish which can be cooked in the same way are sea bass and grey mullet.

Serves 4

4 small sea bream, each weighing up to 350 g (¾ lb); or 1 large bream weighing 1.5 kg (3–4 lb)
salt and freshly ground black pepper
1 bunch parsley
1 bunch green fennel (the tops of the fennel bulbs you will use for the accompanying salad will do if you can't find green fennel)
4 tbs olive oil
4 ripe tomatoes, sliced
4 or 5 leaves fresh basil
1 glass of white wine

Preheat the oven to 200°C (400°F or gas mark 6).

Clean, gut and descale the fish, leaving the head and tail intact. Sprinkle with salt and pepper inside and out. Fill the insides of the fish with the parsley and fennel leaves. Oil an ovenproof baking dish and lay on it the sliced tomatoes, season them with salt and pepper and scatter over them the basil leaves torn into a few pieces. Place the fish on top of the tomatoes, pour over it the remainder of the olive oil and place in a hot oven. After 10 minutes, add the glass of wine, and from this moment on baste the fish frequently with the juice from the bottom of the dish.

Bake for 15 to 20 minutes if you have small fish, longer if you have one large bream. Do not overcook this delicate fish. Test it when basting: when the flesh parts easily from the bone, it is ready. Serve with a fennel salad (Insalata di finocchio) and boiled potatoes.

Right: Baked sea bream

FRITTO MISTO DI PESCE
Mixed Fried Fish

One of the first dishes that I order whenever I set foot in an Italian seaside town is the fritto misto di pesce. I am sure that everyone who has visited Italy at one time or another will have tried this speciality which combines the most tender and delicate Mediterranean fish, and includes shellfish, small soles, squid and any other fresh and tender creatures from the sea – the result inevitably reminds one of good weather and the holidays.

This dish can be found almost anywhere on the coast of Italy as any combination of ingredients may be used.

Serves 4

250 g (½ lb) squid
250 g (½ lb) peeled prawns (shrimp)
250 g (½ lb) whitebait (smelts)
plenty of flour for dusting
olive oil for deep frying
salt and freshly ground black pepper
2 lemons

Shell the prawns if necessary. Wash the whitebait and leave to dry. Clean the squid and cut the body into rings; if they are small, leave the tentacles whole in their bunches. If they are large, cut them into smaller pieces. Thoroughly toss all the fish in plenty of flour, shaking off any surplus. Heat the olive oil in a deep fryer (or a large saucepan), and immerse the fish in it a few at a time. Cook until they have turned golden in colour, drain carefully on kitchen paper and arrange on a large serving dish. Sprinkle with salt and pepper, and decorate with pieces of lemon.

A good rocket salad will complete this excellent meal.

GAMBERI D'ACQUA DOLCE ALLA SVEDESE
Crayfish the Swedish Way

I first discovered how good these freshwater shellfish could be when I was invited to taste them one day by some enterprising farmers who wanted to start breeding these mini-lobsters on a commercial scale. I guess the experiment of importing the small crayfish from their homeland, Sweden, and breeding them in some private pools must have succeeded as I regularly receive from these farmers 20 kg (45 lb) crates full of live crayfish, which are consumed avidly by my clients.

The flesh of these shellfish is very sweet to taste, white in colour and tender. Choose ones that are full and that feel heavy. After they have been cooked they turn a dark red colour not dissimilar to that of a small lobster. In Sweden crayfish are consumed in large quantities throughout the summer (the season in which they are caught). Although this recipe is dedicated to Sweden, the birthplace of crayfish, these shellfish may now be found throughout Europe.

Serves 4

20 crayfish
2 small cans (about 600 ml or 1 pt) light lager beer
2 shallots, sliced
2 carrots, sliced
2 or 3 sprigs of fresh dill (a herb that does not exist in Italy, but is used a lot in northern countries)
salt and freshly ground black pepper

In a large saucepan put the beer, shallots, carrots, dill, salt and pepper, and bring to the boil. Add the crayfish, making sure that they are covered by the beer, and simmer for about 10 minutes. Serve hot with a little of the broth together with some good bread. Follow with a good ripe piece of Cheddar or fresh Parmesan cheese and a couple of glasses of Aquavit from the freezer.

CODA DI ROSPO ALLO ZAFFERANO
Monkfish with Saffron Sauce

Although this fish looks very ugly (in the shops you will only find the edible part, that is to say the tail, on sale) it has quite a firm flesh which is absolutely delicious. Indeed, if monkfish is cut into chunks and fried with bread crumbs, it can easily be confused with prawns. Monkfish can be roasted, boiled or grilled.

This recipe describes a simple yet sophisticated way of cooking monkfish, and is on the menu of the Neal Street Restaurant.

Serves 4

800 g (about 1¾ lb) monkfish, cleaned weight
1 onion
1 celery stalk
1 small carrot
salt
25 g (1 oz or 2 tbs) butter
3 tbs white flour
200 ml (7 fl oz or 1 US cup) good fish stock
2 tbs white wine
2 grates of nutmeg
1 sachet saffron
salt and freshly ground black pepper
8 parsley sprigs

Clean the fish, removing the bones and skin, then cut into serving-size pieces. Make a court bouillon with a litre (2 pt) of water, the celery, carrot and onion. Poach the pieces of monkfish in the court bouillon, without allowing it to boil, for about 15–20 minutes.

Meanwhile, prepare the sauce. Heat the butter in a saucepan, and when it fizzes, add the flour; stir well and allow to cook, not brown, for about 5 minutes. Heat the fish stock in a separate saucepan. Slowly add the hot stock to the flour and butter, stirring all the time; finally add the wine, the saffron and the nutmeg, continue to stir and cook gently for a further 10 minutes. The sauce should be neither too runny nor too thick. Season with salt and pepper to taste.

To serve place 2 or 3 spoonfuls of sauce on to your heated plates, put the monkfish on to the sauce and decorate with sprigs of parsley. Accompany this dish with boiled potatoes and green beans in butter (Fagiolini al burro e pangrattato).

TRIGLIE AL VINO ROSSO
Red Mullet with Red Wine

The only things that mar this beautiful reddish/pinkish coloured fish are the bones. However, if you are enthusiastic enough about your food, you may overcome this obstacle with a little patience.

Mullet is a fish that can be found all over the world, though it is generally admitted that Mediterranean mullet is the best and has the purest taste. The most famous Italian recipe using this fish is called alla livornese, since it is made in Livorno. There are, however, many other variations and here is my own.

Serves 4

4 red mullet weighing up to 250 g (½ lb) each
8 tbs olive oil
12 capers
2 tbs parsley
2 cloves garlic, chopped
4 anchovy fillets
1 small glass red wine
salt and freshly ground black pepper
½ tsp fennel seeds

Wash and gut the fish, removing any loose scales. Preheat the oven to 200°C (400°F or gas mark 6).

Lay the fish side by side in an ovenproof dish. (Use a dish that the fish fit into exactly.) Put into an electric mixer the capers, olive oil, parsley, garlic, anchovies and red wine. Blend together only very briefly to make a thick sauce that still has a texture from the parsley and the capers. Stir in the fennel seeds. Pour the sauce over the red mullet, place them in the hot oven and bake for 15 minutes. Serve with home-made bread (to dip in the sauce) and light red wine. The colours of this dish will astonish you.

Red mullet

FILETTI DI SOGLIOLE CON CANTERELLI
Fillet of Sole with Chanterelles

It is not a widespread practice in Italy to serve fish with mushrooms. Indeed, this particular recipe came to me in England, where there is an abundance of wild mushrooms (which sometimes may even be bought in the markets) and where one may also purchase the famous Dover sole (which is huge when compared with its Mediterranean counterparts, and is endowed with a very delicate flesh).

It is for this last reason that I have chosen to use very delicate mushrooms such as the *Cantharellus cibarius*, more commonly known as the chanterelle mushroom. My first version of the recipe contained the *Lactarius deliciosus*, which is rather hard to find. This recipe can also be made with black Horn of Plenty (*Craterellus cornucopioides*) and Mousseron mushrooms.

Serves 4

750 g (1½ lb) sole fillet (ask the fishmonger if you cannot fillet it yourself)
For the court bouillon:
1 carrot
1 celery stalk
1 bay leaf
1 small onion
1 tsp peppercorns
salt
For the chanterelle sauce:
250 g (½ lb) chanterelle mushrooms
115 g (4 oz or ½ US cup) butter
1 small onion
1 clove garlic
half a glass of dry white wine
2 tbs double (heavy) cream
salt and freshly ground black pepper

Clean the carrot and cut in half. Wash the celery stalk. Fill a fish kettle with water to 6 cm (2½ inches). Put in the carrot, onion, celery, peppercorns, bay leaf and salt and bring to the boil. Meanwhile, roll up each sole fillet and secure with a wooden cocktail stick. When the court bouillon is boiling, add the rolled fillets, then reduce the heat to barely simmering and poach for 10–15 minutes. The moment the sole are cooked remove from the court bouillon and put aside and keep warm.

Clean the chanterelles with a brush, only washing them if really necessary. Slice the onion finely and chop the garlic into small pieces. Heat the butter in a large frying pan and fry the onions; when they begin to turn in colour add the garlic, and after a minute the chanterelles. Keeping the heat up high, fry the chanterelles, stirring gently. Then add the wine and continue to cook until most of the liquid has evaporated. Stir in the cream and season with salt and pepper. Pour the chanterelle sauce over the fillets of sole and serve immediately.

PESCE SPADA AI FERRI
Grilled (Broiled) Swordfish

The swordfish belongs to the family of large fish which, like tuna fish, is sold only in slices. After cooking, and especially if it is fresh, the meat will retain a subtle flavour. Some people compare the texture and the taste to veal.

Swordfish may be cooked in a variety of different ways, such as grilled (broiled) or fried. I prefer, however, to marinate it for about 2 or 3 hours and then to grill (broil) it over charcoal if possible.

Serves 4

4 slices swordfish weighing about 200 g (7 oz) each and about 1 cm (½ inch) thick
6 tbs olive oil
1 tsp dried rosemary
1 clove garlic, finely chopped
½ tsp paprika
salt and freshly ground black pepper

Mix together the ingredients to make the marinade and pour it over the swordfish. Leave to marinate for 3 hours.

Heat the grill to maximum (charcoal, as I have said, is preferable), and grill the steaks for 4–5 minutes on each side. This recipe may be accompanied by fried potatoes with garlic and rosemary (Patate fritte con aglio e rosmarino).

TRANCE DI ROMBO LESSO CON SALSA PICCANTE
Turbot with a Piquant Sauce

Turbot is one of the most delicate and sought-after fish, which is also usually big enough to be cut into slices. Whether it is roasted, poached or stewed, turbot still keeps its immaculate white colour and delicate taste. Owing to this delicate flavour it may be combined with a variety of different ingredients for an excellent result.

In this recipe I have chosen to poach the turbot and to accompany it with a spicy sauce. Turbot should always be eaten with boiled potatoes.

Serves 4

4 slices turbot, each weighing about 200 g (7 oz)
For the court bouillon:
1.5 litres (3 pt) water
2 or 3 bay leaves
1 small onion, cut in half
1 tsp peppercorns
1 carrot, thinly sliced
For the piquant sauce:
300 ml (½ pt or 1¼ US cups) milk
salt
50 g (2 oz) butter
15 g (½ oz) plain white flour
3 tbs dried tomato paste
5 anchovy fillets (cut up into small pieces)
salt
a pinch of cayenne
2 tbs double (heavy) cream

Bring the court bouillon to the boil. When boiling furiously, turn the heat right down, add the slices of turbot and cook very, very gently for 10 minutes.

To make the sauce, heat the milk to hot, not boiling. Melt the butter in a small saucepan, add the flour and stir with a wooden spoon for 3 or 4 minutes to cook the flour – but don't let it brown. Stir in the tomato paste and the pieces of anchovy. Break up the anchovy with the spoon in the pan as you start to add the hot milk, a little at a time, stirring to form a smooth cream. Season with salt and cayenne pepper and stir in the cream at the end. Place the slices of turbot on individual hot plates and pour the piquant sauce over them. Serve with boiled new potatoes and a salad of mâche.

TONNO ALLA SICILIANA
Tuna Sicilian Style

Tuna fish is commonly found in Sicily, where many tales are narrated about the tonnare – fishing trips organized to trap whole shoals of huge tuna fish which are then pulled up into the boats, not without some risk on the part of the fishermen. The tonnare expeditions are considered a kind of ceremony in Sicily and the fish are not only tinned but also eaten fresh, cooked in a variety of ways.

The meat of tuna fish is very substantial and is usually cut into slices so that it may be either fried, grilled or, as in this typical recipe, stewed.

Serves 4

4 steaks fresh tuna, weighing about 200 g (7 oz) each
flour for dusting
salt
4 tbs olive oil
For the sauce:
2 cloves garlic, sliced
1 red pepper
4 tomatoes, skinned and chopped
20 black olives
2 bay leaves
1 sprig of rosemary
a pinch of oregano
1 dried chili pepper
1 small glass of dry Marsala
freshly ground black pepper

Salt the steaks and then dust them with flour on both sides. Slice the red peppers into strips. Chop the garlic finely and skin and roughly chop the tomatoes.

Heat the olive oil in a large frying pan and, when hot, fry the steaks briefly on both sides just to seal in the juices. Remove them from the pan and reduce the heat. Put the red pepper in the frying pan and fry gently for 6 or 7 minutes, then add the garlic. Cook the garlic with the pepper for just a few minutes – they must not brown. Add the tomatoes, olives, rosemary, bay leaves, oregano and crushed chili. Stir the ingredients together, add the Marsala and return the tuna fish steaks to the sauce. The sauce should cover the tuna fish. Simmer gently for a further 15–20 minutes with the lid on the pan. The tuna should be tender, but the sauce should remain fresh-tasting. Season with black pepper and more salt if necessary and serve immediately.

SPIEDINO DI PESCE CON PANCETTA
Marinated Fish on a Skewer

There exist hundreds of ways of combining different types of fish on a spit. One version that is currently very successful in my restaurant consists of three different fishes combined with bacon: monkfish, large shelled scampi and salmon, all marinated for a couple of hours. This is an excellent summer dish, highly suitable for hot days when the fish can be cooked outside on a charcoal grill. If this recipe is accompanied by a fennel salad you will be able to create an instantaneous Mediterranean atmosphere, even if, like me, you only live in Fulham.

Serves 4

12 peeled scampi, weighing about 180 g (6 oz)
about 300 g (½–¾ lb) tail of monkfish
about 300 g (½–¾ lb) fresh salmon
4 slices lean bacon
For the marinade:
1 clove garlic, finely chopped
1 bunch of chives, chopped
1 tbs chopped parsley
3 tbs olive oil
the juice of a large lemon
salt and freshly ground black pepper
1 tsp paprika

Make the marinade by chopping together the garlic, chives and parsley. Mix together with the oil, lemon juice, salt, pepper and paprika.

Cut the salmon and the monkfish into 3 cm (1½ inch) cubes. Cut each slice of bacon into four. Prepare the brochettes by alternating pieces of fish with bacon and scampi. Marinate them for at least 3 hours.

Heat the grill to maximum. Grill the brochettes on all sides, basting from time to time with the marinade. They should take about 3 or 4 minutes on each side. Serve immediately.

PESCE IN CASSERUOLA
Fish Casserole

The principle behind this recipe is a useful one: it doesn't bind you to specific fish, though you should have a mixture of three or more different kinds. Money can also dictate your choice of ingredients – you can include crustaceans from lobster to shrimp, shellfish from scallops to clams, and red mullet or any fish with firm flesh.

Serves 4

250 g (½ lb) large fresh prawn tails (jumbo shrimp)
250 g (½ lb) very small squid
450 g (1 lb) red mullet: 4 small fish, if possible
1 carrot
a large handful of tender celery leaves
1 shallot
4 tbs olive oil
1 tsp fennel seeds
300 ml (½ pt or 1¼ US cups) fish stock

Clean the squid just by removing the transparent bone and cutting off the head; leave the body and the tentacles intact.

Clean and scale the red mullet. Slice the carrot finely and chop the celery leaves roughly. Slice the shallot.

Heat the olive oil in a cast iron casserole and fry the shallot and carrot together. After 2 or 3 minutes add the fennel seeds and the celery leaves, stir to prevent sticking and when the shallot begins to colour add the prawns, red mullet, squid and stock. When the stock reaches boiling, turn down the heat and simmer with the lid on the casserole for 15 minutes. Season with salt and pepper and serve in the casserole at the table. Have plenty of good home-made bread to accompany this marvellous dish.

Fish casserole served with French (green) beans and fried bread crumbs

VELLUTATA DI FRUTTI DI MARE
Shellfish Chowder

This is another favourite dish in my restaurant which is particularly simple to prepare, giving a very satisfying result. If you are unable to buy a great variety of shellfish, this dish may also be prepared with mussels alone. The dish will be more tasty, however, if you are also able to find oysters, large clams, sea truffles, sea dates or any other edible animal with a shell!

Serves 4

1 kg (2 lb) mussels in their shells
1 kg (2 lb) little clams (vongole)
8 oysters
4 scallops
2 leeks
2 carrots
75 g (3 oz or 5 tbs) butter
2 tbs flour
about a wine glass of water
a small glass of white wine
salt and freshly ground black pepper
1 tbs chopped parsley

Thoroughly scrub the mussels and wash the clams, discarding any with broken shells. Take the oysters from their shells, keeping their juice. Take the scallops from their shells.

Put the clean mussels and clams in a saucepan with a lid. Add a wine glass of water. Turn the heat up high and steam the shellfish open, shaking the pan from time to time. The moment the mussels are all open, remove from the heat and put aside to cool. When cool remove the mussels and clams from their shells, filter the liquor that remains in the saucepan and put aside.

Wash and slice the leeks, cut the carrots into oblique fine slices. Heat the butter in a large heavy pan and fry the leeks and carrots together for 5 minutes. Then stir in the flour and cook for a further minute or two, stirring all the time to prevent the flour from sticking. Meanwhile, heat up the strained liquor. You should have about 350 ml (12 fl oz or 1½ US cups) of stock: add water to make it up to that amount if necessary. Slowly add this hot stock to the leeks and carrots, then add the glass of wine. Bring to the boil and put in the scallops and oysters with their juice. Simmer briefly to cook the scallops and oysters for just about 5 minutes, then add the cooked mussels and clams. Season with salt and pepper and add the chopped parsley. Serve with crostini rubbed with garlic.

Different types of seafood

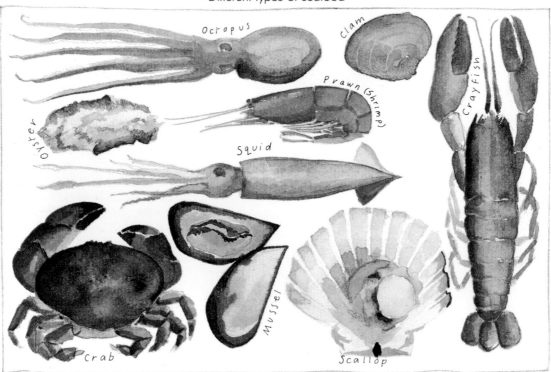

MAPPATELLO DI GRANCHIO
Crab Baked in Pastry

The Neapolitan name of this dish comes from 'mappata', meaning a linen cloth shaped like a huge napkin in which farmers used to wrap their lunch when eating in the fields. The pastry encloses the spiced crabmeat in the same form. Baking crab in this unusual way is impressive in both presentation and flavour.

Serves 4

300 g (10 oz) flaky pastry (the bought frozen kind is very successful)

300 g (10 oz) crabmeat (3 parts of white meat to one of brown)

2 tbs chopped parsley

4 tbs freshly grated Parmesan cheese

2 cloves garlic, finely chopped

salt and freshly ground black pepper

1 egg for sealing

1 tbs oil for oiling the oven dish

Divide the pastry into four equal pieces and roll each piece out to a thickness of 5 mm (¼ inch) or thereabouts. Cut from each piece accurately 20 cm (8 inch) squares. Also cut 4 ribbons of pastry about 1.25 cm (½ inch) wide and about 25 cm (10 inches) long.

Mix the crabmeat with the Parmesan and chopped parsley. Crush the garlic clove with a little salt and then add it to the mixture. Season with freshly ground black pepper.

Preheat the oven to 220°C (425°F or gas mark 7).

Divide the crabmeat mixture into four. Pile the mixture on to the centre of each square of rolled out pastry. Brush a circle of beaten egg round the pile of crab mixture and then pull up the pastry around to enclose the mixture, pleating it together. When you have pulled it up all around, press together with your fingers to seal the pleats, forming a pouch like a gypsy bag. The corners of the squares of pastry should stick up in a bunch, tie the strip of pastry loosely round the top where you pinched the pouch together. Brush the tops and sides of the pouch with beaten egg.

Oil an oven dish, and very carefully place each pouch in the oven dish, not too close as they swell a little when baking. Bake in a hot oven for 20–25 minutes. The pastry should be golden brown, the crab sizzling hot. Serve immediately.

CALAMARI FRITTI
Fried Squid

Even though this dish is sometimes described as alla romana, it is common throughout Italy. For this recipe try and find the longer type of squid, as this will have more effect when it is cut into rings. It is cooked more or less in the same way as the fritto misto and the only slightly more tiresome element in the preparation is the actual cleaning of the squid. In the town of Camogli near Genoa a curious annual celebration takes place when local fishermen organize a fried fish festival. So as to satisfy the thousands of visitors who flock to the town on this occasion, the fishermen install huge frying pans in the market place that are 10 metres in diameter. Several hundred litres of oil are used to fry something like 1,000 kg or more of fish. The whole meal is totally free and, what is more, accompanied by some excellent wine.

Serves 4

1 kg (2 lb) squid, to make about 750 g (1½ lb) cleaned weight

flour for dusting

a generous quantity of olive oil for deep frying

salt and freshly ground black pepper

2 lemons

To clean the squid, first of all divide the animal by pulling its head and tentacles away from its tubular body. This body should then be stripped of its skin and of the internal transparent 'bone'. Cut away the head but keep the tentacles, which will also be fried. Cut the body into rings, cut the bunches of legs only if they are very long.

Heat the oil in a deep fryer or a high-sided saucepan. Flour all the pieces of squid well and deep fry, a large spoonful at a time, so that they don't stick together while cooking. Fry for only 3 or 4 minutes. Drain carefully on kitchen paper, sprinkle with salt and pepper and serve immediately with slices of lemon and a simple lettuce salad.

Overleaf: Crab baked in pastry

Octopus

POLIPI IN UMIDO
Braised Octopus

In Naples octopus are called purpetielli and are cooked in a variety of different ways. The recipe that I am about to describe is one that is quite simple to prepare. Its success depends almost entirely on using very small octopus. I know that outside Italy it is quite difficult to find moscardini, a small type of octopus, but I recommend you to try and buy the smallest variety available, since the larger octopus require a very long cooking time and will still retain a slightly rubbery taste.

Cuttlefish makes a good alternative when octopus is not available.

Serves 4

750 g (1½ lb) very small octopus, or small cuttlefish
250 g (½ lb) onion, finely chopped
2 tomatoes, skinned and chopped
2 cloves garlic, chopped
4 tbs olive oil
25 g (1 oz) pine nuts
6 fresh basil leaves
1 small glass of white wine

Clean the octopus (if they are the very small ones you will not have to remove anything). If you have cuttlefish, remove the bone and cut off the heads, leaving the body and the tentacles.

Heat the oil in a saucepan and fry the onions. When they become transparent, add the garlic and the peeled tomatoes. Cook together for a few minutes, then add the pine nuts and octopus; the heat must be quite strong for a further 2 or 3 minutes. Now pour in the glass of

wine, cover the pan and simmer gently until the octopus is cooked. The small ones will cook in less than 10 minutes. Just before cooking is complete, add the basil leaves, salt and pepper. Serve with rice.

GAMBERONI AGLIO, OLIO E PEPERONCINO
Prawns (Shrimp) in Garlic, Oil and Chili Sauce

Two main advantages are obtained by cooking these prawns together with oil and other ingredients: firstly the delicious juice from the prawns will flavour the broth; secondly the chili, garlic and oil will flavour the prawn meat. The best way of appreciating to the full this inter-reaction is to mop up the sauce with some good bread. With this dish, one's hands prove to be even more useful instruments than either a spoon or fork.

For this recipe you should try and obtain some of those famous red and fleshy prawns, which I came across once in a market in Salerno and which I have already described in the antipasto chapter. An ideal wine to accompany this dish is a good, young red wine, served chilled.

Serves 4

5 or 6 large whole prawns (jumbo shrimp) per person
12 tbs olive oil
2 whole red dried chili peppers, crumbled
4 cloves garlic, chopped fine

Heat the olive oil in a pan, add the crumbled chilies and then immediately the prawns. Fry, turning the prawns over frequently, for 2 minutes. Now add the chopped garlic and allow the flavour to seep into the prawns – this will take only a few seconds. Serve the prawns in warmed individual terracotta bowls. Accompany them with some good bread to dip into the flavoured oil.

Right: Prawns (shrimp) in garlic, oil and chili sauce

INSALATA DI BACCALÀ
Salt Cod Salad

The merluzzo or cod is certainly not a typically Italian fish, as it comes mainly from northern seas; however (perhaps following the example of the Spaniards and Portuguese), the Italians have now fully adopted it in the form of baccalà, or salt cod. Indeed, each region has elaborated its own baccalà speciality. The obvious convenience of salt cod is that it keeps, and therefore may be cooked at any season. Care needs to be taken when buying this fish to ensure that it is both thick and white – two qualities that indicate goodness.

The soaking process (which desalts the fish) should begin at least 24 hours before the preparation is due to start, and the water should be changed three or four times. Try and place the cod pieces in the water with the skin facing upwards, as you will find that the salt is expelled more rapidly this way. In Italy it is possible to buy salt cod that has already been softened and desalted by soaking, though in other countries I have been able to find it only in the dried form.

This dish was a favourite recipe of my mother's. She used to serve it hot as a second course, accompanied by home-made bread.

Serves 4–6

500 g (1 lb) salt cod: soaked weight 1 kg (2 lb)
100 ml (¼ pt or ½ US cup) virgin olive oil
2 tbs finely chopped parsley
2 cloves garlic, sliced
the juice of 1 lemon
freshly ground black pepper

Put the salt cod to soak for 24 hours, changing the water three or four times. Boil the soaked pieces of salt cod in plenty of water until you see that the skin is beginning to come away from the flesh: at least 45 minutes. Drain and remove all the skin and bones, and any tough bits. Flake the fish. Dress with the oil, parsley, garlic and lemon juice. Mix well together, and serve with a generous amount of freshly ground black pepper.

TORTINO DI BACCALÀ
Italian Fish Pie

Here is my own original recipe for salt cod. Apart from soaking the fish (and in Italy this may already have been done when you buy it), the dish does not require a lot of preparation – but it brings out the full flavour of the baccalà.

Serves 4–6

600 g (1¼ lb) good white salt cod: soaked weight 1.2 kg (2½ lb)
45 g (1½ oz or 3 tbs) butter
1 large onion, chopped
2 cloves garlic, sliced
1 carrot, chopped
2 tbs chopped celery leaves
50 g (2 oz) freshly grated Parmesan cheese
200 ml (6 fl oz or ¾ US cup) milk
For the topping:
500 g (1 lb) peeled potatoes
45 g (1½ oz or 3 tbs) butter
4 grates of nutmeg
4 tbs milk
freshly ground black pepper

Put the salt cod to soak for 24 hours as in the previous recipe. Put the soaked pieces of cod in a large saucepan, bring to the boil and simmer for 40–60 minutes, or until the fish is tender and flaking away from the skin. Drain the fish, allow it to cool a little, then remove all skin, bones and tough bits and break it into flakes. Meanwhile, prepare the topping. Boil the potatoes and mash them together with the butter, the nutmeg, 4 tbs milk and some black pepper.

Preheat the oven to 190°C (375°F or gas mark 5). In a small pan, heat a further 45 g butter, and when it has melted, add the chopped onions and fry for 5 minutes. Then add the garlic, chopped carrot and celery leaves. Stir-fry for a further 5 minutes, then add this mixture to the boned and flaked cod. Grate the fresh Parmesan and add it to the fish mixture, stir in the milk and check for seasoning: you will probably not need salt, just freshly ground pepper.

Butter an earthenware oven dish, pour in the fish mixture, and cover with the mashed potato. Place the pie in the medium-hot oven and bake for 30 minutes: the potatoes should be a little crisp on top. Serve immediately.

BACCALÀ IN UMIDO
Salt Cod in Tomatoes

Braising salt cod with tomatoes is common to many regions of Italy. Some people cook potatoes with the fish: I prefer to cook and serve them separately.

Serves 4

500 g (1 lb) salt cod: soaked weight 1 kg (2 lb)
4 tbs olive oil
2 cloves garlic, chopped
1 large can skinned plum tomatoes, chopped in the can with a knife
salt and freshly ground black pepper
8 basil leaves

Put the salt cod to soak for 24 hours, as in the two previous recipes. Remove the biggest bones and any thin dark-coloured pieces from the soaked cod, and cut up into thick smaller portions. You may leave the skin on if you wish: some people like it. Put the cleaned pieces into a large saucepan of cold water and bring to the boil, turn the heat down and simmer gently for 30 minutes.

In the meantime, preheat the oven to 190°C (375°F or gas mark 5) and make a tomato sauce. Heat the olive oil in a large pan, and when hot fry the garlic just for a few seconds; then add the skinned and chopped tomatoes, salt and freshly ground pepper. Bring the sauce to simmering, stirring all the time to break up the tomatoes. Cook for 10 minutes. Add the basil leaves at the end. Drain the salt cod, and arrange the pieces in an ovenproof dish. Cover them with the tomato sauce, season and stew slowly in a moderate oven for an hour, or until the fish is soft: cover the stew for the first half-hour. Make sure the fish is always immersed in the tomato sauce, and add a little extra tomato juice or stock as necessary. Serve with boiled potatoes.

STOCCAFISSO ALLA VICENTINA
Stockfish as in Vicenza

Whereas in most of Italy, baccalà means salt cod, in Vicenza the same word confusingly means cod that has been dried without salt – in other words, stockfish. Like salt cod, stockfish needs to be soaked for a long time in water, which should be changed every so often, before it can be used. Before being left to soak, however, it has to be

beaten with a wooden mallet in order to soften the flesh. You can nowadays buy it already beaten (and since it is popular in Greece, it can often be found in Greek as well as in Italian delicatessens). The resulting tasty dish is even more delicious eaten next day.

Serves 4

400 g (14 oz) dried stockfish: soaked weight 900 g (nearly 2 lb)
1 litre (2 pt) milk
4 tbs melted butter
salt and freshly ground black pepper
1 tbs chopped parsley

Put the beaten stockfish completely covered in water to soak in a large bowl for at least 24 hours, even 2 days. Try to change the water three or four times during that period. After soaking, drain the fish, peel off the skin and tear the flesh away from the bones, breaking it up into shreds. Heat the milk in a large saucepan; when very hot, add the pieces of stockfish, turn the heat down very low and slowly simmer for 2½–3 hours. Stir the fish from time to time to make sure it doesn't stick to the bottom. The fish is cooked when it has totally disintegrated and absorbed all the milk.

At this stage, add the butter, stirring all the time, the salt, a lot of freshly ground black pepper and the parsley. Serve immediately with some Crostoni di polenta.

POLLO AL FORNO CON PATATE
Roast Chicken with Potatoes

This homely dish is known in all the regions of Italy. Chicken used to be a Sunday dish, but is now eaten on any day of the week. As this is an easy recipe which does not require much preparation time, it is highly suitable for a weekday meal.

Serves 6

1 roasting chicken weighing 1.5 kg (3 lb)
1 kg (2 lb) medium-sized yellow waxy potatoes
1 onion
2 sprigs of fresh rosemary
20 unpeeled cloves garlic
salt and freshly ground black pepper
10 tbs olive oil

Preheat the oven to hot (220°C, 425°F or gas mark 7).

Clean the chicken and cut it up into 12–16 pieces. Peel the potatoes and cut them into quarters, then slice the onion. Put the chicken pieces together with the potatoes into a baking tray, mix together with the sliced onion and the whole rosemary leaves. Season with salt and pepper and pour over the olive oil. Scatter the unpeeled garlic cloves on the top and place in the oven. After 20 minutes, turn the heat down to 190°C (375°F or gas mark 5). During the roasting time, turn the chicken and potatoes over occasionally so that they cook evenly on all sides. The potatoes should be golden and the garlic crisp after about 1 hour. Serve with salad.

POLLO IN GELATINA
Chicken in Aspic

This recipe uses one chicken to provide both the meat and the stock. This is an ideal summer dish, as it is eaten cold. All that is needed to accompany it is some salad and good bread.

Serves 6–8

1 large fresh boiling chicken weighing 2.5 kg (5½ lb), cleaned
1 large onion
4 carrots
4 bay leaves
4 celery stalks
20 whole peppercorns
salt
For the jelly:
1 litre (2 pt) chicken stock
10 leaves gelatine, or an equivalent amount of packet gelatine
the juice of 2 lemons plus the grated rind of 1
1 tbs chopped parsley

Put the whole chicken in a large saucepan, cover with cold water and bring to the boil. Add the onion cut in half, the whole carrots and the bay leaves, turn the flame down and simmer for about an hour. Now add the celery stalks, peppercorns and salt and continue to simmer until the chicken is cooked. If it is a proper boiling chicken it will take at least 2 hours.

When cooked, the meat on the legs should begin to come away from the bone, but not fall apart. Remove the chicken, carrots and celery from the stock and put aside to cool.

Make the jelly by adding the leaves of gelatine to 1 litre of strained hot chicken stock. (If using packet gelatine follow the instructions on the packet.) Add the juice of both lemons and the grated rind of one to the gelatine solution, stir well and leave to cool, not solidify.

When the chicken is cold, carve the flesh off the bones. Slice the cooked carrots and celery into thin slivers and lay them in a decorative pattern in a shallow dish. Lay the slices of chicken on top. Mix the chopped parsley into the cooled gelatine mixture and pour this over the chicken and vegetables. Leave to set. When absolutely cold, turn out on to a plate. Cut into slices to serve.

POLLO FARCITO
Stuffed Boned Chicken

The most important thing in this recipe is to remove the chicken bones without cutting the skin. It takes some skill to do this, but if you use a very sharp knife and keep the cutting edge facing the bone rather than the flesh you reduce the risk of piercing the skin.

Serves 6

1 chicken weighing 1 kg (2 lb), cleaned
For the stuffing:
60 g (2 oz or 1½ US cups) fresh white bread crumbs: include some crust
100 ml (4 fl oz or ½ US cup) milk
30 g (good 1 oz or 2 tbs) butter
1 small onion, sliced
250 g (½ lb) field mushrooms, sliced
1 clove garlic, chopped
1 tbs finely chopped fresh rosemary
30 g (good 1 oz or 6 tbs) freshly grated Parmesan cheese
2 tbs chopped parsley
salt and freshly ground black pepper
3 eggs
For roasting:
2 tbs olive oil

First bone the chicken. Holding it with its breast downwards, slit the skin and flesh along the backbone from neck to tail. With your sharp knife, work the flesh away from the rib cage on either side. When you come to the ball joints where the wings and legs join the carcass, cut through them and continue down either side of the breastbone. Lift the rib cage and free it by cutting very closely against the ridge of the breastbone – be especially careful not to puncture the fine skin here.

Cut off the two lower joints of each wing. From the inside, work the flesh off the bone and pull it out, turning it inside out in the process. Repeat for the legs.

Preheat the oven to 200°C (440°F or gas mark 6) while you make the stuffing. Put the bread crumbs to soak in the milk. Meanwhile, heat the butter in a pan and fry the sliced onion and mushrooms for 5 minutes, then add the chopped garlic clove and stir-fry for a further 5 minutes to reduce any liquid. Remove from the stove and leave to cool.

In a separate bowl mix together the soaked bread crumbs, squeezed of any excess milk, the rosemary, grated Parmesan cheese, parsley and the salt and pepper. Beat the eggs and add them to the bread crumb mixture and finally stir in the cooled mushrooms, onions and garlic. The mixture should be fairly dry in texture.

Heap the stuffing lengthwise along the centre of the boned chicken, fold the skin up over it to enclose it and sew up with a kitchen needle and fine string. Place the bird in an oven dish with the olive oil and bake in the hot oven, basting now and again. Turn the chicken over for the last 15 minutes of cooking; the bird should take about 1 hour altogether.

When fully cooked, let the chicken cool down slightly before removing the string and cutting it into slices. Accompany with new potatoes and Piselli con cipolle e prosciutto.

SALTIMBOCCA DI POLLO
Chicken Saltimbocca

This is yet another extremely simple and economical dish which produces a good result. It is ideally suited to light lunches where the food is prepared immediately before eating. As this dish contains fontina cheese which dissolves on cooking, serve it without any delay.

Serves 4

3 large chicken breasts
100 g (4 oz) prosciutto
100 g (4 oz) prosciutto crudo (Parma ham)
12 sage leaves
45 g (1½ oz or 3 tbs) butter
salt and freshly ground black pepper

Cut each chicken breast into four diagonal slices. Flatten the slices by lightly beating them between sheets of plastic. Slice the fontina cheese into 12 pieces. Cut the prosciutto into pieces the same size as the flattened chicken slices. Now place on each chicken slice a piece of fontina cheese and season with salt and freshly ground pepper and one sage leaf. Cover with the prosciutto.

In a large pan heat the butter until it fizzes, place the saltimbocca prosciutto-side-down into the hot butter and fry briefly, hardly for a minute, before turning them over. Continue to fry gently until you see the fontina has melted and the chicken has cooked. Serve immediately, three per person, accompanied by beans and bacon (Fave fresche alla pancetta).

SUPREME DI POLLO AL LIMONE
Chicken Supreme with Capers and Lemon

Chicken meat is very delicate and is suitable for almost any diet. This way of cooking it contrasts the tenderness of the breast with the intense flavour of the capers and the acidity of the lemon. This is an extremely easy recipe, and chicken breasts can be found anywhere.

Serves 4

4 chicken breasts
white flour for dusting
salt and freshly ground black pepper
45 g (1½ oz or 3 tbs) butter
1 tbs capers (salted if possible)
the grated rind and juice of 1 large lemon

Season the flour with salt and pepper and roll the chicken breasts lightly in it. Put the capers to soak in a little water.

Heat the butter in a large pan and when it is hot, not brown, add the chicken breasts. Fry gently on each side until they are cooked and golden-brown – about 15 minutes. Remove the chicken to a heated serving dish. Now add to the same pan the capers (chopped into pieces if they are the large variety), the grated rind of the lemon and all its juice. Stir well to deglaze the pan, season with salt and pepper and pour over the chicken breasts. An ideal side dish to accompany this recipe is Jerusalem artichokes (Topinambur con cipolle) or deep-fried cauliflower (Fioretti di cavolfiore fritti).

Previous page: Stuffed chicken legs

COSCIA DI POLLO RIPIENA
Stuffed Chicken Legs

With a little skill and patience you will be able to amaze people with what it is possible to do with a mere chicken leg. This is a good example of a dish which may be prepared in advance.

Serves 4

4 whole chicken legs
4 thin slices of back bacon
3 tbs olive oil
kitchen string
For the stuffing:
50 g (2 oz or 1½ US cups) fresh white bread crumbs
75 g (2½ oz) mortadella, cut into strips
¼ nutmeg, grated
1 tbs chopped parsley
1 clove garlic, finely chopped
2 eggs
salt and freshly ground black pepper

Take the legs, cut off any adjoining backbone and knuckles (use these pieces in stock). Now with a very sharp small knife cut down the length of the bones on the inside and ease the flesh away, taking care not to puncture the skin. (Discard the bones.) You will obtain a sort of tapering rectangle of flesh, which should be flattened out on your work surface, skin side down.

Make the stuffing by mixing together the bread crumbs, sliced mortadella, nutmeg, parsley and garlic. Beat the eggs, season with salt and pepper and mix with the other ingredients.

Place a spoonful of this mixture in the middle of each rectangle of chicken. Fold the rectangle into a sausage-shaped parcel. Put a piece of bacon lengthwise along each 'sausage' to close the join and flap over the end to close the parcel. Bind with kitchen string to make an even shape and so that the stuffing cannot escape.

Meanwhile, preheat the oven to 200°C (400°F or gas mark 6).

Heat the oil in a heavy casserole and fry the stuffed chicken legs on all sides, browning them gently. Now place the pan in the oven and bake for 15 minutes. Remove the string and leave the parcels to cool slightly before slicing them. Serve with French beans and fried bread crumbs (Fagiolini al burro e pangrattato) or with spinach and Patate all'aglio. They are equally good served cold.

PETTO DI TACCHINO FARCITO
Stuffed Breast of Turkey

For this dish you will need a large turkey breast, easily found in Britain and in America, where these birds can be up to 14 kg (30 lb) in weight. A turkey breast in itself is slightly dry, and so the addition of other ingredients renders it much more tasty, hot or cold. You may accompany this dish with some broccoli spears with ginger (Broccoli allo zenzero) or with carrot and celeriac purée (Pure di carote e sedano rapa).

Serves 8

1 whole side of a turkey breast weighing about 1.5 kg (3 lb)
salt and freshly ground black pepper
¼ nutmeg, grated
1 tbs French mustard
100 g (4 oz) smoked ham, thinly sliced
1 sprig of rosemary, finely chopped
30 g (good 1 oz or 2 tbs) butter
8 large leaves raw spinach
kitchen string
2 tbs olive oil
a further nut of butter
1 glass of dry white wine

Slice the turkey breast on one side only and then almost right through the whole length in such a way that it opens up like a book into one large slice of about 3 cm (1½ inches) thick. Preheat the oven to 200°C (400°F or gas mark 6).

First sprinkle the whole of the inside of the breast with salt, black pepper and grated nutmeg. Then spread one side of the breast only with the French mustard and lay on this the slices of smoked ham. Sprinkle the ham with the chopped rosemary and dot with little pieces of butter. On the facing side lay the washed raw spinach leaves. Now fold together the two halves and roll up into a neat parcel, tying securely with string. Put the olive oil into an ovenproof dish and place the rolled turkey into it. Spread the butter over the top and season with salt.

Bake the roll in the medium oven for 1½ hours. Add the glass of wine after the first half-hour. Baste continually during cooking, turning the roll from time to time. Leave for at least 10 minutes before cutting into slices if you wish to serve it hot.

TACCHINO AL FORNO
Roast Turkey

Other people may consider this way of cooking turkey slightly sacrilegious. In Italy we not only roast turkey in the conventional way, but also cook it cut into smaller pieces. This is possible as Italian turkeys are usually of a smaller size than English or American ones. It is customary to eat this dish at Christmas as a complement to other meat dishes.

Serves 6

1 turkey weighing 3–4 kg (6–9 lb), including the liver and giblets
4 onions
4 carrots
2 large sprigs of fresh rosemary
8 tbs olive oil
salt and freshly ground black pepper
2 glasses of white wine

Preheat the oven to hot (220°C, 425°F or gas mark 7).

Cut the turkey into portions: cut each leg into 4 pieces and each breast into 8 or 10 pieces. Place all the turkey pieces, including the whole liver and giblets, in a large baking tray. Slice the onions and carrots and mix them together with the turkey. Pour over this the olive oil, sprinkle with the whole rosemary leaves and season with salt and pepper. Place in the oven. After half an hour turn the heat down to 190°C (375°F or gas mark 5), turn over the pieces of turkey and add the wine. Continue to roast at this lower temperature for a further hour, turning the turkey pieces over from time to time. The turkey should be cooked after an hour and a half, but you should taste for yourself in order to judge. Serve with the juices from the pan, accompanied by cabbage with bacon or by peas with ham (Cavolo verza con pancetta or Piselli con cipolle e prosciutto).

PETTO D'ANITRA AL MANGO
Duck with Mango

It is quite usual to see duck accompanied by some sort of fruit – be it cherries, grapes, dates or, of course, oranges – in recipes that seem mostly to be of French origin. I do not wish to start heated discussions with our French friends, but le canard à l'orange was a dish served up in the Tuscan courts in 1600 – a fact upheld by several menus from that period.

I have preferred to use mango (all the better if it is not totally ripe), as it adds a touch of acidity to the duck meat which is usually rather fatty. This is another favourite dish in my restaurant where whole ducks are used (for obvious reasons). This gives us the additional advantage of obtaining an excellent demi-glace of duck which will be used later as a sauce. However, if you are preparing this recipe at home I suggest you use only the duck breast, one per portion.

Serves 4

4 duck breasts with their skin
salt and freshly ground black pepper
3 or 4 tbs stock
30 g (good 1 oz or 2 tbs) butter
1 large mango (not too ripe)
a further 30 g (good 1 oz or 2 tbs) butter
2 tsp brandy
1 tbs mango chutney
1 tsp potato starch

Salt and pepper the duck breasts. Heat the first 30 g of butter in a heavy pan which has a fitting lid, and quickly fry the breasts, skin-side down, for 5 or 6 minutes. Turn the duck breasts over, add the stock, cover with the lid and cook for a further 10 minutes, lowering the heat slightly.

Meanwhile, cut the mango in two halves, peel off the skin and cut the flesh from the stone in thin slices. When the breasts are cooked, remove them from the pan and keep warm.

Put the pan back on a moderate heat and add the second 30 g of butter. Stir it well into the duck juices and add the brandy, the mango chutney and some salt and pepper. Cook for a moment, then stir in the potato starch, mixed to a paste in a little of the sauce.

To serve, cut the duck breasts slantwise into slices and arrange them on warm plates alternating with slices of fresh mango. Pour a little of the sauce over the breasts and serve with spinach (Spinaci, olio e limone) and new potatoes.

QUAGLIE CON UVETTA ALLA GRAPPA
Quails with Grappa Raisins

A little planning is necessary for this dish, as you should put some raisins to soak in the grappa a couple of days beforehand. (Unless, of course, you have some already made. This is extremely simple: all you need is a jar filled with seedless raisins and topped up with grappa.)

Quails these days are easy to find all the year round as they are now bred for consumption. They represent a light but elegant dish for people without much appetite.

Serves 4

50 g (2 oz or ⅓ US cup) seedless raisins, soaked in a small glass of grappa
8 plucked quails
salt and freshly ground black pepper
2 tbs olive oil
45 g (1½ oz or 3 tbs) butter
3–4 tbs stock
1 tbs chopped parsley

Put the raisins to soak in a small glass of grappa, if possible two or three days ahead.

Preheat the oven to 200°C (400°F or gas mark 6). Clean the quails thoroughly, and rub with salt and pepper both inside and out. Heat the olive oil in a heavy pan or casserole over a strong flame, and fry the quails until they become golden on all sides: this will only take a few minutes. Place the open casserole into the hot oven and bake the birds for a further 10 minutes. When the quails are cooked, remove them from the casserole and keep them warm. Skim away any excess oil. Put the casserole back on a high flame, add the butter and with a wooden spoon stir it into the juices. Remove the raisins and add the grappa to the quail juices and butter in the pan; allow to evaporate for a minute, then add the stock, stir to deglaze the quail juices and now add the raisins and the chopped parsley. Season with salt and pepper and pour over the quails. Serve with fried carrots (Carote fritte).

FAGIANO FARCITO AL FORNO
Stuffed Roast Pheasant

In Italy pheasant is considered the prince of all feathered game. However, whereas in Italy this bird is consumed almost immediately it is caught, in Britain and America it is more usual to let the bird hang and season for seven to eight days after it is killed.

Whenever I visit my English brother-in-law, who has a dozen or so pheasants running around in his artichoke patch, I always have to stop myself from laughing as I think of the many Italian hunters who would give their right arm to come across one of these rare birds. Here in England, they can be found almost anywhere. The unfairness of it all!

The recipe that I am about to describe uses the female pheasant which is generally more tender and succulent than the male of the species. You may accompany this dish with some beautiful yellowy-orange chanterelle mushrooms if they are in season.

Serves 4

2 female pheasants weighing about 750 g (1½ lb) each when cleaned
2 slices fatty bacon (in many cases pheasant is sold trussed with bacon)
For the stuffing:
1 small onion, finely chopped
1 clove garlic, chopped
2 tbs olive oil
250 g (½ lb) minced (ground) pork
the livers from the pheasants, chopped
2 whole cloves, crushed
1 tbs chopped parsley
1 sprig of rosemary, finely chopped
1 tbs dry bread crumbs
2 tbs mostarda di Cremona (the fruit cut into small pieces)
¼ nutmeg, grated
a nut of butter
For the sauce:
45 g (1½ oz or 3 tbs) butter
½ tbs flour
half a glass of white wine
salt and freshly ground black pepper

Thoroughly clean the pheasants. Preheat the oven to 200°C (400°F or gas mark 6).

To make the stuffing, fry the chopped onion and garlic in the oil and add to it the chopped pheasant livers and the minced pork, plus the crushed cloves. Continue cooking together for 8 minutes, then remove the mixture from the flame. Let it cool down and then add the chopped parsley, rosemary, bread crumbs, nutmeg and mostarda di Cremona. Mix all these ingredients together thoroughly and season with salt and pepper.

Stuff the pheasants with this mixture and tie in the stuffing with the pieces of bacon. Place a knob of butter on each bird and put in a hot oven for 1½ hours. Baste the birds every now and again with the juices in the baking pan. When cooked, remove from the pan and keep hot.

To prepare the sauce, heat up the pheasant juices in the roasting pan, skim away any excess bacon fat, then stir in the butter and the flour. After a few minutes, pour in the wine and continue to stir over the heat for a minute or two. Season with salt and pepper.

To serve, cut the pheasants into quarters, with the stuffing, and pour the sauce over.

FARAONA AL MELOGRANO
Guinea Fowl (Guinea Hen) with Pomegranate

As they are now artificially bred, you will find no difficulty in acquiring this bird, which is a more sophisticated version of the chicken. In order to underline this degree of sophistication I have chosen to prepare this dish with pomegranate. I find this slightly sour ingredient makes the guinea fowl all the more interesting to savour, and the combination of tastes is reminiscent of Renaissance recipes.

Serves 4

2 guinea fowl (guinea hen) weighing about 1 kg (2 lb) each, complete with livers and giblets
2 tbs olive oil
30 g (good 1 oz or 2 tbs) butter
1 small onion
1 carrot
50 g (2 oz) prosciutto crudo
1 large ripe pomegranate
1 glass of dry Marsala
salt and freshly ground black pepper

Preheat the oven to 200°C (400°F or gas mark 6).

Clean the guinea fowl and lightly singe them to remove any bristles. Brush over with a little olive oil, salt inside and out and roast in the oven for 1 hour. In the meantime, chop the onion and cut the carrot into thin slices. Heat the butter in a heavy pan and gently fry the onion and carrots. Cut the giblets and liver into small pieces and add to the frying pan, stir and fry for a few minutes before adding the sliced prosciutto. Now pour in the glass of wine, allow it to bubble for a few minutes then turn down the flame and simmer the sauce while you peel the pomegranate. To open the pomegranate, score the skin round once and split open with your hands. Take out the grains by breaking away the yellow membrane and skin: do this over a bowl so that you collect all the juice as well as the seeds.

When the guinea fowl are cooked, remove them from the roasting pan, pour away any excess fat and deglaze with a tablespoon of water. Add to these juices the liver, carrot and prosciutto mixture and, finally, the pomegranate seeds. Stir very briefly and do not cook, but keep hot.

Carve the breasts and legs from the birds and place on a warm serving dish (the carcasses may be used to make an excellent broth). Pour over them the pomegranate sauce, and serve with potato croquettes and sautéed wild mushrooms (Funghi misti in umido).

PICCIONI CON OLIVE NERE
Pigeons with Black Olives

Tuscany can perhaps be considered the homeland of game. In this region recipes abound for all types of birds, and domestic or wild pigeons are often to be found on the menu. It is often possible to find pigeons (or wood pigeons) in Britain when they are in season. These are preferable to the domestic variety as they are slightly more flavoursome.

Don't be surprised when you find that this is yet another recipe for a stuffed bird. In my view, stuffing is the simplest, easiest way to render a game dish more attractive and satisfactory.

Serves 4

4 pigeons, complete with giblets
2 tbs olive oil
For the stuffing:
1 small onion, finely chopped
2 tbs olive oil
the pigeon giblets and liver, chopped
100 g (4 oz) fresh pork sausage
1 tbs raisins
150 g (6 oz or 2¼ US cups) fresh bread crumbs
salt and freshly ground black pepper
1 tbs chopped parsley
2 egg yolks
For the sauce:
2 tbs olive oil from frying the pigeons
2 cloves garlic, chopped
1 glass red wine
1 medium can plum tomatoes
20 black olives, pitted
salt and freshly ground black pepper

Clean and gut the pigeons (taking care not to throw away the giblets). Salt them inside and out, then fry them on all sides in a large pan for about 15 minutes. Keep the frying oil for the tomato sauce.

To make the stuffing, fry the finely chopped onion in the oil, adding the chopped giblets and liver and the crumbled sausage meat. Continue to fry these ingredients for 15 minutes, then withdraw the pan from the heat and let it cool down a bit. Next add to this the raisins, the bread crumbs, salt, pepper and parsley. Mix in the egg yolks and then proceed to stuff the pigeons.

For the sauce, use the oil you fried the pigeons in to fry the chopped garlic until golden. Add the glass of wine to deglaze the pan, and reduce before adding the tomatoes, which you can chop in their can with a long knife. (You may strain the tomatoes if there seems to be too much liquid.) Cook, stirring, for 5 minutes and then add the pitted olives and season with salt and pepper.

Place the stuffed pigeons in a casserole, pour the tomato sauce over them, cover and simmer gently for at least 1 hour, or until the pigeons are tender. Serve with baked potatoes and onions (Patate al forno).

Right: Pigeon with black olives

LE PERNICI CON LE PERE
The Partridge and the Pear

One of the best game birds is the partridge. With its delicate flavour, it is an excellent autumnal dish. In my restaurant I serve it in the simplest way possible: baked in the oven and accompanied by a pear in sweet-and-sour syrup. The pears can, naturally, be prepared well in advance, as they are served cold. I would recommend that you make a few extra ones and keep them for use at a later date.

Serves 4

4 partridges, ready larded if possible, plus giblets
1 tbs brandy
1 ladleful of broth
60 g (2½ oz or 4 tbs) butter
salt and freshly ground black pepper
For the pears:
2 not-too-ripe pears
10 cloves
4 grates of nutmeg
2 cm (1 inch) stick cinnamon
100 g (4 oz or ½ US cup) sugar
1 small wineglass of wine vinegar
1 small wineglass of water
salt and freshly ground black pepper

First prepare the pears. Peel them, halve them and remove the seeds. Place in a saucepan the water, vinegar, sugar and spices, and bring to the boil. Immerse the pears in this liquid and cook for 15 minutes, depending on their texture: by the end of this time the pears should still be quite firm. Allow to cool.

Remove the liver and giblets from the partridges and put them to one side. Salt and pepper the partridges inside and out.

Preheat the oven to 200°C (400°F or gas mark 6). Take a casserole, heat it thoroughly on the stove and then add half the butter – which should melt immediately. Place the four partridges and their giblets in the pan and fry over a high flame to seal in the juices for 5 minutes on all three sides and 5 minutes on their backs. Throw away the larding and take out the giblets and liver, which should now be cooked. Replace the partridges in the same pan together with the second half of the butter, the brandy and broth, and put in a very hot oven for 15–20 minutes. When cooked, remove the partridges and keep them warm while you make the sauce. Use the partridge juices to make the sauce: purée

the liver and giblets and stir into the roasting juices over a low flame, then season with salt and pepper.

Serve the partridges with the pears and a little sauce. Ideal vegetables to serve with this dish are potato and cheese croquettes (Crocchette di patate al formaggio) and baked celery (Sedani al forno), which can be cooked in the hot oven at the same time.

CONIGLIO S. ANGELO
Rabbit St Angelo

Normally I never give a proper name to a recipe as I consider the name should reflect the ingredients used in the dish. This, however, is an exception and is dedicated to a man who lived alone on an island facing St Angelo of Ischia and was renowned for preparing rabbit in an interesting way. I don't know if this man is still living as he was when I heard of him 30 years ago. I have tried to recreate as near as possible his recipe.

Serves 4

1 young rabbit weighing 1 kg (2 lb) when cleaned
flour for dusting
3 tbs olive oil
1 clove garlic, sliced
3 or 4 ripe seedless tomatoes, skinned, or 1 large can peeled plum tomatoes drained of their juice
1 sprig of rosemary
pinch of thyme
1 glass of dry white wine
some fresh basil leaves
salt and freshly ground black pepper

Cut the rabbit into smallish pieces and try to take out as many bones as possible. Lightly salt and flour the pieces, then fry them in the oil in a deep saucepan so that every side is well browned. Next add the garlic, the roughly chopped tomatoes, rosemary, thyme and white wine. Add the basil after half an hour. Cook these ingredients with the lid on the saucepan over a moderate flame. Every now and again stir the sauce and add the rest of the tomato juice or some water if you find it is becoming too thick. It will be ready after about 1 hour. Season with salt and pepper and serve hot, accompanied by some fried courgettes (zucchini) and boiled new potatoes or polenta.

CONIGLIO ARROSTO CON PATATE E CARCIOFI
Roast Rabbit with Potatoes and Artichokes

Rabbit meat is similar to chicken in that it is tender and white. It will usually need some additional flavours to make it more interesting: artichokes and capers are ideal.

Serves 6

1 young rabbit weighing about 1 kg (2 lb) when cleaned
6 young and fresh artichokes
1 bunch or 4 large spring onions (scallions)
18 small new potatoes
1 medium can peeled plum tomatoes
5 tbs olive oil
1 tbs capers
salt and freshly ground black pepper

Clean the rabbit and cut it into smallish pieces. Clean the artichokes and divide them into quarters (leave only the most tender leaves – if they are big artichokes, use only the heart). Preheat the oven to 220°C (425°F or gas mark 7).

Clean the spring onions and slice them, including the tender part of the stalk. Clean and peel the new potatoes. Place all these ingredients in a casserole dish, adding the tomatoes, oil, capers and some salt and pepper. Cover and put in a hot oven for 15 minutes. Remove the lid and reduce the oven to 190°C (375°F or gas mark 5). Stir from time to time so that all the contents cook evenly and simmer gently for a further hour or until the rabbit is cooked.

This dish requires some good bread and a good fresh salad to go with it, for instance Cicoria e radicchio con rucola.

LEPRE AL BAROLO
Hare in Red Wine and Grapefruit

Luckily the hare, proverbially known for its astuteness, is able to avoid being caught by swarms of covetous hunters eager for its skin, otherwise it would undoubtedly be extinct by now. As hare is similar to wild rabbit, the meat has to be marinated overnight, like other types of game. In the olden days the marinade used to be composed of a sweet and sour mixture, and this idea may still be appreciated today.

Serves 8

1 big hare weighing 2 kg (4 lb)
flour for coating
8 tbs olive oil for frying
For the marinade:
juice of 2 pink grapefruit
500 ml (18 fl oz or 2¼ US cups) red wine, preferably Barolo
50 g (2 oz) raisins
5 cloves
the grated peel of an orange
10 bay leaves
1 large sprig of thyme
1 sprig of fresh rosemary
2 cloves garlic
1 tbs honey
1 bunch of celery leaves
1 large carrot, chopped fine
1 tsp mustard
For the sauce:
25 g (1 oz) dried ceps
30 g (good 1 oz or 2 tbs) butter
1 small onion, finely chopped
50 g (2 oz) prosciutto crudo

Prepare the marinade and leave the hare (cut into pieces) to marinate for 24 hours.

Take the hare from the marinade and dry with a cloth. Dust with some flour and fry in the hot oil on all sides. Heat up the marinade. Remove the pieces of browned hare from the pan and deglaze with a ladleful of the hot marinade.

Place the pieces of hare in a cast-iron casserole and pour over them the deglazed juices and enough marinade to cover. Bring to the boil, turn down the heat and simmer gently for 2 hours, until the hare is tender. After 1 hour of cooking add the dried ceps, crumbled in your hand.

Meanwhile, to make the sauce, fry the chopped onion in the butter until it becomes transparent, then add the prosciutto crudo cut into strips. Take the pieces of hare from the casserole. Strain the liquid and add it to the onion and prosciutto; stir well and simmer for a few minutes longer, seasoning to taste. Pour the sauce over the hare and serve yet again with polenta crusts (Crostoni di polenta).

CAMOSCIO IN SALMÍ
Venison Steak with Wild Mushrooms

This is a typical dish of the Aosta Valley region where it is still possible to hunt deer with a licence that is rather hard to come by. In the rest of Europe it is much easier than in Italy to come across this king of the mountains; in America it is easier still.

The recipe requires that you marinate the meat for a long time in a rather complex marinade. This is to take away the too intense gamy flavour of the meat and to make it more tender. It is traditional to serve the venison with polenta, which turns it into a princely dish.

Serves 4

4 1 cm (½ inch) thick slices from a venison leg or fillet, weighing a total of 600 g (1¼ lb)
flour for dusting
For the marinade:
1 litre (2 pt) good red wine
1 small onion, chopped
5 bay leaves
1 sprig of rosemary
2 cloves of garlic, chopped
2 carrots, chopped
2 celery stalks, chopped
1 sprig of thyme
5 cloves
10 juniper berries
1 tbs split black peppercorns
salt
For the sauce:
45 g (1½ oz or 3 tbs) butter
1 small onion, sliced
100 g (4 oz) smoked bacon, chopped
350 g (¾ lb) mushrooms, sliced

Marinate the venison for three days before you are to cook the dish.

Take the meat from the marinade, keeping the marinade to add to the sauce later, and dry with a cloth. Lightly dust the slices with flour and then fry for 5 minutes in the butter until brown on each side, and put aside to keep hot. Then, in the same butter, fry the sliced onion and the smoked bacon cut into small pieces. Now add the sliced mushrooms and fry all together for a few minutes until golden, then add 2 glasses of the strained marinade, allow to bubble and reduce briefly. Add the venison pieces, coat with the sauce and serve with Crostoni di polenta.

Beef and Veal

CARNE ALL'ALBESE
Raw Beef with Alba Truffles

In the region of Alba this dish would normally be considered an antipasto. By increasing the quantities used, however, it can be transformed into a cold main course. It is an excellent dish which, in pairing raw beef with the white truffle, results in a culinary triumph. Some people wrongly call this recipe 'carpaccio', but the only thing they have in common is raw beef. It is necessary to use a slicing machine in order to obtain very thin slices: if you do not happen to possess one of these, ask your butcher to slice the meat for you. You may even have to beat the meat out still thinner.

Serves 4

350 g (¾ lb) fillet beef, sliced very thinly
salt and freshly ground black pepper
juice of a lemon
2 tbs olive oil
2 or 3 tender white celery stalks, finely sliced
60 g (2 oz) fresh Parmesan cheese, cut with a knife into thin slivers
1 white truffle weighing about 50 g (2 oz)

Beat the meat between two sheets of plastic with a meat-beater. Spread the slices of meat out on four large flat plates. Season with salt and pepper and divide out the juice of one lemon equally among the four. Trickle the oil over the meat and sprinkle on it the very finely sliced celery and the slivers of Parmesan cheese. Only when the plates are on the table should you slice the truffle very finely using a mandolin, and distribute the pieces over the meat.

You may accompany this dish with some grissini and a salad such as Insalata capricciosa.

TARTARA A MODO MIO
Steak Tartare My Way

I always prepare this excellent cold dish a couple of hours before serving so that the full flavour of the meat is brought out. Accompanied by some pieces of garlic toast, steak tartare is not only a simple recipe to prepare but also an easily digested one. Evidently you have to like raw meat in order to appreciate this speciality.

Serves 4

8 small gherkin pickles
40 g (1½ oz) capers
2 spring onions (scallions)
2 tbs parsley
4 anchovy fillets
600 g (1¼ lb) fillet of beef (sirloin), finely chopped
3 tbs olive oil
2 egg yolks
10 drops Tabasco
a sprinkling of Worcestershire sauce
1 tbs brandy
the juice of 1½ lemons
salt and coarsely ground black pepper
sprigs of parsley for decoration
For the garlic toast:
8 slices of (preferably) home-made bread
1 clove garlic
30 g (good 1 oz or 2 tbs) butter

Finely chop the gherkins, capers, spring onions (scallions), parsley and anchovies and mix them in with the chopped fillet of beef, olive oil, egg yolks, Tabasco, Worcestershire sauce, brandy and lemon juice. Add salt and pepper. Thoroughly stir these ingredients so as to obtain an even mixture, then spoon it out on to a serving dish and decorate with some sprigs of parsley. Toast the bread and rub the clove of garlic over it, taking care not to press the garlic too much. Butter the prepared toast and serve with the meat and a carrot and coriander salad (Insalata di carote e coriandolo).

FILETTO FREDDO CON SALSA VERDE
Cold Fillet of Beef with Green Sauce

To conclude the cold meat dishes, here is a classical recipe which, incidentally, is also very popular in my restaurant.

It is vital that you like your meat cooked rare, as the fillet will be all the more tender and succulent if prepared in this way.

Serves 4

2 Châteaubriands weighing 350 g (12 oz) each
kitchen string
salt
30 g (1 oz or 2 tbs) butter
For the green sauce:
6 tbs chopped parsley
8 small gherkin pickles
30 g (1 oz) capers
8 anchovy fillets
5 tsp green peppercorns preserved in brine
the grated rind of 1 lemon
6 tbs olive oil

Tie the Châteaubriands with kitchen string in such a way that they keep their round shape, and salt them. In a steak pan, heat the butter and fry the steaks fiercely for a few minutes on each side, so that they appear almost charred on the outside but are still rare towards the centre. Put them aside to cool.

To make this green sauce the simplest way, place all the ingredients in an electric blender and purée quite briefly until you have a smooth sauce. Alternatively, chop the parsley, gherkins and capers as fine as you can. Cut the anchovy fillets into small pieces and place them in a mortar. Begin by pounding the anchovies to a paste and then add in this order the green peppercorns, gherkins, capers, lemon peel and parsley. The sauce will now be thick and bitty. At this stage start adding the olive oil, dribble by dribble as for making mayonnaise, until you have a smooth sauce.

Remove the string from the cold Châteaubriands. Slice them and arrange on a serving dish, spooning the green sauce over them. In summer, serve this dish with a salad made from new potatoes. Beans with garlic and oil (Fagioli aglio e olio) or dandelion salad (Insalata di cicoria di campo) make a good accompaniment.

Overleaf: Cold fillet of beef with green sauce

BRASATO AL BAROLO
Braised Beef with Red Wine

The Barolo, king of Italian wines, is supposed to give the maximum flavour to meat and other dishes. Piedmontese beef, full of wonderful taste and tenderness, combines perfectly with the wine, producing this outstanding dish.

Serves 6

1300 g (3 lb) rump steak cut thick in one piece
30 g (good 1 oz or 2 tbs) butter
30 g (good 1 oz or 2 tbs) lard
1 large spring onion, sliced
2 cloves garlic, roughly chopped
1 carrot
2 celery stalks
small sprig of fresh rosemary
2 bay leaves
1 sprig fresh thyme
5 sage leaves
1 cinnamon stick, 4 cm (1½ inches) long, or 1 pinch ground cinnamon
the grated peel of ¼ lemon
600 ml (1 pt or 2½ US cups) Barolo wine
salt and freshly ground black pepper
a little stock (optional)

In a heavy casserole just bigger than the piece of steak, heat the butter and the lard together. When very hot add the steak and brown on all sides to seal in the juices. Remove the meat and put to one side. Fry the sliced onion, garlic, the split carrots and the celery stalks for a few minutes, then add the herbs, cinnamon, lemon peel and the Barolo wine. Stir well, deglazing the sides and bottom of the casserole.

Now replace the steak in the sauce, season with salt and pepper and cover the casserole. Simmer very gently for 1½ hours. Turn the steak frequently so that it cooks evenly, and make sure that it is always covered by the sauce. Add a ladle of stock if necessary. When the steak is cooked, leave it to cool. Strain the sauce to remove the herbs, cinnamon, lemon peel and vegetables. (You may wish to reduce the sauce by increasing the heat and boiling for 5 minutes or more before adding the steak.)

Very gently reheat the steak in the sauce just before serving with new potatoes and a mushroom dish – Prataioli al burro, aglio e prezzemolo, or Funghi misti in umido, depending on the ingredients available.

INVOLTINI DI CARNE
Beef Roulade

This delicious recipe may be found in all regions of Italy with a variety of different fillings and cooked in different ways. Its unchanging feature is that it must be made from thin slices of mature well-flavoured meat that can be rolled up. The topside is perhaps the most suitable meat to use. This is another extremely simple dish to prepare.

Serves 4

4 thin slices of topside (beef round) weighing a total of 650 g (about 1½ lb)
4 slices prosciutto crudo
salt and freshly ground black pepper
For the filling:
2 tbs chopped parsley
1 tsp chopped fresh rosemary
5 small gherkin pickles
1 tbs raisins
For the sauce:
3 tbs olive oil
1 small onion, thinly sliced
1 medium carrot, chopped
2 celery stalks, chopped
1 glass of white wine
150 ml (¼ pt or ½ US cup) stock

Beat the slices of beef with a meat-beater between sheets of see-through plastic as thin as you can, being careful not to break them. Spread the slices of beef out on a working surface, sprinkle them with salt and pepper and lay the slices of prosciutto on top. Finely slice the small gherkins and scatter these on to the prosciutto with the parsley, rosemary and raisins. Roll the meat up and secure each piece into a roulade with two wooden cocktail sticks.

Heat the olive oil in a cast-iron casserole and fry the roulades so that they are well browned on all sides. Remove them from the casserole and put to one side. In the same oil fry the sliced onion for a few minutes, then add the chopped celery and carrot and continue to fry, stirring from time to time, for about 10 minutes. Now pour in the glass of wine and allow it to reduce.

Return the roulades to the casserole. Add the stock, salt and pepper, cover and simmer for about an hour or until the meat is tender. Fried potatoes with garlic and rosemary (Patate fritte con aglio e rosmarino) and sautéed aubergines (Melanzane al funghetto) make good accompaniments.

MEDAGLIONI CON CANTERELLI
Beef Medallions with Chanterelles

The word medallion means, as the name itself suggests, slices of fillet (sirloin) cut to the size of a large medallion. This is yet another extremely simple dish to prepare but, like many simple things, it is also sophisticated – doubly so owing to the addition of the chanterelles, or gallinacci as they are called in some parts of Italy.

If you are unable to obtain any chanterelles you may substitute oyster mushrooms, which are somewhat easier to acquire, since they are cultivated.

Serves 4

12 slices of beef fillet (sirloin) cut 1 cm (½ inch) thick, total weight 400 g (10 oz)
flour for dusting
3 shallots
400 g (10 oz) chanterelles or oyster mushrooms
45 g (1½ oz or 3 tbs) butter
half a glass of white wine
4 tbs double (heavy) cream
salt and freshly ground black pepper
1 tbs chopped parsley
2 tbs olive oil

Flour the medallion fillets. Chop the shallots and clean the mushrooms, cutting them in slices. Melt the butter in a heavy pan and gently fry the shallots until they become golden. Now add the mushrooms and stir-fry over a medium heat until most of the liquid from the mushrooms has evaporated away. Next add the wine, allow it to bubble and penetrate the mushrooms for a few minutes before adding the cream. Stir in the cream but do not allow it to boil, season with salt and pepper and sprinkle in the chopped parsley.

Heat the olive oil in a steak pan until it is very hot and fry the beef medallions briefly on both sides. Serve the medallions on heated plates with the mushrooms on top.

This dish is ideally accompanied by some new potatoes and French beans.

POLPETTONE AL SUGO
Meat Loaf in Tomato Sauce

I confess that I have had to telephone my mother on more than one occasion in order to gather the exact ingredients to make up this economical recipe.

I distinctly remember the tremendous satisfaction with which this dish used to appease our appetites when my brothers and I were young. It had two advantages: the sauce in which it was cooked provided an excellent dressing for the pasta which was served up as a first course. Then the meat loaf – cut into slices – appeared as a tasty main course accompanied by peas with ham.

Serves 8

1 kg (2 lb) minced (ground) beef
150 g (6 oz or 5 US cups) bread crumbs made from stale bread
2 tbs finely chopped parsley
60 g (2 oz or ¼ US cup) freshly grated Parmesan cheese
salt and freshly ground black pepper
4 eggs
oil for frying
For the tomato sauce:
1 onion, finely chopped
4 tbs olive oil
1 clove garlic
2 large cans peeled plum tomatoes
10 fresh basil leaves
salt and freshly ground black pepper

Mix the minced meat together with the bread crumbs, add the parsley, Parmesan cheese, salt and pepper and thoroughly mix so that the meat is well incorporated. Lightly beat the eggs and add to the meat mixture. The mixture should stick together and you can now form it into a large oval meat loaf. If you have difficulty in shaping the meat loaf and it is falling apart, add a few more bread crumbs to the mixture. (It is a good idea to fry a small meatball first to check the seasonings before you make the meat into a loaf.) In a large oval cast-iron casserole, heat the olive oil and fry the meat loaf until it is a crisp golden-brown all over and retains the juices of the meat inside. Take great care not to break the loaf as you turn it in the casserole. Set the casserole aside while you make the tomato sauce.

In a separate pan, fry the finely chopped onion

in the olive oil. When the onion has become golden, add the garlic and fry only briefly before adding the tomatoes, drained of some of their liquid. Cook the sauce over a medium flame for ten minutes, stirring to break up the tomatoes. Season with salt and pepper and add the basil leaves.

Now add the sauce to the meat loaf, put the lid on the casserole and return it to the stove. Simmer gently for about 1 hour. Alternatively, you can place the casserole in a fairly hot oven (200°C, 400°F or gas mark 6) for an hour. While it is cooking, gently turn the loaf from time to time. Remove the lid after 30 minutes to allow the sauce to thicken. When the loaf is cooked you may use the rich tomato sauce to dress some pasta prepared in the meantime. The meat loaf should be allowed to cool for 10 minutes before it is sliced. Serve with peas and ham (Piselli con cipolle e prosciutto) and fried potatoes (Patate fritte con aglio e rosmarino).

MANZO BOLLITO IN INSALATA
Boiled Beef Salad

This is a typical example of 'recycling' meat to create an unpretentious but delicious cold dish. This is an excellent recipe to make in the summer and should be accompanied by a mixed salad and some good bread.

For this recipe you will need some beef that has been used to make a good broth. Although it may appear to you that this meat is no longer up to much, it will be extremely tender and tasty.

Serves 4

500 g (1 lb) boiled beef: silverside (bottom round), brisket or topside (beef round or top round)
4 spring onions (scallions)
1 tbs chopped parsley
salt and freshly ground black pepper
4 tbs olive oil
1 tbs balsamic or red wine vinegar

Trim the pieces of cooked beef, removing all the fat and nerves and leaving only the lean meat. Slice this into 1 cm (½ inch) slices and then cut the slices into strips. Chop the spring onions, including the green part. Mix the strips of beef in a bowl with the chopped onion, parsley, salt and pepper and then add the olive oil and the vinegar. Toss a few times.

If you wish to increase the volume of this dish, add a few boiled potatoes. Leeks in vinaigrette (Porri all'agro) make a good accompaniment.

BOLLITO MISTO ALLA PIEMONTESE
Boiled Mixed Meat from Piedmont

This is perhaps the most famous of all Piedmontese dishes as it invariably figures in most good Italian restaurants abroad. It is a classic autumn or winter dish.

In Piedmont there are many ingredients available for the bollito, such as calf's head and feet which, when boiled, will become gelatinous. Make sure to include the famous zampone (stuffed pig's trotter). You can easily obtain this speciality from any good Italian delicatessen, only be sure to examine the 'sell-by' date.

Serves 8

1 ox tongue weighing about 1.5 kg (3 lb), preferably one that has been soaked in brine
1 zampone
1 boiling chicken weighing about 2 kg (4 lb)
500 g (1 lb) beef brisket
4 carrots
5 stalks of celery
2 medium onions
1 large sprig of rosemary
8 medium potatoes
salt and freshly ground black pepper
mostarda di Cremona for serving
For the green sauce:
10 anchovy fillets
50 capers
40 g (1½ oz or 1¼ US cups) bread crumbs
1 large bunch flat-leaved parsley
1 clove garlic
2 tbs wine vinegar
about 400 ml (14 fl oz or 2 US cups) olive oil

Clean the ox tongue of any excess fat and gristle. Clean and wash the chicken.

Into a very large saucepan (big enough to take the chicken, tongue and beef), put the ox tongue, cover with cold water and bring to the boil. Skim away the froth that comes to the surface every now and again. Boil the tongue for an hour, then add the piece of beef and the boiling chicken, the carrots, celery, onions, rosemary and a little salt. Continue to boil the meats together for a further 2 hours. The boiling chicken and the beef should be tested to see if they are cooked after 1½ hours, as it is important that your meats are tender but not falling apart. During the final half-hour of boiling add your potatoes.

In a separate saucepan boil your zampone. The cooking time is usually specified on the package, and most zampone are precooked so that 20 minutes is sufficient. When the tongue, chicken and beef are cooked, remove them from the saucepan. Allow the tongue to cool a little before peeling off the skin. Allow all the meats to stand for 10 minutes before carving. Arrange slices of all the different meats on a large hot serving plate. You may ladle a little of the stock on to the serving dish to keep the meats moist. Arrange the potatoes and other vegetables with the meats and serve with green sauce.

To make the green sauce, put all the ingredients except the olive oil into your electric blender and mix until you get a thick paste. Then slowly add the olive oil, intermittently blending, until you obtain a beautiful thick sauce. The amount of oil used depends upon the size of your bunch of parsley. You may wish to add salt and pepper, but usually the capers and anchovies are seasoning enough.

In some regions of Piedmont this dish will also be served accompanied by mostarda di Cremona (crystallized fruits in mustard syrup). You can obtain this from many Italian delicatessens.

LA PIZZAIOLA
Beef Steak with Pizzaiola Sauce

'La Pizzaiola' is another classic name together with 'alla scapece' and 'al funghetto': the words alone indicate the way a certain food is cooked. La pizzaiola probably comes from how the pizza-making woman would have cooked with tomatoes, garlic and oregano in olive oil. La pizzaiola sauce can equally successfully be served with fish such as swordfish and tuna.

Serves 4

500 g (1 lb) beef sirloin steak cut from the bone into 4 slices, each about 1.5 cm (¾ inch) thick
1 medium can tomatoes, chopped in the can (Cirio make a brand ready chopped)
4 tbs olive oil
2 pinches of oregano
2 cloves garlic
flour for dusting
salt and freshly ground black pepper

Salt the meat on both sides and then dip into the flour. Heat the olive oil in a heavy pan over a high flame. Fry the steak as you like it on both sides. Remove from the pan and keep warm. Slice the garlic and add it to the olive oil, reduce the heat a little and almost immediately, before the garlic starts to brown, add the tomatoes, oregano, salt and pepper. Stir and cook for 5 minutes, incorporating the meat juices into the tomato sauce. Return the steaks to the sauce, and let them soak up the flavour of the tomatoes for a minute before serving.

NODINO AL VINO
Veal Cutlets with Wine and Sage

Because veal is considered a rather tasteless meat on its own, it is usually accompanied by either a herb or a sauce which will enhance the flavour of the dish.

The main virtues of veal, however, are its tenderness and the facility with which it is cooked. It is for this reason that most Italian restaurants have a variety of veal escalopes on their menu.

The chop or nodino of veal is a typical Piedmontese or Lombardian speciality. The best known is 'alla Sassi', so called because it originated in the Villa Sassi restaurant, situated in the hills of Turin.

Serves 4

salt and freshly ground black pepper
4 large veal chops, including the tenderloin
flour for dusting
45 g (1½ oz or 3 tbs) butter
1 glass of dry white wine
10 fresh sage leaves
2 tbs stock (optional)

Salt the veal and dust with flour. Heat the butter in a large pan; when hot, put in the chops and fry over a medium flame until golden on both sides. This takes about 10 minutes. Now add the glass of wine, and allow to evaporate before adding the roughly cut sage leaves. Turn the heat down and cook gently for a further 10 minutes, if necessary adding a little stock to keep the chops moist. Season and serve with the juices from the pan.

Fennel prepared 'au gratin' (Finocchi gratinati) is an excellent vegetable to serve as an accompaniment.

SCALOPPINE ALLA TIROLESE
Veal Escalopes (Scallops) from the Tyrol

I have already hinted that escalopes may be prepared in a hundred and one ways. The most remarkable feature of this meat is that it can be cooked in seconds and may be flavoured by a variety of herbs and spices. The most famous ways of flavouring escalopes are: marsala, lemon, white wine, cream, truffles. However, the simplest of all these versions, the 'paillard', is merely a thinly sliced escalope, grilled, and which requires no added flavouring.

Escalopes can be made from any cut of veal (but ideally from the topside); the main thing is that they should be beaten flat with a meat-beater.

Serves 4

12 veal escalopes (scallops) weighing a total of 600 g (1¼ lb)
salt and freshly ground black pepper
flour for dusting
45 g (1½ oz or 3 tbs) butter
3 carrots, thinly sliced lengthwise
80 g (3 oz) speck tirolese affumicato, sliced

Beat the escalopes flat between two sheets of see-through plastic. Spread them on your working surface, season with salt and pepper and dust them with flour. Heat the butter in a large flat frying pan. When it begins to fizz, add the escalopes; fry for only a few minutes on each side, remove from the pan and keep warm in a serving dish. In the same butter fry the slivers of carrot, when al dente add the sliced speck. Toss for a few minutes together, season and spread over the veal escalopes. Serve with boiled new potatoes and courgettes (Pasticcio di zucchini) or asparagus (Asparagi al parmigiano), if in season.

LA MILANESE
Veal Escalope (Scallop) Milanese

The veal escalope Milanese is similar to the escalope Viennese in that they are both cooked in bread crumbs. The Viennese, however, is almost always served with a slice of lemon and a rolled anchovy, which is not the case with the Milanese.

In this recipe I have deviated slightly from the classical method of preparing the escalope Milanese by adding some finely chopped basil

and some grated Parmesan cheese with the egg. This addition renders a hitherto rather boring dish more interesting!

Serves 4

4 veal chops with their bones, each weighing 200 g (7 oz)
1 egg
60 g dry bread crumbs
4 tbs freshly grated Parmesan cheese
5 fresh basil leaves, chopped
salt and freshly ground black pepper
oil for frying
4 lemon slices for garnish

Flatten the chops, leaving the bone, and trim away the fat. Beat the egg, add the finely chopped basil, the grated Parmesan cheese and some salt and pepper. Dip each of the escalopes in the egg and then roll them immediately in the bread crumbs. Heat the oil in a large pan and fry the escalopes over a gentle flame. When the bread crumbs turn a deep golden colour take the escalopes out of the pan and serve garnished with a slice of lemon with Zucchini alla scapece, turnips with butter (Rape al burro) or dandelion salad (Insalata di cicoria di campo).

MEDAGLIONI AL SUGO DI NOCI
Veal Medallions with Walnut Sauce

This is another classic recipe which I have developed in my restaurant and whose simplicity is much appreciated by my clients. The combination of meat and walnuts owes its success to the juxtaposition of the neutral flavour of the veal with the distinct flavour and texture of the nuts. This is another dish which may be cooked in a couple of minutes.

Serves 4

600 g (1¼ lb) fillet (sirloin) of veal, cut into medallions
flour for dusting
salt
45 g (1½ oz or 3 tbs) butter
1 tsp brandy
250 ml (8 fl oz or 1 US cup) double (heavy) cream
50 g (2 oz) walnut halves
salt and freshly ground black pepper

Dust the medallions in flour and salt. Heat the

butter in a heavy pan and when it fizzes, fry the medallions on both sides for only a few minutes. Remove the veal and put it on a heated serving dish.

To make the sauce, add the brandy to the butter in the pan and stir briefly to incorporate the juices from the veal. Now add the cream and the walnuts, stirring all the time and cooking very gently until the cream has thickened. Season the sauce with pepper and (if necessary) salt, and pour it over the medallions. Serve hot with Jerusalem artichokes and onions (Topinambur con cipolle).

CIMA ALLA GENOVESE
Stuffed Breast of Veal

This dish, usually eaten hot but also excellent cold, is derived from the famous Ligurian speciality called Cima alla genovese. It is an ideal dish for picnics and also for cold buffets. As it is almost impossible to prepare the pocket for only 4 people, this recipe gives quantities for 8–10 people, or you may wish to eat the portions for a couple of days afterwards. It is very important that you try and find a piece of breast of veal large enough to be cut into the shape of a pocket – with only one open side which will be sewn up when the stuffing has been inserted.

Serves 8–10

1½ veal (calf's) brains, cleaned
a boned breast of veal, cut into a tapered rectangle and weighing about 900 g (2 lb)
80 g (3 oz) pork fillet (tenderloin)
50 g (2 oz) smoked bacon
50 g (2 oz) mortadella
50 g (2 oz) fresh bread crumbs
1 tbs fresh thyme leaves
1 tbs chopped parsley
30 g (1 oz) freshly grated Parmesan cheese
200 g (7 oz) shelled fresh peas (alternatively, frozen)
2 eggs
1 tbs black olive paste
half a small nutmeg, grated
salt and freshly ground black pepper
2 celery stalks
2 carrots
2 bay leaves
salt
a piece of muslin and kitchen string, or a barding needle and thread

Put the brains to soak in cold water for half an hour.

With a very sharp knife cut a pocket in the breast, leaving only one side open. Remove any extra layers of fat and any small bones or gristle that may remain. Be careful not to damage the middle part of the pocket or puncture the outside. Use an electric blender to make the stuffing. Cut the pork fillet and the bacon into pieces, roughly chop the mortadella and put them in the blender with the fresh bread crumbs. Blend only briefly as you want to keep a texture to this stuffing. Now add the fresh thyme, the parsley and the Parmesan and blend again briefly.

In a small saucepan bring 500 ml (1 pt or 2 US cups) of water to the boil and poach the brains for 5 minutes, adding a little salt. Allow to cool and roughly chop them. If you are using frozen peas, cook them for a couple of minutes. If you have fresh peas, do not cook them. Beat the eggs together in a large bowl, incorporate the bread crumb and meat mixture from the blender, then stir in the chopped brains and the peas, and finally add the olive paste. Grate into this mixture the nutmeg and season generously with salt and pepper.

Bring to the boil a large saucepan of water (big enough to take the stuffed veal pocket). Add to the water the celery, carrots, bay leaves and plenty of salt. Meanwhile, stuff the pocket with the mixture: you may need help, as the easiest way is for one person to hold the pocket open like a bag while the other person spoons the stuffing in. The pocket should be completely full so that it appears quite swollen. Wrap the pocket tightly in muslin and tie up with kitchen string, or sew up to form an oblong parcel. Place the pocket in the boiling water, reduce the heat and simmer gently for 2 hours. When cooked remove from the water and leave to drain for 5 minutes. Now very carefully remove the muslin, place the pocket into an oval pot approximately the same size as the stuffed pocket, which is the typical shape of the 'cima' dish. Weight it down and leave to cool. Serve cut into 1 cm (½ inch) slices.

OSSOBUCO MILANESE
Veal Marrow-bone Milanese
(Braised Veal Shanks)

Together with risotto and cutlets, this way of preparing ossobuco is a typical speciality of Lombardy and more precisely of Milan.

It is a particularly filling dish which is usually eaten during the colder months. Of great importance is to find a butcher who will supply you with the marrow-bones or ossibuchi – so called because they are derived from the tibia of the calf which, when cut, reveals a bone with a hole filled with the marrow. I have based this recipe on the marrow-bones served at Badia a Coltibuono when I was the guest of Lorenza de Medici.

Serves 4

4 marrow-bones (cross-cut veal shanks), 3–4 cm (1½ inches) thick, cut from the middle of the shin where the bone is rounded on both sides and the meat is dense
flour for dusting
salt
4 tbs olive oil
1 small onion, sliced
1 large can Italian peeled tomatoes, strained of half their juice
the juice and half the grated peel of a large orange
1 glass of dry red wine
salt and freshly ground black pepper

Dust the marrow-bones with salt and flour. Heat the olive oil in a cast-iron casserole and fry the marrow-bones two at a time on both sides, taking great care not to damage the marrow in the centre of the bone or allow it to fall out. Remove the marrow-bones from the casserole and put to one side. In the same oil, fry the onion until transparent then add the tomatoes, breaking them up in the casserole with a wooden spoon while cooking. Keep the heat up high so that the tomatoes reduce. After 5 minutes add the orange juice, the grated peel and the glass of wine. Continue to cook fast and return the marrow-bones to the sauce. Season the sauce with salt and pepper and then reduce the heat, cover the casserole and simmer for an hour to an hour and a half or until the meat has begun to come away from the bone. Serve with saffron rice (Risotto milanese).

Lamb

NOCCIOLE D'AGNELLO CON CARCIOFI
Noisette of Lamb with Artichokes

Noisettes are the most tender cut of lamb and, in this recipe, they should be accompanied by equally tender artichokes. It is during the spring that you will be able to find these tender artichokes, which in Pinzimonio can even be eaten raw. If you are unable to obtain any of these, you may substitute artichoke hearts.

Serves 4

4 small artichokes
400 g (14 oz) lamb fillet (sirloin or noisette)
1 tbs capers, preferably salted
1 bunch of spring onions (scallions)
4 tbs olive oil
50 g (2 oz) prosciutto crudo, with fat, cut into strips
a ladle of stock
2 tbs chopped parsley
salt and freshly ground black pepper
a slice of lemon

Wash the artichokes and pull off the tough outside leaves. Trim off the tops and cut into quarters. If the artichokes have spiny centres, remove these with a sharp knife. Put aside in a bowl of cold water with a slice of lemon.

Cut the lamb fillet into 2 cm (1 inch) thick noisettes. Put the capers to soak in cold water to wash off surplus salt or vinegar. Chop the spring onions. Now heat the olive oil in a medium-sized saucepan and fry the noisettes, turning them over so that they brown on each side, remove them from the pan and place them in a hot dish to keep warm. Add to the pan the spring onions and the prosciutto cut into strips, fry briefly over a strong flame and then add the pieces of artichoke. Stir-fry all together for 5 or 6 minutes. Now add a ladle of stock and the capers, turn the heat down and cook gently for a further 10 to 15 minutes or until the artichokes are cooked. Return the noisettes to the pan, add the parsley, black pepper and salt, (if necessary), mix the meat together with the artichokes and serve straight away.

Right: Noisette of lamb with artichokes

AGNELLO AL FORNO CON PATATE
Roast Lamb with Potatoes

This is a dish which does not require any side-dishes or other vegetables as it is a meal in itself. Even the cooking itself does not require much attention as it is entirely left up to the oven. Aside from this, it is an extremely economical dish, as you may use the cheaper cuts of lamb. In addition to all these advantages, this recipe yields an excellent result.

Serves 6

1200 g (2¾ lb) boned shoulder of lamb, cut into medium-sized pieces
1 kg (2 lb) yellow waxy potatoes, peeled weight
1 medium onion, sliced
1 sprig of fresh rosemary
5 tbs olive oil
salt and freshly ground black pepper

Preheat the oven to 200°C (400°F or gas mark 6).

Peel the potatoes and cut them into thick slices. Slice the onion. Place the pieces of lamb in a baking tray, add the onions, potatoes and the sprig of rosemary broken into 3 or 4 pieces. Pour over the olive oil, season with salt and pepper and then mix all together with your hands so that both the meat and the potatoes are evenly coated.

Place the baking tray in the oven and bake for an hour and a half. Half-way through cooking, thoroughly stir the ingredients so that the meat and potatoes brown evenly. Serve hot, taking care to give everyone equal portions of potatoes and meat.

AGNELLO ALLA GIUDEA
Lamb with Lemon and Egg

Why my mother used to call this recipe 'alla Giudea' I do not know as a similar sauce is prepared in Greece and is called avgolemono. All I know, however, was that when it was prepared with exceptionally young and tender lamb it was an exquisite dish. The same recipe can use chicken instead of lamb.

Serves 4

600 g (1¼ lb) very lean lamb (preferably from the leg), cut into 3 cm (good 1 inch) pieces
4 tbs olive oil
4 eggs
the juice of 3 medium lemons
the grated peel of 1 lemon
2 cloves garlic, crushed to a pulp
1 tbs chopped parsley
4 tbs stock

Heat the olive oil in a saucepan, add the pieces of lamb and brown them on all sides. When the meat is sealed, put a lid on the saucepan and reduce the heat. Cook for 15–20 minutes, shaking the pan from time to time. The resulting moisture will cook the meat.

Beat the eggs and add the lemon juice, grated peel, parsley and crushed garlic. Once the lamb is cooked, remove the saucepan from the heat, add the stock, stir well and then pour in the egg mixture. Continue to stir all the time so that the sauce thickens with the heat of the meat. Take care not to take too long as the sauce will curdle if it begins to cook. You may accompany this recipe with fried potatoes and salad, or with baked celery (Sedani al forno).

SCOTTADITO
Barbecued Lamb Cutlets

This is a typical Roman recipe whose success depends on two things: some good cutlets from a young lamb and, if possible, a charcoal grill.

Apart from these two factors the secret of this dish lies in its simplicity: it should be eaten with the fingers immediately after being cooked (the Italian name scottadito means burnt fingers!).

Serves 4

12 good best end lamb cutlets (rib lamb chops)
50 g (2 oz) pork lard
salt and freshly ground black pepper

Melt the pork lard in a small saucepan. Remove from the stove. Flatten the lamb cutlets with a meat-beater, and dip them into the melted lard. Season each side of the cutlets with salt and pepper and place them on a charcoal grill. Grill briefly on both sides and decorate the bones with paper frills that can be found in any good stationers. Serve accompanied by fried potatoes with garlic and rosemary (Patate fritte con aglio e rosmarino) and French bean salad (Insalata di fagiolini alla menta).

A variation of this dish is obtained by substituting goat's meat for lamb, though this may be a little difficult to find outside Italy.

AGNELLO CON CICORIA
Lamb Casserole with Belgian Chicory (Endive)

It has been claimed that this method of cooking lamb originated from the town of Taranto in the region of Puglia. I first tasted this excellent dish when I was travelling through Lecce, one of the most beautiful towns in southern Italy. I remember I was invited to eat this dish by some peasants whose house was situated in the middle of an expanse of olive trees set off by the beautiful dark red soil typical of the area. The bread that accompanied the 'stew' was also home-made . . . what memories!

In the effort to reconstitute this dish I have had to substitute Belgian chicory for the wild chicory used in the original. In my opinion wild dandelion is still the best.

Serves 4

800 g (1¾ lb) boned leg of lamb, cut into pieces
1 medium onion, sliced
4 tbs olive oil
1 large can Italian peeled tomatoes
salt
2 small hot red chili peppers, crumbled
400 g (14 oz) Belgian chicory (endive), cut in halves
100 ml (4 fl oz or ½ US cup) stock
2 tbs chopped parsley

If you have an earthenware casserole with a lid, use it for this dish; otherwise use an ovenproof casserole. Preheat the oven to 200°C (400°F or gas mark 6).

Place the pieces of lamb, the sliced onion, olive oil, tomatoes and their juice into the casserole. Season with salt and crumbled chili and place in the oven with the lid on. Bake for 1½ hours.

Clean and wash the chicory and cut the heads in half. Core the stalk, as that part of the chicory is very bitter.

After 1 hour of cooking, arrange the halves of chicory over the lamb, pour over the stock, sprinkle with parsley and return to the oven for the final half-hour. Serve with toasted home-made bread rubbed with garlic and spread with pork lard.

COSCIA MARINATA ALLA GRIGLIA
Grilled Lamb Steak

A good lamb steak cooked over a charcoal grill has an exquisite taste. The meat for this dish needs to be prepared the day before to allow it to become more tender and to absorb all the flavours.

Serves 4

4 slices of lamb cut from the leg where the bone is quite thin, each slice weighing 150–180 g (about 6 oz)
For the marinade:
1 tbs chopped fresh rosemary
1 tbs chopped fresh marjoram
1 tbs chopped parsley
1 tbs chopped chives
6 tbs olive oil
the juice of 2 lemons
salt and freshly ground black pepper

Prepare the marinade by mixing together the chopped herbs with the oil, lemon juice and seasoning. Spoon the marinade on to each of the steaks and place them stacked one on top of the other in a small dish. Leave the lamb to marinate in a larder or refrigerator overnight.

The next day, cook the steaks, without any further preparation, over a charcoal grill. They will cook very quickly and be deliciously tender. Serve with a tomato, onion and fresh basil salad or with French bean salad with mint (Insalata di fagiolini alla menta).

Pork

COTOLETTE ALL'ARANCIO
Pork Cutlets with Orange Sauce

Although pork itself is a tasty meat, accompanied by orange it becomes doubly delicious – the acidity of the fruit counteracts the fattiness of the pork. This is an extremely simple recipe which for once makes use of the stock cube to flavour not only the sauce but also the meat.

Serves 4

4 lean pork cutlets (loin chops)
the juice of 3 oranges and the grated peel of one
45 g (1½ oz or 3 tbs) butter
1 bouillon cube
salt and freshly ground black pepper

Heat the butter in a large pan, fry the cutlets for 10 minutes on each side and then remove from the pan. Deglaze the pan with the orange juice, then add these juices to the cutlets in a saucepan with a lid. Add the grated peel, the bouillon cube and salt and pepper. Cover the saucepan and simmer the cutlets for 20 minutes or until the pork is tender. Serve with cabbage and bacon (Cavolo verza con pancetta).

FILETTI ALLO SPIEDO
Marinated Pork Fillet (Tenderloin) on Skewers

As the fillet is the most tender part of the pig, it only requires a very brief cooking time. It is ideal grilled (broiled), especially over charcoal. The longer you marinate it, the better the result will be.

Serves 4

500 g (1 lb) pork fillet (tenderloin)
150 g (5–6 oz) lean bacon
For the marinade:
1 tbs finely chopped fresh rosemary
1 tbs chopped parsley
1 tbs finely chopped fresh sage
2 cloves garlic, finely chopped
3 tbs olive oil
the juice of 2 lemons

Cut the pork fillet into medallions 1 cm (½ inch) thick. Make the marinade by mixing the chopped herbs with the garlic, olive oil and lemon juice in a ceramic or glass dish. Immerse the medallions in the marinade and turn them over from time to time: if possible leave to marinate overnight. Cut the bacon into pieces the same size as the medallions. Take 4 long skewers and push pieces of pork alternating with pieces of bacon on to each skewer. Grill the skewers (preferably over some charcoal) until the meat is cooked. Serve with an interesting salad, such as roast peppers with garlic and parsley (Insalata di peperoni arrostiti).

SPEZZATINO CON PEPERONI
Pork Fillet with Preserved Peppers

This is both a rustic and a ceremonious recipe. The slaughtering of the pig which is to provide food for the country families for months to come is usually celebrated in winter, when this activity takes place. It is somewhat difficult to explain to vegetarians the nature of this celebration, which smacks of a pagan rite! It is only natural that this ceremony does not weigh on the country folks' conscience, since it is a matter of survival to them.

Serves 4

400 g (14 oz) pork fillet
30 g (1 oz or 2 tbs) pork lard
3 tbs olive oil
4 cloves garlic
200 g (7 oz) large red bell peppers (preserved in vinegar, if possible), drained weight. Alternatively, 2 small whole fresh red peppers plus 2 tbs red wine vinegar
1 dried hot red chili pepper, crumbled
salt and freshly ground black pepper

Melt the lard with the olive oil in a large pan. When very hot add the pieces of pork fillet and fry, turning all the time, for about 10 minutes. Slice the red peppers and cut the cloves of garlic into slivers. Add these to the pork fillet and continue to cook over a reduced flame for as long as it takes to cook the garlic. The preserved red pepper merely requires heating up: if you do not have preserved peppers, sliced fresh red peppers will take at least 10 minutes longer to cook. You will also need to add 2 tbs of vinegar at the end. Season the meat mixture with the crumbled red chili, salt and pepper, and serve piping hot. The country folk would accompany this dish with some good home-made bread. I will leave it up to you to chance an alternative.

Right: Pork fillet with preserved red peppers

SCALOPPINE DI MAIALE ALLO ZENZERO
Escalope (Scallop) of Pork with Ginger

Although ginger is not a typically Mediterranean root, it was introduced in the past into Venetian and Florentine cooking probably, like saffron, by merchants returning from their long voyages to the East. Today in some places in Italy ginger has been rediscovered and its distinct, strong flavour coupled with garlic is used to set off many a dish.

Serves 4

4 pork escalopes (scallops) weighing about 150 g (6 oz) each
salt and freshly ground black pepper
2 tbs olive oil
4 cloves garlic, sliced
30 g (1 oz) fresh ginger, cut into strips
2 tbs chopped parsley

Season the pork with salt and pepper. Heat the olive oil in a heavy pan. Fry the meat on all sides on a medium flame until it is brown – it takes only about 10 minutes. Add the garlic and ginger 5 minutes before serving and the parsley at the last minute. Turn the meat over so that the pieces are well covered with garlic, ginger and parsley. Serve with a Savoy cabbage salad (Insalata di cavolo verza).

ZAMPONE CON LENTICCHIE
Stuffed Pig's Trotter with Lentils

The stuffed pig's trotter or 'zampone' is a typical speciality from Modena. The skin of the trotter is stuffed with a selection of minced meats, skin and spices. The stuffed trotters sold by butchers in Italy require more than 2 hours' cooking time; however, it is possible to buy specially packaged products which need to be cooked for only 20 minutes in boiling water. You will probably find the latter in Italian delicatessens. I suggest that you cook the lentils separately and that you add them to the trotter at the end.

Serves 4

1 zampone weighing about 600 g (1¼ lb)
400 g (14 oz) lentils (large brown type)
3 tbs olive oil
2 cloves garlic
1 medium can peeled plum tomatoes
good pinch oregano
salt and freshly ground black pepper

Put a large saucepan (big enough to take the zampone) of water on to boil. In a separate saucepan, simmer the lentils in plenty of salted boiling water for 15 minutes.

Slice the cloves of garlic. In a large pan heat the olive oil and briefly fry the garlic; the moment it begins to turn in colour, add the tomatoes. Roughly break up the tomatoes as they fry in the pan. Cook over a medium flame for 10 minutes, reducing the tomatoes to a sauce. At this point put the zampone in the large saucepan of boiling water and simmer for 20 minutes or as instructed on the packaging. When the lentils are cooked, drain them well and add to the tomatoes and garlic in the pan, season with salt and pepper and oregano. Stir well and continue to cook for a further 10 minutes, testing the lentils, which should not be reduced to a mush but retain a 'bite'.

Serve the zampone, sliced into slices 1 cm (½ inch) thick, with the lentils and possibly some mostarda di Cremona. A wonderful winter dish.

Stuffed pig's trotter with lentils served with fruits in mustard syrup.

149

ARROSTO DI MAIALE
Roast Pork with Garlic

For this recipe it is best to use the hind leg of the pig (otherwise known as the ham) with its delicious skin.

Serves 6

1 piece of leg of pork weighing about 1.8 kg (4 lb)
sea salt
2 tbs olive oil
2 carrots
15 cloves garlic
a large glass of dry white wine
freshly ground black pepper

Preheat the oven to 220°C (425°F or gas mark 7).

Score the skin of the piece of pork with a very sharp knife to make a grid pattern of little squares (your butcher may do this for you). Now rub the skin with sea salt and grease all sides with the olive oil. Place the meat in a baking tray and put in the hot oven for 25 minutes.

In the meantime, finely dice the carrots and chop the garlic into little pieces. Mix these together with the white wine and season with black pepper. After roasting the pork for 25 minutes, take it out of the oven and pour over it the carrot, garlic and wine mixture. Turn the oven down to 190°C (375°F or gas mark 5), replace the roasting pan and cook at this temperature for a further 2 hours. Every now and again baste the pork with the juices in the pan. Don't let the garlic stick to the skin of the pork or it will burn.

Before carving, leave the meat to rest in its juices for 10 minutes. Accompany this dish with red cabbage (Cavolo rosso) and mashed potatoes.

COSTINE DI MAIALE CON CECI
Spare-Ribs with Chick Peas

Here is another rustic pork recipe which – although it could never feature as nouvelle cuisine – is tasty enough to be appreciated by even the most delicate of palates.

Serves 4

1 kg (2 lb) pork spare-ribs with plenty of meat on them
250 g (8 oz) dried chick peas, or 2 medium cans of chick peas
3 tbs olive oil
5 cloves garlic, chopped
2 stalks of celery, chopped
2 carrots, chopped
1 large can Italian peeled plum tomatoes
salt and freshly ground black pepper
a little stock (optional)
5 or 6 fresh basil leaves

Put dried chick peas to soak in a lot of water (remember they will increase their volume threefold) for 24 hours. Strain the chick peas and add to a saucepan of boiling salted water. Boil gently for 1½ hours or until the chick peas are cooked al dente.

Take a thick-bottomed saucepan or casserole large enough to contain both the meat and the chick peas. Heat the olive oil in this pan and thoroughly brown the spare-ribs: this will take at least 15 minutes. Move the spare-ribs around in the pan so that they do not stick. Chop the garlic, the celery and the carrots and add to the spare-ribs. Fry very briefly, just coating the vegetables with oil, and then add the tomatoes and all their juice and season with salt and pepper. Cook the spare-ribs in the tomato sauce for about 20 minutes, then add the drained chick peas. If there is not sufficient liquid in the pan to cover the spare-ribs and chick peas, add a ladle of stock or tomato juice.

Cover the pan and simmer for 45 minutes or until the spare-ribs are cooked: the meat should be coming away from the bones. Add the basil leaves 5 minutes before serving. Home-made bread, as usual, is a good accompaniment to this wholesome dish.

Offal

SOFFRITTO ALLA NAPOLETANA
Mixed Offal in Hot Tomato Sauce

This is a typically Neapolitan recipe which is considered more a soup than a proper dish. I remember my mother used to prepare large quantities of the soffritto in advance, so that it could be consumed little by little. Although it is rather rich and heavy, the soffritto is also very flavoursome. It is ideal for offal enthusiasts.

Serves 6

500 g (1 lb) pork liver
250 g (½ lb) pork lung
250 g (½ lb) pork heart
2 tbs olive oil
150 g (6 oz) pork lard
1 large glass of red wine
4 tbs tomato purée
1 tbs Harissa
2 whole hot red chili peppers
5 bay leaves
salt and freshly ground black pepper
For serving:
1 litre (2 pt) stock or water
6 slices wholemeal toast

Wash all the offal under running water. Remove any fat and gristle. Cut into small chunks about 2 cm (1 inch) square. In a heavy casserole heat the oil and lard together, add the pieces of offal and fry over a strong flame, browning all sides: this will take about 10 minutes. Now add the glass of wine, allow it to evaporate for a bit before adding the tomato purée, the Harissa, the crumbled chilies, the bay leaves, salt and freshly ground black pepper. (If you have difficulty in finding Harissa, use two extra chili peppers and another teaspoon of tomato purée.) Reduce the heat and cook over a moderate flame for a further 30 minutes, or until all the pieces of offal are cooked. Leave the soffritto to set overnight in a cold larder or refrigerator.

To serve the following day or whenever (the soffritto is excellent for freezing), spoon the solid soffritto into a saucepan, add a litre (2 pt) of stock and bring to the boil: the proportions are two heaped tablespoons of soffritto to 150 ml (5 fl oz or ⅔ US cup) of stock or water. Make some thick slices of toast from a good wholemeal loaf. Put a slice in the bottom of each soup bowl and pour over it the hot melted soffritto.

FEGATO BURRO E SALVIA
Calf's (Veal) Liver with Butter and Sage

I don't know if this can be even described as a recipe, it is so simple. All I know is that it can be found in most Italian restaurants, for the combination of liver and sage is delicious.

Serves 4

500 g (1 lb) calf's (veal) liver, cut into 4 slices
salt and freshly ground black pepper
flour for dusting
45 g (1½ oz or 3 tbs) butter
12 fresh sage leaves

Season the pieces of liver on both sides and then dust with flour. Heat the butter in a large saucepan. Fry the liver slices in the butter: being tender, they will only require cooking for a couple of minutes on each side. Add the sage leaves once one side is cooked.

Any kind of delicate vegetable can be used to accompany this delicious dish: broad (fava) beans and bacon (Fave fresche alla pancetta) are an example.

FEGATO ALLA VENEZIANA
Calf's (Veal) Liver Venetian Style

This typical Venetian recipe has become a classic Italian dish which may be found on the menu of any good Italian restaurant.

Serves 4

400 g (14 oz) calf's (veal) liver, sliced into thin strips
300 g (10 oz) onions
4 tbs olive oil
flour for coating
salt and freshly ground black pepper
2 tbs wine vinegar
1 tbs finely chopped parsley

Coarsely slice the onions and fry in a pan with the olive oil. Slowly cook the onions until they become transparent, but do not let them burn. When they are cooked, remove the onions from the pan and put them aside while you cook the liver in the same pan. Roll the pieces of liver in the flour and shake off the excess, then and fry over a medium flame, turning frequently. Return the onions to the pan. Season with salt and pepper and then add the wine vinegar, which should be left to reduce a little. Serve with a sprinkling of parsley and a fennel salad (Insalata di finocchio).

FEGATELLI DI MAIALE CON ALLORO
Pork Faggots with Bay Leaves

This recipe, which is popular throughout Italy, is only possible to make if you are able to find the reticella, or caul, in which the stuffing is wrapped. Reticella is a delicate net of membrane and threads of fat from the stomach of the pig.

Serves 4

500 g (1 lb) pork liver
250 g (½ lb) reticella or caul
salt and freshly ground black pepper
half a nutmeg, grated
24 fresh bay leaves
12 wooden cocktail sticks (to fix the parcels)
45 g (1½ oz or 3 tbs) pork lard

Thoroughly clean the liver, taking off all membranes and nerves. Cut it into 12 large chunks weighing about 40 g (1½ oz or so) each.

Spread the reticella out in warm water to soak for 10 minutes and cut it into 12 squares big enough to wrap each chunk of liver. Sprinkle the pieces of liver with salt, pepper and a pinch of nutmeg. Place a bay leaf on each side and wrap up with the reticella. (Instead of using cocktail sticks, my mother used to close the parcels with bits of twig from the bay tree, and these imparted extra flavour.)

Heat up the lard in a large pan and fry the fegatelli over a moderate flame. Serve when the liver is a golden-brown colour on each side and fully cooked. The bay leaves will have become crisp and brown as well. The fegatelli take about 10 minutes on each side. Endive and cannellini beans (Cicoria e fagioli) go very well with this.

TRIPPA ALLA GENOVESE
Tripe Genoese Style

All the different kinds of offal represent true delicacies for countries such as France and Italy. In Britain and the USA, however, fanatics of these dishes are decidedly less numerous, perhaps owing to the fact that many butchers do not sell offal directly to the public. They may be found, though, in the larger more specialized

Tripe

shops. Tripe (or busecca, as it is called in Milan) is a part of a cow's stomach. Before being sold it has been blanched to a creamy white by being boiled for a short period.

Serves 4

500 g (1 lb) fine-textured tripe
1 carrot
2 celery stalks
4 shallots
2 cloves garlic
45 g (1½ oz or 3 tbs) pork lard
3 tbs olive oil
1 glass of white wine
800 ml (1¾ pt) stock
1 tbs chopped parsley
5–6 fresh basil leaves
salt and freshly ground black pepper
60 g (2 oz or ¼ US cup) freshly grated Parmesan cheese.

Clean the tripe and dry it with a cloth. Chop the celery, shallots and garlic and cut the carrot into strips. Heat the lard and oil in a terracotta pot (one that has a lid) if you have one, otherwise a thick casserole is suitable. Gently fry the shallots, celery and carrot together, add the garlic and before it turns in colour add the glass of wine. Allow the wine to bubble for a minute and then add the tripe and the stock, cover the pot or casserole and simmer gently for at least 1½ hours (the tripe should be slightly al dente). Just before serving add the parsley, basil, salt and pepper. Serve in soup bowls with a generous amount of freshly grated Parmesan cheese.

Right: Pork faggots with bay leaves with the caul in which the meat is wrapped

TRIPPA A MODO MIO
Tripe Prepared My Way

Tripe is yet another of my favourite dishes, and here is my own way of preparing it. Choosing tripe from your butcher is a difficult task in countries other than Italy, as it is often overcooked and bleached in the original cleaning. Try to find tripe that has been blanched, not overcooked.

Serves 6

1 kg (2 lb) tripe (different textured cuts, including honeycomb, etc)
2 carrots
3 celery stalks
2 cloves garlic
5 tbs olive oil
2 large ripe tomatoes or 1 medium can peeled plum tomatoes
2 bay leaves
1 sprig of rosemary
2 dried red chili peppers
half a glass of white wine
200 ml (7 fl oz or 1 US cup) stock (made from a bouillon cube if you wish)
2 medium cans drained borlotti beans
salt and freshly ground black pepper

Thoroughly clean the tripe and cut it into slices at least 1 cm (½ inch) thick. Chop the carrot and celery and slice the garlic. Heat the olive oil in a large saucepan, add the carrots, celery and garlic and fry together until they are well coated with oil, then add the tomatoes and their juice, the bay leaves, rosemary, salt and the chili peppers, bring to the boil, turn down the heat and simmer for 20 minutes. Add the tripe and the wine and, if necessary, some of the stock: the tripe should be covered with liquid while cooking. Leave to simmer for at least an hour.

Drain the borlotti beans and wash them under cold water. Add to the tripe after 45 minutes of simmering, and season with salt and pepper. The tripe should be cooked after 1 hour, but the whole cooking time depends on how cooked the tripe was when bought from your butcher. I like my tripe al dente. Test throughout simmering, as overcooked tripe becomes slimy in texture. Eat together with some good home-made bread.

FRATTAGLIE MISTE FRITTE
Deep-fried Mixed Offal

This is a very substantial dish because not only is it fried but also the brains and sweetbreads are both quite rich ingredients. It is, however, a particularly delicious dish which does not require much preparation. The fritto misto from the Piedmont region, presented as an antipasto, would also include these three specialities amongst many other ingredients. This recipe could be described as a smaller version of this fritto misto, but I would suggest that you serve it up as a main course.

Serves 4

200 g (7 oz) calf's (veal) brain
200 g (7 oz) calf's (veal) sweetbreads
200 g (7 oz) calf's (veal) liver
1 egg
salt and freshly ground black pepper
oil for frying
100 g (4 oz or 3 US cups) fresh bread crumbs
1 large bunch of parsley, washed and thoroughly dried
olive oil for deep-frying the parsley
2 lemons

Put the brains and sweetbreads to soak in cold water for about 1 hour, so that most of their blood is lost. Bring a small saucepan of water to the boil and poach the sweetbreads and brains for only a couple of minutes. Remove from the boiling water and leave to cool before removing the skin and nerves. Cut the calf's liver into slices 1 cm (½ inch) thick. Cut the brains and sweetbreads into equally thick slices.

Beat the egg and season with salt and pepper. Heat the oil, which should be 1 cm (½ inch) deep in your pan, until hot. Dip the slices of sweetbread first into the egg and then into the bread crumbs, fry until they become golden, turning them over so they are cooked on both sides. Remove from the pan and keep warm. Next fry the brains, coating them in the same way, and finally the liver. In a separate pan heat up the olive oil and fry sprigs of parsley until they become crisp. Serve the fritto misto on a heated dish surrounded by the parsley and slices of lemon. Good companions include mushrooms (Prataioli al burro, aglio e prezzemolo), and spring salad (Insalata primaverile).

ANIMELLE CON LIMONE E CAPPERI
Sweetbreads with Lemon and Capers

This combination successfully contrasts the richness of the sweetbreads with the taste of the lemon and capers. This is one of the favourite recipes in my restaurant.

Serves 4

400 g (14 oz) calf's (veal) sweetbreads
flour for dusting
salt and freshly ground black pepper
60 g (2 oz or 4 tbs) butter
25 g (1 oz) salted capers (alternatively, capers preserved in vinegar)
the juice of a lemon
1 tbs chopped parsley

Put the capers to soak in a small bowl of water. Prepare the sweetbreads by saoking and poaching them as in the previous recipe. Season the slices of sweetbread with salt and pepper and dust them in the flour. Heat the butter in a pan until it fizzes. Add the sweetbreads and fry over a gentle heat until a good golden colour on each side. Drain the capers and add them to the sweetbreads along with the lemon juice. Serve immediately with the sauce from the pan, sprinkled with chopped parsley.

FEGATELLI DI POLLO AL MARSALA
Chicken Livers with Marsala

Although chicken liver is not usually paid much attention, it is a simple food, which, with a little care, may whet the appetite even of a king. In the days when the battery-raised chicken was unheard of, this dish was considered delicacy. Let us then try and return to the spirit of the olden days.

Serves 4

500 g (1 lb) well-cleaned chicken livers
100 g (3½ oz) smoked bacon
1 small onion
45 g (1½ oz or 3 tbs) butter
salt and freshly ground black pepper
a small glass of dry Marsala
1 tbs finely chopped parsley

Cut each chicken liver into two, the bacon into matchsticks, and slice the onion. Heat the butter in a pan and fry the onion until golden, then add the bacon and continue frying for a minute or two. Add the chicken livers, season with salt and pepper and fry over a low flame, turning the livers over until they are cooked on all sides. Pour the Marsala into the pan, raise the flame and allow it to bubble, then reduce for a few minutes. Sprinkle over the chopped parsley and serve immediately, perhaps with a dish of beans, such as Fagiolini al burro e pangrattato.

ROGNONI DI VITELLO TRIFOLATI
Calf's (Veal) Kidneys with Garlic and Parsley

The word trifolati originally indicated the addition of truffles (from the Piedmontese trifola, meaning truffle). As the truffle is a rare commodity the word has assumed a secondary, more popular meaning – denoting that something is fried together with butter, garlic and parsley.

This recipe is based on veal kidneys which are the tenderest of them all. Anyone fortunate enough to come by some truffles may add slices of these to the kidneys, thereby transforming them into a more sophisticated meal.

Serves 4

600 g (1¼ lb) calf's (veal) kidneys
flour for coating
45 g (1½ oz or 3 tbs) butter
2 cloves garlic, sliced
half a glass of dry white wine
salt and freshly ground black pepper
2 tbs chopped parsley

Thoroughly clean the kidneys, removing all the fat and gristle from the middle. Slice them finely, then roll them in the flour before frying in the butter over a high flame. Cook these for around 5 minutes, turning constantly or stir-frying, before adding the sliced garlic which should also be lightly fried for a moment or so. Next add the white wine and the salt and pepper and reduce for a minute or so. Just before serving, sprinkle with the fresh parsley. Accompany the dish with potato croquettes or fried potatoes (Patate fritte con aglio e rosmarino) and a green salad or, perhaps, a vegetable such as spinach (Spinaci, olio e limone).

I VEGETALI

—————— VEGETABLES ——————

As you look around an Italian food market at the abundance of fresh, beautifully displayed vegetables, it is easy to imagine the amazing variety of wonderful dishes that you can prepare from them. I will never forget visiting the San Lorenzo market in Florence one spring – it was impossible to resist buying ingredients for an Insalata primaverile or a good Pinzimonio, such was the quality and quantity of the produce on display. There were at least twelve salad vegetables on one stall, and I saw five different types of artichokes each of which suited a different cooking method.

Vegetables are regarded as very important by the Italians and sometimes are even served as il secondo in place of meat or fish, especially during the hot weather. The vegetables must always be very fresh, of course. If they are less than perfect they will ruin the dish. The only time I have ever broken this rule was once when I used an artichoke with slightly withered outer leaves. Since I needed the heart only, it was an acceptable compromise – just.

Italian salads are artful mixtures of cultivated and wild plants – one salad may contain ten, or even more, different types of foliage, including cress, lettuce, endive, chicory, lamb's lettuce, radicchio, dandelion and beet leaves, wild fennel and unfamiliar plants gathered from the woods and fields. The dressing will be simple – a good olive oil with lemon juice or either wine vinegar or balsamic vinegar, and sometimes garlic or onion will be added or a handful of fresh herbs. When I was young, I used to collect new dandelion leaves in springtime. They made a wonderful salad combined with a couple of anchovies, a hard-boiled egg or two, and maybe some spring onions. And true nature-lover that I was, sometimes I would gather wild violets and dandelion heads to add to it. Collecting wild rucola just before lunch was also one of my regular tasks when I was a boy.

The salad is never eaten by itself. It is usually served as part of il secondo, although some people eat the cheese and salad together. And it is very rarely served as an antipasto; the most notable exceptions are Bagna cauda – raw vegetables dipped into hot garlicky olive oil and eaten with bread, and Pinzimonio, where they are dipped in virgin olive oil.

Courgette (Zucchini)

borlotti bean

bean

Radish

Pea

pepper

bean

Chilli

Aubergine (Eggplant)

cep

Florence Onion

Florence Fennel

Black Truffle

Leek

Asparagus

Vegetable dishes

FAGIOLINI ALLA NAPOLETANA
French Beans with Tomato

This excellent marriage of typically Neapolitan ingredients provides us with a simple but delicious speciality. It is an excellent starter, but it can be eaten as an accompaniment to a main course, either hot or cold.

Serves 4

500 g (1 lb) very tender French beans (or Bobby beans), topped and tailed
4 tbs olive oil
2 cloves garlic, finely chopped
600 g (1 ¼ lb) ripe tomatoes, skinned, or 1 large can peeled plum tomatoes
salt
10 fresh basil leaves
freshly ground black pepper

Heat the olive oil in a saucepan, add the chopped garlic but don't let it colour: just fry for half a minute or less. Chop the tomatoes roughly and add to the oil and garlic. Cook the tomatoes fiercely for 5 minutes, reducing the liquid, then add the beans and salt. Cover the pan, reduce the flame and simmer for a further 5–10 minutes or until the beans are al dente. Shortly before the end of cooking, add the whole basil leaves and black pepper. Serve on slices of toast.

MINESTRA DI PUNTE DI ZUCCHINI
Courgette (Zucchini) Top Soup

This is a rather unusual starter: you use only the tops of the plant (i.e. the most tender part with the new leaves and tiny courgettes still attached), so you can gather this only at the end of the summer, when the plant will no longer produce fruits that will reach maturity.

In Italy it is possible to obtain this ingredient in the markets, but I have never come across it in Britain. Perhaps you could ask a favour from someone with an allotment.

Serves 4

750 g (1 ½ lb) courgette (zucchini) tops
750 g (1 ½ lb) ripe tomatoes, skinned, or 1 large can peeled plum tomatoes
4 tbs olive oil
2 cloves garlic, finely chopped
a few fresh basil leaves
salt and freshly ground black pepper
200 ml (8 fl oz or 1 US cup) water

Wash the courgette tops thoroughly. Heat the olive oil in a saucepan, fry the garlic for a minute or two then add the roughly chopped tomatoes. Cook for 5 minutes then add the courgette tops and the water. Cover the saucepan and cook until tender. Add salt and pepper and the basil leaves just before the end. Serve with the liquor in bowls, accompanied by good bread.

CIME DI RAPE CON PIZZA DI POLENTA
Rape Tops with Polenta Cake

Like the first two, this recipe is one of those tasty rural recipes that are fast disappearing because they are considered simple and of little value. Yet the ingenious ways in which country cooks use local produce have given great chefs useful hints more than once. This recipe teams the succulent green leaves of rape with a crispy polenta cake.

Serves 6

1 kg (2 lb) rape tops, cleaned, washed and trimmed
6 tbs olive oil
100 g (4 oz) smoked bacon, sliced into matchsticks
4 cloves garlic, sliced
2 small hot red chili peppers
Pizza di polenta (see recipe, page 88)

Make the polenta cake according to the recipe. While it is cooking, wash the rape and trim off any rough stalks. Bring a large saucepan of water to the boil, cook the rape for 2 minutes or thereabouts, drain and put aside.

In a large frying pan, heat 4 tbs of olive oil and fry the bacon. When it is crisp and golden, add the garlic and chili peppers. Stir-fry the garlic without browning it, and then add the drained rape. Continue to cook, stirring from time to time, until the rape is thoroughly mixed with the bacon, oil and garlic: the rape takes 10–15 minutes to cook, less if it is very tender. Serve in soup bowls with a slice of polenta cake, the rape and its cooking liquor.

PANZANELLA O FRESELLA
Bread and Tomato

This is a typical summer dish from the region of Campania. It combines a salad and a snack. Made from twice-baked granary bread called fresella, it has a delicate toasty taste. The genuine product may be bought in Italian delicatessens.

Serves 4

8 slices fresella or granary bread
8 small ripe tomatoes
4 generous pinches of dried oregano
salt
2 cloves garlic, finely chopped (optional)
4 tbs virgin olive oil

To make your own fresella, cut thick slices of granary bread about 4 cm (1½ inches) thick and bake in a moderate oven for 15–20 minutes. They must not burn, just become crisp and completely dry. Allow to cool, then pass the fresella under running cold water for a few seconds to dampen, not soak. Shake off the water and place on a large plate.

Chop the tomatoes and put them on top of the pieces of bread along with their juice and seeds. If you have very ripe tomatoes you may crush them directly on to the bread with your hand, as I prefer to do. Sprinkle the tomatoes with oregano, salt and chopped garlic if you wish and then pour the olive oil over them. Fresella should be enjoyed with some young fresh wine.

PEPERONCINI AL POMODORO
Peppers in Tomato Sauce

A recipe typical of the south of Italy, using small peppers which are similar to chili peppers, but very sweet. They are green and about 7 or 8 cm (around 3 inches) long. The whole pepper is eaten – even the seeds, as they are very tender. If you buy them outside Italy, make sure they are the right ones. Sometimes they can be found in markets abroad, but in Italy they are commonplace and are called peperoncini. They should be served with good bread such as fresella made as in the previous recipe.

Serves 4

600 g (1¼ lb) sweet baby peppers (peperoncini)
6 tbs olive oil
2 cloves garlic, chopped
3 large ripe tomatoes or 1 medium can tomatoes drained of their juice
4 fresh basil leaves
salt and freshly ground black pepper

Heat the olive oil in a heavy pan and when hot put in the peppers. Fry for 5 minutes, stirring from time to time, so that the peppers fry on each side. Their skins will begin to blister; at that point add the garlic, and almost immediately the tomatoes. Stir to break up the tomatoes and cook together for 10 minutes. Finally add the basil leaves, salt and pepper. Serve hot or cold.

POMODORI RIPIENI DI RISO
Tomatoes Stuffed with Rice

A typically Roman recipe, cooked in various ways with different ingredients, but always with excellent results. I also like to eat this dish cold as a starter.

Serves 4

4 ripe beef tomatoes (the height should be greater than their width)
120 g (4 oz) long-grain rice
1 tbs chopped chives
1 tbs chopped mint
1 tbs chopped basil
2 tbs olive oil
salt and freshly ground black pepper

Preheat the oven to 200°C (400°F or gas mark 6).
Cut the tops off the tomatoes to form lids. Without breaking the tomatoes, scoop out the insides with a teaspoon. Wash the rice and then mix it with the chopped herbs, salt, pepper and the chopped insides of the tomatoes. Add to this mixture the olive oil and then fill the tomato shells. They should be only three-quarters full, as the uncooked rice has to have room to expand. Put on the lids, place in an ovenproof dish and bake in the oven, basting occasionally with the juices, until the rice has absorbed all the liquid – for approximately 45 minutes.

CIPOLLE RIPIENE
Stuffed Onions

This can be used as a starter too, and calls for those lovely big Spanish onions which have plenty of room for the filling, which may be based on vegetables or meat, or a mixture of the two.

Serves 4

4 medium white Spanish onions
For the stuffing:
15 g (½ oz) dried ceps
3 tbs olive oil (1 for greasing)
100 g (4 oz) minced (ground) pork, or other meat
50 g (2 oz) fresh button mushrooms, chopped
1 egg
4 grates of nutmeg
2 tbs chopped parsley
salt and freshly ground black pepper

Put the dried ceps to soak in warm water.

Cut the tops off each onion a third of the way down, so as to make a lid. Remove the dry outer skin. With a small knife and a spoon, scoop out the centre of the onion, leaving a shell at least 1 cm (⅓ inch) thick. Keep the onion pulp. Bring a large saucepan of water to the boil, drop the onion shells and their tops in, and boil for 5 minutes. Remove from the water, drain well and place in a greased ovenproof dish (use olive oil for greasing). Preheat the oven to 200°C (400°F or gas mark 6).

To make the stuffing, heat the remainder of the olive oil in a small pan and fry the inside pulp of the onions. When transparent, add the minced pork, stir-fry for a few minutes to brown the meat, then add the chopped mushrooms, the soaked dried ceps and a tablespoon of their liquor. Fry all together until the mushrooms are cooked. Remove from the heat and leave to cool.

Beat the egg, season with salt and pepper and mix it well with the mushrooms and pork, grate the nutmeg into the mixture and add the chopped parsley. Now fill the onion shells with the mixture, which may be heaped into pyramids on top of each onion. Put the onions in the oven without their lids for 15 minutes. Hollow out the lids so that they fit neatly over the mounds of stuffing. After 15 minutes put the lids on the onions, baste with olive oil from the baking dish and bake for further 30 minutes. They should be golden-brown and just cooked.

Vegetables

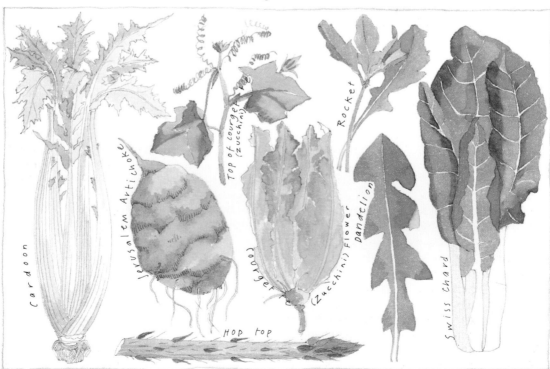

LA PARMIGIANA DI MELANZANE
Timbale of Aubergines (Eggplants)

I've never known whether this dish is called parmigiana because it comes from Parma, or because it's made with Parmesan cheese. It is cooked all over Italy and can be an excellent main course. The aubergines (eggplants) should be nice and firm, with not too many seeds. I use fontina cheese instead of mozzarella, as good mozzarella which remains soft when cooked is hard to find outside Italy. Another of my variations is to coat the aubergine slices in flour and egg before frying: I've discovered that in this way they absorb less oil, and even with the egg, are lighter and tastier. A good result is obtained by using courgettes (zucchini) in place of aubergines.

Serves 8 as a main course or 10–12 as a starter

4 large aubergines (eggplants) weighing altogether 1100–1200 g (about 2½ lb)
salt
flour for coating
4 eggs
plenty of olive oil for frying
For the sauce:
1½ large cans peeled plum tomatoes
1 clove garlic, chopped
4 tbs olive oil
300 g (10 oz) fontina cheese
100 g (4 oz) freshly grated Parmesan cheese
10 fresh basil leaves
salt and freshly ground black pepper

Slice the aubergines about 1 cm (½ inch) thick. Sprinkle the slices with salt and put them to stand for half an hour stacked one on top of the other with a weight on top, so that their juice can drain away. Wipe the slices dry and dust them on both sides in flour. Beat the eggs, season with salt, dip the floured aubergine slices into the egg, then fry 3 or 4 at a time in hot oil. Brown on both sides, remove and drain on kitchen paper. This is a slow process, so allow plenty of time. Now make your tomato sauce. Chop the tomatoes with their juices in the can. Chop the garlic. Heat the olive oil in a large pan and gently fry the garlic, allow it to colour but not brown. Add the tomatoes and cook for 15 minutes, adding salt, pepper and the basil leaves towards the end. Slice the fontina cheese. Preheat the oven to 200°C (400°F or gas mark 6).

Put two or three spoonfuls of tomato sauce in the bottom of a large ovenproof dish, then arrange a layer of the aubergine slices, placed as close together as possible. Cover the aubergines with some pieces of fontina cheese, spoon a little tomato sauce on the cheese and then a sprinkling of Parmesan. Continue with another layer of aubergine slices, arranging them in the opposite direction to the layer below, cover with fontina cheese, tomato sauce and Parmesan. The final layer should be of tomato sauce dotted with fontina and a generous amount of Parmesan. Bake in a medium-hot oven for 25–30 minutes. Leave the dish to sit for 15 minutes before cutting up to serve.

As a main course, serve with a salad. La parmigiana di melanzane is also very good cold.

ACQUA COTTA
Cooked Water

An extremely easy Tuscan speciality made with a few variations all over the region. It is essentially an autumn dish, made when the wild mushrooms needed for this recipe are plentiful.

Serves 4

600 g (1¼ lb) fresh young ceps, or 600 g (1¼ lb) flat field mushrooms plus 10 g (½ oz) dried ceps
3 tbs olive oil
2 cloves garlic, chopped
1 medium can peeled plum tomatoes
600 ml (1 pt or 2½ US cups) stock
5 fresh basil leaves
salt and freshly ground black pepper
4 slices toast
60 g (2 oz or ¼ US cup) freshly grated Parmesan cheese

If you are using field mushrooms put dried ceps to soak in warm water for 15 minutes. Wipe the fresh mushrooms clean and slice them. In a large pan heat the oil and fry the garlic very briefly, then add the sliced mushrooms and sauté for 10 minutes or thereabouts. Add the soaked ceps and their liquid at this point. Sieve the tomatoes and add them and their juice to the mushrooms. Cook, stirring over a medium flame, for 10 minutes. Heat the stock in a separate pan and when hot add to the mushroom and tomato mixture, and season with salt and pepper.

Make the toast and place one piece in each bowl. Pour the mushroom soup over them and immediately sprinkle with Parmesan.

MELANZANE E PEPERONI RIPIENI
Stuffed Peppers and Aubergines (Eggplants)

My mother was always good at making this recipe. I remember it was delicious in summer when the heat was intense and it wasn't so necessary to eat large quantities of protein. This dish was nearly always served cold, but still crispy on the top, and accompanied by plain bread, even though the filling contained bread crumbs.

She used to prepare more than was needed. This was greatly appreciated by my brother and me at around one in the morning, when we returned from our summer escapades to raid the fridge!

Serves 4

2 large yellow or red bell peppers
2 medium-sized aubergines (eggplants)
2 tbs olive oil
400 g (14 oz) ripe tomatoes, skinned and finely chopped
40 g (1½ oz) finely chopped capers (salted if possible)
12 anchovy fillets
2 cloves garlic, very finely chopped
4 tbs finely chopped parsley
80 g (3 oz or 2½ US cups) fresh white bread crumbs
50 g (2 oz) freshly grated Parmesan cheese
3 grates of nutmeg
salt and freshly ground black pepper
5 tbs olive oil

Preheat the oven to 200°C (400°F or gas mark 6). Slice each of the peppers and the aubergines in two lengthwise. Remove the stalks and the seeds from the peppers, leaving a clean cavity for the filling. Scoop out as much as you can of the flesh of the aubergine with a knife, taking care to leave the skin intact. Chop the scooped-out pulp finely and fry it in 2 tablespoons of oil for 5–6 minutes, until it is soft. Remove from the heat and leave to cool.

Chop the tomatoes, capers, anchovies, garlic and parsley finely. Then take the bread crumbs, Parmesan and nutmeg and mix well with the chopped ingredients and the aubergine pulp, including the oil in which it was cooked. When it is well mixed, fill the aubergine and pepper shells with this mixture. Put 2 tablespoons of oil in the bottom of an oven dish large enough to hold the eight halves and arrange them in it.

Pour the 3 remaining tablespoons of oil over the stuffed vegetables and bake in a hot oven for around 40 minutes. Serve hot or cold.

CARCIOFI IN UMIDO
Stewed Artichokes

I know it is hard to buy the small tender artichokes needed for this recipe although they are easily found in Italian markets. But just in case you are able to find one or two particularly tender ones, this recipe is ideal. It's strange, but it seems that in Britain artichokes are nearly always boiled or served with a vinaigrette or hollandaise sauce, and this is why the importers bring in all those big, slightly hard ones. I hope people start asking for the smaller ones, as more dishes can be prepared with them.

Serves 4

1 kg (2 lb) fresh artichokes
the juice of half a lemon
400 g (14 oz) onions
60 g (2 oz) smoked bacon
8 tbs olive oil
2 cloves garlic, sliced
40 g (1½ oz) capers
salt and freshly ground black pepper
2 tbs chopped parsley

Clean the artichokes, pulling off all the tough outer leaves. Cut off the tops and the stalks about 2 cm (1 inch) from the base. (If the artichokes are large, cut them in half and then in quarters, cutting away the prickly choke with a sharp knife.) Put the thus prepared artichokes in a bowl of water with the juice of half a lemon to prevent them from going black where you have cut them. Slice the onion finely and chop the bacon into matchsticks. In a medium-sized saucepan heat the olive oil, add the bacon and fry for a couple of minutes. Then add the onion and when it begins to colour add the garlic and the capers. Cook together just for a minute over a medium flame before adding the artichokes and a ladle of hot water. Season with salt and pepper and turn the heat down low. Simmer for 20 minutes or until the artichokes are cooked. Bigger ones take longer – up to 40 minutes. Add the chopped parsley before serving. This dish is excellent cold.

Right: Stuffed peppers and aubergines (eggplants)

Artichokes

CARCIOFI ALLA GIUDEA
Artichokes the Jewish Way

A typically Roman recipe, probably with a Jewish origin. It is very easy to prepare, but bear in mind it requires a lot of good olive oil which will add flavour to the artichoke. Any left-over oil can be used for other purposes.

Serves 4

12 tender medium artichokes
12 cloves garlic
3 tbs parsley
salt
freshly ground black pepper
as much good olive oil as is needed to cover the artichokes – about 400 ml (¾ pt)

Clean the artichokes: pull off the tough outside leaves, cut off the tips, peel away with a knife any dark green left at the base of the bud. Cut the stalks about 5 cm (2 inches) from the head. Now halve the artichokes and if they are large ones cut into quarters. With a sharp knife cut away any choke at the centre.

Peel the garlic: if you squeeze it gently between the palms of your hands, the skin comes off easily. Put the garlic and artichokes in a pan with a tight-fitting lid and cover with good olive oil. (If you pack the artichokes tightly, you will save on the olive oil.) Add salt, close the lid tightly and very gently heat up the oil and cook on a low heat for 40 minutes. The oil must not be allowed to fry, and the garlic must not brown. Drain off the oil, add the parsley and serve immediately. Keep the oil to cook with later.

ASPARAGI PASTICCIATI CON UOVA
Asparagus with Scrambled Eggs

A good summer recipe using those lovely green asparagus tips with their own special flavour. Obviously, if you use the locally grown sort in season, it tastes better than the cultivated sort from who-knows-where. And if you add to all this good fresh farm eggs, it will be delicious!

Serves 4

400 g (14 oz) fresh green asparagus (cleaned weight)
1 onion, sliced
12 fresh eggs
50 g (2 oz) freshly grated Parmesan cheese
2 tbs double (heavy) cream
45 g (1½ oz or 3 tbs) butter
salt and freshly ground black pepper

Peel the asparagus stalks, removing any woody bits. Cut into 5 cm (2 inch) lengths, putting aside the tips. Boil the asparagus in lightly salted water until tender for about 15 minutes, adding the tips 5 minutes before the end. Carefully drain and put aside. Melt the butter in a large pan and add the sliced onion, which should be fried gently until cooked through but not browned. Add the asparagus stalks (not tips) and gently heat – don't fry. Beat the eggs, season them with salt, pepper and grated Parmesan cheese. Raise the heat and add the egg mixture to the onion and asparagus. Stirring all the time, cook the eggs to a scrambled consistency, add the cream and serve immediately, with the tips arranged on top.

ASPARAGI CON PROSCIUTTO DI SAN DANIELE
Asparagus with San Daniele Ham

The idea for this came to me in Germany, where the smoked ham from the Black Forest is eaten along with German asparagus, which is usually white. The combination of green asparagus with a San Daniele ham gives an exceptional result.

Serves 4

600 g (1¼ lb) tender green asparagus
salt
500 g (1 lb) new potatoes
200 g (7 oz) San Daniele prosciutto
60 g (2 oz or 4 tbs) unsalted butter

Peel and trim the asparagus stalks, keeping only the green parts. Scrape or scrub the new potatoes. Cook the asparagus whole in slightly salted boiling water until tender. Boil the new potatoes. Melt the butter. Arrange the slices of ham on individual plates. Lay the asparagus and potatoes, with a spoonful of melted butter on them, beside the ham, and serve as a main course.

TORTA DI SPINACI
Spinach Tart

This type of dish, based on shortcrust pastry and vegetables, is ideal for picnics, or as a main course if eaten straight from the oven. You can also use frozen pastry which is readily available in the shops.

Serves 4–6

For the pastry:
200 g (7 oz) plain white flour
100 g (3½ oz or ⅓ US cup) butter
up to 100 ml (¼ pt or ½ US cup) iced water
salt
alternatively 400 g (14 oz) frozen short crust pastry, thawed
For the filling:
500 g (1 lb) spinach
4 eggs, beaten
200 g (7 oz or scant 1 US cup) fresh ricotta
50 g (2 oz) freshly grated Parmesan cheese
4 or 5 grates of nutmeg
salt and freshly ground black pepper

Preheat the oven to 200°C (400°F or gas mark 6).

Wash the spinach and cook in a little salted boiling water for 2 minutes. Drain, squeeze dry, and allow to cool.

Make the pastry by crumbling together the flour, salt and butter very lightly with your fingers. Add enough iced water to keep the pastry together and shape into a ball. Take a 25 cm (10 inch) flan tin and spread the pastry out directly over the base and sides of the flan tin with your hands, making sure you have an even thickness. (Roll out the thawed ready-made pastry if you are using that.) Trim the edges, prick the surface, fill with dried beans and bake blind for 10 minutes. Remove the dried beans.

In the meantime, chop the cooled spinach. Beat the ricotta cheese with a fork, add the beaten eggs, the grated Parmesan, the spinach,

Asparagus

nutmeg, salt and pepper. Pour the mixture into the pastry shell, spread it out evenly and bake in the moderate oven for 25 minutes. When cooked, the tart should be golden on top and set.

TORTA DI PATATE
Potato Cake

A very economical recipe, which allows us to use any leftover bits of cheese and salami.

Serves 6

2 kg (4 lb) good floury potatoes
4 eggs, beaten well
75 g (3 oz or 5 tbs) butter
4 grates of nutmeg
50 g (2 oz) grated Parmesan cheese
100 g (4 oz) cooked ham or salami, or both mixed
100 g (4 oz) fontina cheese, Fior di Maggio, or any other soft cheese
20 g (scant 1 oz or 2 tbs) dry bread crumbs
salt and freshly ground black pepper

Peel and boil the potatoes. When cooked mash them thoroughly and mix with half the butter, the grated Parmesan, nutmeg, beaten eggs, salt and pepper. Preheat the oven to 200°C (400°F or gas mark 6).

Butter a deep oven dish, and place in it half the potato mixture. Cut the fontina cheese into thin slices and the ham and salami into strips. Cover the potato with the cheese, salami and ham and dot with some of the remaining butter. Put the remainder of the potato mixture on top, dot with the rest of the butter, shake the bread crumbs over the top and bake for 25 minutes in a moderately hot oven. Serve after cooling for 5–10 minutes.

TORTA PASQUALINA
Easter Cake

This Genoese speciality is usually eaten at Easter, but there is no reason to stop us eating it during the rest of the year. It is really excellent and the ingredients used by my mother offer a spicy alternative to the original recipe. It is especially suited to picnics; in fact it shouldn't be forgotten that Italians cook it for the traditional trip to the country on the day after Easter, which is called Pasquetta. As the recipe is quite elaborate, I have used frozen pastry, thereby cutting down on preparation time.

Serves 8

650 g (1 lb 6 oz) frozen puff pastry
750 g (1½ lb) scarola (curly endive, escarole, or prickly lettuce)
50 g (2 oz) lean smoked bacon
3 tbs olive oil
2 ripe tomatoes
25 g (1 oz) capers
1 clove garlic, finely chopped
500 g (1 lb or 2½ US cups) ricotta
50g (scant 2 oz or ¼ US cup) grated Parmesan cheese
10 eggs
salt and freshly ground black pepper
milk for glazing

Wash the scarola and cut into 6 cm (2½ inch) lengths. Cut the bacon into matchsticks. Peel and roughly chop the tomatoes. Chop the garlic finely. Heat the olive oil in a large saucepan that has a fitting lid. Fry in the hot oil the bacon, and after a minute add the garlic – the bacon must become quite crisp and the garlic must not go brown. Add the chopped tomatoes and when they have begun to bubble put in the scarola and the capers, and stir so that all the ingredients are well mixed.

Cover the saucepan and simmer for 15 minutes – the scarola should be cooked. Drain away any excess liquid and put aside to cool. Preheat the oven to 190°C (375°F or gas mark 5).

In the meantime, roll out the pastry into two large rectangles, one large enough to fit inside a baking tray about 20 × 30 cm (8 × 12 inches) and at least 7 cm (2½ inches) deep; the other slightly smaller for the top. Line the baking tray with the larger piece of pastry and trim the top and sides.

Now beat the ricotta cheese with a fork, add two of the eggs and continue to beat until the mixture becomes lighter, then add the Parmesan, salt, pepper and finally the cooked scarola mixture. Gently mix all together and then spoon the mixture into the pastry case. Make 8 wells in the ricotta mixture and put a fresh shelled egg in each. Season the top with salt and pepper before covering with the second piece of pastry, pricking holes here and there to allow steam to escape. Pay attention not to prick holes in the pastry where the eggs are or you will break the yolks. Decorate the top with strips of pastry, brush with milk and put in a moderate oven for 45 minutes to 1 hour. Excellent served hot or cold.

FRITTATA DI PUNTE DI LUPPOLO
Omelette of Wild Hops

Being an impassioned lover of nature and the countryside, I always tend to gather things when on walks and bring them back to the kitchen – aromatic herbs, wild vegetables or mushrooms according to the season. The first spring walks are already tinged with success. Some of the first things to gather are the shoots and tops of wild hops which can be found along country hedgerows. Picking off the tops only, i.e. the most tender part, means that the plant is not harmed and will still sprout new shoots. It has a very particular flavour, which might not appeal to everyone. In Italy hop shoots are sold in bunches tied with a blade of grass by those famous old women who, apart from that, sell bunches of parsley, sage and beet greens in the markets.

Serves 4

2 handfuls wild hop shoots weighing about 150–200 g (around 6 oz)
2 tbs oil for frying
6 eggs, beaten
4 tbs freshly grated Parmesan cheese
salt

Wash the hops and cut them into shorter lengths.

Heat the olive oil in a medium-sized frying pan. Over a high flame fry the hops; as soon as they begin to become tender, which will take only a minute or two, add the beaten egg mixed with the Parmesan and salt. Cook the omelette on both sides.

CARCIOFI E PATATE AL FORNO
Baked Artichokes and Potatoes

Only small tender artichokes, which unfortunately are rarely seen in markets outside Italy, are suitable for this recipe. If you must use the bigger ones, make sure to remove all the hard bits which, even when cooked, contain tough threads. It is possible to use artichokes that seem too old for boiling, since all but the centre is peeled away. It is an ideal dish for vegetarians.

Serves 4

350 g (¾ lb) potatoes (peeled weight)
250 g (½ lb) artichokes (peeled weight)
a slice of lemon
1 medium-sized onion
50 g (2 oz) capers (salted if possible)
5 tbs olive oil (1 tbs for greasing the pie dish)
25 g (1 oz or ⅔ US cup) fresh bread crumbs
100 ml (¼ pt or ½ US cup) stock
salt and freshly ground black pepper

Preheat the oven to 190°C (375°F or gas mark 5). Put the capers to soak in a small bowl of water. Peel and slice the potatoes 5 mm (¼ inch) thick. Wash the artichokes, pull off the tough leaves, cut away the top, slice into quarters (or eighths if

they are big artichokes) and remove any choke from the centre. Put aside in a bowl of cold water with a slice of lemon in it. Slice the onion finely. Grease an ovenproof dish with olive oil, then make alternating layers of potato, onion and artichoke. Sprinkle each layer with a few capers, salt and pepper. Pour in the stock, cover the top with bread crumbs and trickle with olive oil. Cover the dish with foil and bake in the medium-hot oven for 40 minutes. Remove the foil and bake for a further 20 minutes until crisp and golden on top. Serve at once.

FRITTO MISTO DI VEGETALI
Fried Mixed Vegetables

The Mediterranean diet is based on lots of fresh vegetables, which when cooked with care, supply all the goodness that nature gives us.

Vegetables that can be used raw include courgette (zucchini) flowers; spinach and Swiss chard; quartered radicchio; sliced aubergines (eggplants); mushrooms and small artichokes which have been cleaned and trimmed. Cut courgettes (zucchini) lengthwise into slices.

Firmer-textured vegetables need blanching beforehand to make them tender. Asparagus stalks can be kept whole; celeriac, celery, fennel and Jerusalem artichokes should be sliced. Separate cauliflower and broccoli into florets.

With the exception of mushrooms, which simply need wiping, all the vegetables should be washed and thoroughly drained dry before being dipped in the batter.

Serves 6

1 kg (2 lb) prepared mixed vegetables
4 small eggs
130 g (4½ oz or 1 US cup) flour
60–70 ml (2–3 fl oz or ¼–⅓ US cup) milk
salt
enough corn oil or olive oil to deep fry
3 lemons

Take a combination of four or five different vegetables and prepare them as described above.

Heat the oil in a deep fryer. Make the batter by sieving the flour into a large bowl, add the eggs to the centre and mix gently incorporating the flour. When all the flour is blended with the egg add the milk and salt. Dip the vegetables in the batter and deep fry until golden. Drain on kitchen paper and decorate with lemon wedges.

CAPPELLE DI PORCINI FRITTE
Fried Cep Caps

As you probably know by now, I am a fanatical wild mushroom gatherer! While writing this book, I am in fact preparing material for my next one which will be dedicated entirely to mushrooms. So it is not difficult for me to find the ingredients for this recipe – all I have to do is go into the woods at the correct time: if the season is right, the woods are full of them. However, in countries where mushrooms are regarded with suspicion, it will be easier for you to use large cultivated field mushrooms. Even though the taste is not as good, you can console yourself with the fact that you haven't contracted toadstool poisoning!

Serves 4

4 large cep caps, 10 cm (4 inches), or 8 small caps, 5 cm (2 inches) in diameter, or large open field mushrooms
4 tbs fresh bread crumbs
1 egg, beaten
salt and freshly ground black pepper
4 tbs olive oil for frying

Clean the ceps by wiping rather than washing them. Beat the egg and season with salt and pepper. Dip the caps in the beaten egg and coat in bread crumbs. Heat the oil in a large pan and fry until the caps become light brown on both sides.

CAPPELLE DI PORCINI ALLA GRIGLIA
Grilled (Broiled) Cep Caps

The wonderful flavour from grilling over charcoal comes from the oil dripping down on to the hot coals and the resulting smoke penetrating the mushrooms. If you can't get hold of any ceps, use large open field mushroom caps.

Previous page: Fried mixed vegetables. Top left to right: asparagus tips, fennel, mushrooms, artichokes, asparagus stalks. Bottom left to right: radicchio, spinach, courgettes (zucchini), cauliflower and celery; celeriac, broccoli.

Serves 4

4 large cep caps, 10 cm (4 inches) or 8 small caps, 5 cm (2 inches) in diameter, or large open field mushrooms
2 tbs olive oil
salt and freshly ground black pepper

Clean the ceps with a brush, cut off the stems and use them for another recipe. Preheat the grill. Brush the top surface of the caps with oil and sprinkle with salt. Place top side upwards on the grill and grill for about 4 or 5 minutes. Turn the caps over, pour the remainder of the olive oil into the centres of each, sprinkle again with salt and continue to grill until cooked. According to their size they may take up to 10 minutes. Season with freshly ground black pepper.

ASPARAGI AL PARMIGIANO
Asparagus with Parmesan

This dish can be served as an antipasto, but can also accompany meat dishes, veal in particular. It is essential to buy very tender asparagus and use freshly grated Parmesan from a recently cut cheese.

Serves 4

500 g (1 lb) fresh asparagus
45 g (1½ oz or 3 tbs) unsalted butter
50 g (2 oz) freshly grated Parmesan cheese
salt and freshly ground black pepper

Peel the base and cut away any woody bits from the asparagus. Bring to the boil a large saucepan of salted water. Cook the asparagus in the boiling water with a lid on until tender: depending on the size of the asparagus, about 15–20 minutes.

Serve with a light meat dish, adding the melted butter and the grated Parmesan – if the Parmesan is very fresh, grate it coarsely.

CICORIA E FAGIOLI
Curly Endive (Chicory) and Cannellini Beans

This is a good accompaniment for stronger tasting meats such as pork or lamb. I use the wild field chicory, which is related to the dandelion, but you can use scarola, or the curly-leaved endive type.

Serves 4–6

400 g (14 oz) curly endive, scarola, or dandelion leaves
200 g (7 oz) dried cannellini beans, or 1 medium can
6 tbs olive oil
2 whole small red chili peppers
4 cloves garlic, sliced
salt and freshly ground black pepper
500 ml (about 1 pt or 2½ US cups) water

Put the dried cannellini beans to soak for 12 hours or more in a large bowl as they do increase in size. Drain them and boil for 2 hours in fresh unsalted water. Salt at the end of the cooking time. If using canned beans, drain them from their liquid and wash them before using them. Wash the endive and cut it up into short lengths.

Heat the olive oil in a large saucepan, fry the garlic (not letting it brown) and then add the washed endive and the crushed chili peppers. Keeping the heat up high, stir-fry for a minute or two, coating the endive with the oil, then add the drained cannellini beans, some salt and the water. If you are using canned beans, you will find that they absorb less liquid, so reduce the amount of water slightly. Bring to the boil, cover the saucepan and reduce the heat. Simmer until the endive is tender and most of the liquid has evaporated, but the consistency is slightly soupy.

Swiss chard

PISELLI CON CIPOLLE E PROSCIUTTO
Peas and Ham

This recipe enhances the very ordinary frozen garden pea by cooking it in olive oil with onion and adding pink cooked ham. The combination is complementary in both colour and taste. It is a pity that this delicious dish, which is well known in Italy, is hardly known abroad. It has a very distinctive flavour and can accompany both meat and fish.

Serves 4

1 small onion
300 g (10 oz) fresh or frozen peas
3 tbs olive oil
150 g (5 oz) cooked ham
salt and freshly ground black pepper

Slice the onion finely, dice the ham into small pieces. Heat the olive oil in a medium saucepan and fry the onion for a few minutes. When it begins to colour, add the peas, stir and cook for 8–10 minutes on a low flame. Finally add the diced ham, salt and pepper. Stir, mixing well together and serve. If you are lucky enough to have fresh and tender peas, cook for only 2–3 minutes.

BIETOLE AL BURRO
Swiss Chard with Butter

Whenever possible, I try to avoid cooking vegetables in water and then putting butter on them. Instead, I prepare them in a way that conserves the vitamin content which remains in the cooking liquid and that at the same time enhances their flavour.

Serves 4

500 g (1 lb) Swiss chard, with stalks
45 g (1½ oz or 3 tbs) butter
200 ml (7 fl oz or 1 US cup) water or stock
salt and freshly ground black pepper

Wash and cut the chard, including the stalks, into 2 cm (1 inch) thick slices. Heat the butter in a large saucepan, and when melted add the chard. Increase the heat and stir to combine the butter with the chard, then add the water and salt. Cover the pan and cook for about 7 minutes. This vegetable has a taste similar to spinach.

FAVE FRESCHE ALLA PANCETTA
Broad (Fava) Beans and Bacon

This recipe, again, is only good if you can find the smaller fresh, tender broad beans. They are difficult to find, as the growers prefer to sell the bigger variety. The frozen ones need an extra minute or two of cooking time.

Serves 4

500 g (1 lb) fresh broad beans (fava beans), podded weight, or 500 g (1 lb) frozen broad beans
1 small onion
50 g (2 oz) smoked bacon
3 tbs olive oil
100 ml (¼ pt or ½ US cup) water
salt

Chop the onion and cut the bacon into matchsticks. Heat the olive oil in a saucepan and fry the onion until transparent, add the bacon and stir-fry together until golden. Put in the broad beans and the water and cook, covered, until tender: probably about 5–7 minutes. Broad beans like this make a good accompaniment for game and other strongly flavoured dishes.

FIORETTI DI CAVOLFIORE FRITTI
Deep Fried Cauliflower Florets

The cauliflower should be nice and white. Even the common cauliflower assumes a sophistication cooked in this way.

Serves 4

300 g (10 oz) cauliflower florets
flour for dusting
50 g (2 oz or ¾ US cup) dry bread crumbs
2 eggs
salt and freshly ground black pepper
1 lemon
plenty of oil for deep frying (olive oil is best)

Separate the cauliflower florets and boil in salted water until al dente. Drain and cool. Beat the eggs and season with salt and pepper. Dip the florets in the flour, then in the beaten eggs and finally roll in the bread crumbs.

Heat the oil in a deep fryer and fry the florets three or four at a time. Serve with slices of lemon.

FAGIOLINI AL BURRO E PANGRATTATO
French (Green) Beans and Fried Bread Crumbs

Make your own fresh bread crumbs for this delicious way of serving French beans. The crunchiness of fried bread crumbs combined with the tender beans is a surprising texture.

Serves 4

300 g (10 oz) French (green) beans, topped and tailed
100 g (4 oz or ½ US cup) butter
100 g (4 oz or 3 US cups) fresh bread crumbs
salt and freshly ground black pepper

Preheat the oven to 230°C (450°F or gas mark 8).

Crumble the bread into coarse crumbs, best done in a food processor, where you can use both the crust and the crumbs. Lay the crumbs in an oven tin and roast for 5–6 minutes. They should become golden, not brown.

Drop the beans in boiling salted water and cook until al dente. Meanwhile, melt the butter in a small frying pan. When fizzing, add the roasted bread crumbs and stir until they have soaked up the butter and turned a lovely brown. Season with salt and pepper. Cover the boiled beans with the bread crumb mixture. This is an excellent recipe to go with chicken or fish.

SPINACI, OLIO E LIMONE
Spinach with Oil and Lemon

This is one of the best ways of using an oil and lemon dressing. The oil gives a certain softness, and the sharpness of the lemon brings out the flavour of the vegetables.

Serves 4

600 g (1 ¼ lb) washed spinach
3 tbs olive oil (virgin if possible)
the juice of half a lemon
salt and freshly ground black pepper

Wash the spinach thoroughly and leave whole. In a large saucepan put water up to 5 cm (2 inches) deep, add salt and bring to the boil. When boiling, add the spinach, cook for 2 minutes or less if the spinach is very tender, drain immediately and pour over it the oil mixed with the juice of half a lemon. Freshly ground black pepper is excellent added to the dressing.

False fish or Russian salad

FINTO PESCE O INSALATA RUSSA
False Fish or Russian Salad

The name of this recipe is misleading: there is no fish in this well-known simple combination of vegetables and mayonnaise. My mother used to shape it into a fish to make it a more exciting dish for us as children.

Serves 6

300 g (10 oz) carrots
300 g (10 oz) celeriac
300 g (10 oz) potatoes (the yellow waxy ones)
150 g (5 oz) fresh peas (if not fresh use frozen, but not canned)
300 g (12 fl oz or 1½ US cups) mayonnaise (see recipe on page 32)

Peel the celeriac and cut into slices about 1.5 cm (a good ½ inch) thick. Peel the carrots and leave whole. Peel the potatoes.

Boil the vegetables together in salted water, adding the peas in the last two minutes. The vegetables should all be cooked al dente: if they have become soft you can't use them. Drain the vegetables and leave them to cool for 5–10 minutes. Meanwhile, make your mayonnaise.

Cut the cooled vegetables into 5 mm (¼ inch) cubes. Mix with the mayonnaise, to which you may wish to add extra lemon juice. Season with salt and pepper. Arrange on an oval flat dish in the shape of a fish.

PURÉ DI CAROTE E SEDANO RAPA
Carrot and Celeriac Purée

This is a speciality of my restaurant and judging by the number of times it is asked for, it seems to be popular.

Serves 4

300 g (10 oz) celeriac (peeled weight)
300 g (10 oz) carrots (peeled weight)
3 tbs double (heavy) cream
4 grates of nutmeg
salt and freshly ground black pepper

Slice the celeriac into 2 cm (1 inch) thick slices, cut each carrot lengthwise into four. Boil together in salted water for 20 minutes. They should be soft. Drain and put them through a mouli while they are still hot. Add the cream, grated nutmeg and salt and pepper.

173

CAROTE FRITTE
Fried Carrots

Frying unpeeled cloves of garlic along with the carrots imparts a special light flavour to them. (Eating garlic fried in its skin is not as dangerous as you may think!) This dish goes very well with Spinaci, olio e limone.

Serves 4

600 g (1¼ lb) carrots (peeled weight)

4 cloves garlic, unpeeled

3 tbs olive oil

salt

Wash and slice the carrots lengthwise. Bring a saucepan of water to the boil, add salt and the carrots. Cook, just boiling, for 7–8 minutes, remove and drain. Heat the olive oil in a frying pan and gently fry the carrots with the unpeeled cloves of garlic. Cook until brown; both the carrots and the garlic should be tender.

CIME DI RAPE AGLIO E OLIO
Rape Tops with Garlic and Oil

This inexpensive dish made from everyday ingredients has a slightly bitter taste that doesn't appeal to everyone. But, served with a good steak, especially a charcoal-grilled one, it is extraordinary. Try to buy tender rape: only the tops are used, as the main part is inedible.

Serves 4

900 g (2 lb) rape tops, cleaned

4 cloves garlic, sliced

2 small hot red chili peppers

6 tbs olive oil

Wash the rape tops very thoroughly and cut away any tough stalks or leaves.

Steam or boil the rape in salted water for only 3–4 minutes and drain. Heat the olive oil in a large pan, fry the sliced garlic and when it begins to turn in colour add the crushed chili and the rape tops. Stir-fry for a few minutes, season with salt and pepper and serve.

SEDANI AL FORNO
Baked Celery

The intensity of the taste of baked celery wonderfully complements the flavour of game.

Serves 4

750 g (1½ lb) celery, either 1 big head or 4 smaller heads

45 g (1½ oz or 3 tbs) butter

salt and freshly ground black pepper

Preheat the oven to 190°C (375°F or gas mark 5). Wash the celery heads and cut off the tops, leaving the young green leaves. Cut each head lengthwise in half and boil in salted water for 20–25 minutes. Drain and place the celery halves in an ovenproof dish. Pack the butter in each half, season with black pepper and bake in a medium to hot oven for 15 minutes.

FINOCCHI GRATINATI
Fennel au Gratin

It is a pity that this most delicious dish, very well known and appreciated in Italy, is hardly known abroad. It has a very distinctive flavour and can accompany both meat and fish.

The preparation is similar to the preceding recipe, with the addition of bread crumbs. Choose round, fat, firm bulbs of fennel.

Serves 6

1 kg (2 lb) fennel bulbs

45 g (1½ oz or 3 tbs) butter

20 g (scant 1 oz or 2 tbs) dry bread crumbs

salt and freshly ground black pepper

Wash and clean the whole fennel bulbs. Cut off the top stalks and the hard base, and cut each bulb in two lengthwise.

Preheat the oven to 200°C (400°F or gas mark 6). Boil the fennel halves in salted water for 15 minutes, drain and leave to cool a bit before slicing. Butter an ovenproof dish, slice the fennel into 1 cm (½ inch) slices and lay them in the dish, slightly overlapping each slice. Dot with pieces of butter, season with salt and pepper, and sprinkle over the bread crumbs. Bake in the medium hot oven for 15–20 minutes until brown and crispy.

CAVOLO VERZA CON PANCETTA
Savoy Cabbage with Bacon

Bacon, especially if it is smoked, seems to give an excellent flavour to vegetables, and cabbage makes a perfect companion to it. Roast pork is well complemented by this recipe. It is essential to have a good firm Savoy with enough white in it, although the green parts are tasty.

Serves 4–6

500 g (1 lb) Savoy cabbage (cleaned weight)
60 g (2 oz) smoked streaky bacon
4 tbs olive oil
1 clove garlic, chopped
1 dried red chili pepper
300 ml (½ pt or 1¼ US cups) water
salt and freshly ground black pepper

Slice the cabbage very thinly. Chop the garlic and cut the bacon into matchsticks. Heat the oil in a large saucepan. Fry the bacon, adding the garlic and crushed chili, for 2 minutes: the garlic must not brown. Put in the cabbage, add salt, pepper and the water. Stir to mix and then cook with the lid on for 10–15 minutes until the moisture has evaporated and the cabbage is cooked.

BROCCOLI ALLO ZENZERO
Broccoli with Ginger

Another recipe traditionally served in my restaurant. Both the broccoli and the ginger should be fresh.

Serves 4

500 g (1 lb) broccoli heads
2 cloves garlic
a piece of ginger the size of a walnut
4 tbs olive oil
salt and freshly ground black pepper

Wash the broccoli and separate into heads. Slice the garlic, peel the ginger and cut it into thin strips.

Boil the broccoli in salted water until cooked al dente, then drain. Heat the oil, fry the garlic and ginger together, taking care not to let the garlic brown, for a few minutes and then pour over the broccoli and serve.

PASTICCIO DI ZUCCHINI
Courgettes (Zucchini) Stewed with Tomatoes

As this is a summer dish, try to find some small fresh courgettes, sun-ripe tomatoes and fragrant basil.

Serves 4

500 g (1 lb) courgettes (zucchini)
1 medium-sized onion
1 clove garlic
2 tomatoes
3 tbs olive oil
3 or 4 fresh basil leaves
salt and freshly ground black pepper

Skin the tomatoes by immersing them for a minute or two in boiling water, and chop them roughly. Slice the onion finely. Chop the clove of garlic and finely slice the courgettes.

Heat the oil in a saucepan, fry the onion and when it begins to turn in colour add the garlic and almost immediately the tomatoes. Allow to bubble for a minute then add the courgettes. Simmer all the ingredients together for about 20 minutes. The courgettes should be soft. Add the basil leaves, salt and pepper and serve.

PEPERONATA
Stewed Peppers

This is a typically Piedmontese dish based on peppers, tomatoes, onions and celery.

Serves 4

1 medium-sized onion
2 large red peppers
2 celery stalks, with leaves
4 ripe tomatoes
5 tbs olive oil
salt and freshly ground black pepper

Prepare the vegetables; chop the onion, dice the red peppers, slice the celery and skin and roughly chop the tomatoes. Heat the oil in a large frying pan. When hot fry the onion, and as it begins to turn in colour add the peppers and celery. Fry together for 2 or 3 minutes. Now add the tomatoes and turn the heat down so that you slowly simmer the vegetables until they are reduced and resemble a ratatouille. This may take 35–40 minutes. Season with salt and pepper and serve either hot or cold.

Red peppers

PEPERONI ROSSI E GIALLI IN ACETO
Red and Yellow Peppers Preserved in Vinegar

My mother used to have a damigiana with a huge cork about 15 cm (6 inches) across. In the late summer she used to fill the whole jar with special fleshy round red peppers like huge tomatoes. She preserved them whole, not cut into pieces as I suggest in the following recipe. The amount my mother made lasted our family the whole winter. We ate them usually dressed with beautiful virgin olive oil and also as an accompaniment to pork dishes.

In Italy there are many varieties of red peppers. The little round ones are quite common; if you can find them, try them.

Makes 1 litre (2 pt) preserving jar

3–4 red and yellow bell peppers weighing in total 800 g (1¾ lb)
1.5 litres (3 pt) white wine vinegar
1 spray fresh bay leaves
salt

If the peppers are large, cut them lengthwise into four and remove the seeds, pith and stalks.

In a saucepan large enough to take the vinegar and the peppers, bring the vinegar to the boil. Add the peppers and salt and boil gently for 15 minutes. Sterilize your preserving jar, place the bay leaves on one side of the jar and fill up with the peppers and hot vinegar. Allow to cool before sealing the jar. Make sure the vinegar completely covers the peppers. Leave for two months before using.

PEPERONI FRITTI CON AGLIO, CAPPERI E ACETO
Fried Peppers with Garlic, Capers and Vinegar

The most important feature of this recipe is the slightly burnt taste of the peppers (red and yellow if possible) which is obtained by frying the vegetables so that the skin is scorched.

If I was ever late coming home, I was always glad to find a dish of fried peppers in the fridge!

Serves 4–6

800 g (1¾ lb) whole red and yellow bell peppers
4 cloves garlic
1 tbs salted capers (alternatively capers in vinegar)
4 tbs olive oil
2 tbs wine vinegar
salt

Cut the peppers into strips. Slice the garlic and put the capers to soak in a bowl of water. Heat the oil in a large frying pan and fry the strips of pepper. The oil should be quite hot. Stir while frying the peppers: their skins should begin to scorch at the edges. Then add the slices of garlic and the capers, drained and dried before being added. While these ingredients are sizzling, add the vinegar and salt, stir well and let the vinegar evaporate for a minute. Serve immediately if you like, but an excellent dish cold.

PORRI ALL'AGRO
Leeks in Vinaigrette

This recipe is ideal for accompanying cold meat and makes an excellent part of an antipasto.

Serves 4

1 kg (2 lb) leeks (ones that are not too thick)
6 tbs olive oil
2 tbs wine vinegar, if possible balsamic vinegar
salt and freshly ground black pepper

Wash the leeks thoroughly and cut off the tough dark green leaves and the roots.

Bring a large saucepan of water to the boil and add the leeks; boil them gently for about 10 minutes. They are cooked if when pierced with a fork they offer no resistance. Drain and while still hot pour over the olive oil and vinegar mixed together, season with salt and pepper and serve hot or cold.

CAVOLO ROSSO CON LE MELE
Red Cabbage

This recipe improves with being made the day before you wish to serve it. The flavours go particularly well with roast pork or goose.

Serves 6–8

1 kg (2 lb) red cabbage
100 g (3½ oz) smoked bacon
150 g (5 oz) leeks
50 g (2 oz) pork lard or goose dripping
4 cooking apples
500 ml (about 1 pt or 2½ US cups) cider
10 whole cloves
2 cm (1 inch) stick cinnamon
salt and freshly ground black pepper

Peel the apples and cut into quarters. Wash and slice the white part of the leeks; slice the red cabbage into strips. Cut the smoked bacon into matchsticks. In a large saucepan heat, over a medium flame, the lard or goose dripping. Fry the bacon in the hot fat until golden, then add the leeks and stir-fry for a few seconds so that they absorb some of the fat. Now add the cabbage, turn up the flame and stir continually, coating with the fat, for 2 or 3 minutes before adding the apples, the cider, salt, pepper, cloves and cinnamon.

Now cover the pan and when it has come to the boil turn down the heat and simmer gently for 50 minutes to 1 hour.

PATATE AL FORNO
Baked Potatoes and Onions

This simple but effective dish is a typically Italian way to cook potatoes, making the perfect accompaniment to all kinds of roast meat.

Serves 4–6

800 g (1¾ lb) potatoes (peeled weight)
150 g (6 oz) Spanish onions
1 sprig of fresh rosemary
salt and freshly ground black pepper
6 tbs olive oil

Preheat the oven to 200°C (400°F or gas mark 6).

Slice the onions and cut the potatoes into 1 cm (½ inch) thick slices. Mix the potato and onion together and put in an ovenproof dish. Pour over the olive oil and scatter the rosemary leaves.

Season with salt and pepper, stir all the ingredients together with your hands and place in the medium hot oven. Bake for 20 minutes and stir all the ingredients again. Replace and bake for a further 30–40 minutes, stirring once more. The potatoes should be cooked and slightly crisp on top.

PATATE FRITTE CON AGLIO E ROSMARINO
Fried Potatoes with Garlic and Rosemary

This is another wonderful recipe containing simple but effective ingredients. The combination of rosemary and garlic give an unmistakably Italian flavour.

Serves 4

500 g (1 lb) peeled potatoes
8 large cloves garlic, unpeeled
8 tbs olive oil
1 sprig of fresh rosemary
salt and freshly ground black pepper

Cut the potatoes into cubes 1.5 cm (½ inch) square. Heat the olive oil in a large frying pan, and when hot add the potato cubes. Spread them well out over the pan, but do not stir-fry until they form a golden crust. Turn the potatoes over and add the unpeeled garlic. Fry together to brown on all sides. Just before the end add the rosemary, salt and pepper.

RAPE AL BURRO
Turnip with Butter

A typical winter dish that is having a revival outside Italy.

Serves 4

600 g (1¼ lb) young tender turnips
100 ml (¼ pt or ½ US cup) stock
60 g (2 oz or 4 tbs) butter
salt and freshly ground black pepper

Peel and slice the turnips. In a saucepan with a fitting lid, melt the butter, add the turnips and fry for a minute or two, then pour in the stock. Bring to the boil, turn down the flame and simmer for approximately 10 minutes, covered. Season with salt and pepper and serve.

FAGIOLI AGLIO E OLIO
Beans with Garlic and Oil

Ideally, this recipe should be prepared with fresh borlotti beans, which are very tasty indeed. But as these are hard to come by, I will allow (as I do for tomatoes), the use of canned borlotti beans, or alternatively dried borlotti beans. Cannellini beans are another possibility.

Serves 4

200 g (7 oz) dried borlotti beans or 2 medium cans of borlotti beans
2–3 cloves garlic, chopped
4 tbs olive oil
1 tsp dried oregano
salt and freshly ground black pepper
Optional: 2–3 fresh or 10 g (½ oz) dried ceps

The dried beans should be put to soak in a large bowl of water for at least 12 hours before you are ready to cook them. Drain them and boil for 2 hours in fresh unsalted water. Season with salt at the end. If using canned beans, drain them of their liquid, run them under a tap for a minute, and leave in a colander to dry.

Heat the olive oil in a large pan, and fry the garlic for a minute or two. Before it browns, add the oregano and the drained borlotti beans, stir to heat up the beans and let the garlic and oil flavour them. Season with salt and pepper and serve.

If you have two or three fresh ceps, slice them and fry in the oil with the garlic before adding the borlotti beans. If you are using dried ceps, allow them to soak for 15 minutes before adding them, chopped into small pieces, to the oil and garlic. Cook these dried ceps for a little longer before adding the borlotti beans.

MELANZANE AL FUNGHETTO
Sautéed Aubergines (Eggplants)

Funghetto suggests a cooking method similar to that for preparing mushrooms. Aubergines cooked in this way do taste like funghi. An ideal accompaniment for that veal dish, 'La milanese'.

Serves 4

500 g (1 lb) aubergines (eggplants)
8 tbs olive oil
2 cloves garlic, sliced
1 tsp salt
freshly ground black pepper
2 tbs chopped parsley

Peel and dice the aubergines. Heat the olive oil in a large frying pan and when hot add the cubed aubergine and slices of garlic. Cook over a medium heat, stirring frequently, until they look cooked – this will take about 10 minutes. Mix the parsley with the aubergines and season with salt and pepper.

PRATAIOLI AL BURRO, AGLIO E PREZZEMOLO
Mushrooms with Butter, Garlic and Parsley

Field mushrooms can be found everywhere, and when cooked in the following way, provide an alternative to the usual mushroom flavour. Try to find button mushrooms that are still closed. You can also cook other types of wild mushrooms this way, for example, ceps, chanterelles, horn of plenty, etc. The result will be excellent.

Serves 4

350 g (¾ lb) button mushrooms
1 clove garlic, chopped
60 g (2 oz or 4 tbs) unsalted butter
3 tbs chopped parsley
salt and freshly ground black pepper

Slice each mushroom into three. Heat the butter until it fizzes, add the mushrooms and fry over a fierce heat until golden at the edges and all moisture has evaporated. Now add the chopped garlic, fry for only a minute, sprinkle with parsley and season with salt and pepper. Serve immediately.

FUNGHI MISTI IN UMIDO
Mixed Sautéed Wild Mushrooms

I cook this recipe every time I have had an unsuccessful mushroom hunt. I find that even the small amount of mushrooms I have gathered provide an opportunity to have a colourful, flavourful recipe, ideal to accompany autumn game dishes.

Serves 4–6

750 g (1½ lb) mixed mushrooms – oyster, field, ceps, hedgehog
1 small onion
1 large tomato
5 tbs olive oil
1 sprig of rosemary
2 bay leaves
salt and freshly ground black pepper

Clean the mushrooms, wiping them rather than washing them if possible. Slice the onion and peel and chop the tomato. Heat the oil in a large pan, fry the onion and when it becomes golden add the tomato, the bay leaves and the sprig of rosemary. Cook the tomato for a minute or two and then add the mushrooms. Continue cooking for 20 minutes more on a low heat, stirring occasionally. Season with salt and pepper.

TOPINAMBUR CON CIPOLLE
Jerusalem Artichokes with Onion

Artichokes cooked in this way are delicious served with delicate meats such as veal or chicken.

Serves 4

650 g (1 lb 6 oz) Jerusalem artichokes (peeled weight)
the juice of half a lemon
150 g (6 oz) onion
45 g (1½ oz or 3 tbs) butter
200 ml (7 fl oz or 1 US cup) water or stock
salt and freshly ground black pepper
2 tbs chopped parsley

Peel the artichokes and put in water with the lemon juice to prevent discolouring. Slice the onions finely and roughly chop the artichokes. Heat the butter and fry the sliced onion. When the onion is transparent, add the artichokes together with the water or stock and some salt

and pepper. Simmer gently for 30 minutes; the liquid should become syrupy when the artichokes are cooked. Serve sprinkled with parsley.

CROCCHETTE DI PATATE AL FORMAGGIO
Potato and Cheese Croquettes

It takes a fair bit of work to make these special favourites of my childhood. My mother always found it difficult to produce enough for the meal: she would watch us stealing them the moment they came out of the pan.

Serves 4

600 g (1¼ lb) potatoes (peeled weight)
45 g (1½ oz or 3 tbs) butter
50 g (2 oz) freshly grated Parmesan cheese
2 eggs
80 g (3½ oz or 2½ US cups) fresh bread crumbs
4 grates of nutmeg
salt and freshly ground black pepper
oil for deep frying

Boil the potatoes in salted water until cooked, drain and mash them together with the butter and the Parmesan. Season this with freshly ground black pepper, nutmeg and salt. Beat this mixture very thoroughly and then roll into sausages 4 × 10 cm (1½ × 4 inches). Lightly beat the eggs and dip the croquettes first into the egg and then roll them in bread crumbs.

Heat the oil in a deep fryer and fry the croquettes two at a time. They should be crisp and golden on the outside. These can accompany any dish or be eaten on their own – best very hot.

INSALATA PRIMAVERILE
Spring Salad

The spring salad, in short, should be a mixture of vegetables: obviously all the things that can be found in abundance in spring – young red lettuce, the small shoots from perennial plants in your garden such as mint, chives, parsley, etc. If you cannot find these, then buy some fresh spinach. The only rule is that everything should be perfectly fresh.

Serves 6

75 g (3 oz) radicchio
75 g (3 oz) white lettuce
100 g (4 oz) small spinach leaves
1 small bunch of watercress
1 small bunch of chives
2 or 3 sprigs of mint
1 small bunch of flat-leaved parsley
4 or 5 tbs olive oil (virgin if possible)
the juice of half a large lemon
salt and freshly ground black pepper

Wash and dry all the salad ingredients very thoroughly. Slice the radicchio and white lettuce into strips 1 cm (½ inch) wide. Leave the spinach leaves whole, but remove any long stalks. Cut the stalks off the watercress. Chop the chives into short lengths. Roughly chop the parsley and tear the mint leaves off their stalks. Choose a large salad bowl and mix all the leaves together in it. Make the dressing by mixing together the olive oil and lemon juice seasoned with salt and pepper. Only pour over the salad seconds before serving, so as to avoid the vegetables being 'cooked' by the acid in the lemon: even the freshest salad can be destroyed by being dressed too early. A delicious alternative to lemon juice in the dressing is balsamic vinegar (aceto balsamico) – a mild and sweet fragrant vinegar.

INSALATA DI CICORIA DI CAMPO
Dandelion and Violet Salad

A nice country walk gives us the chance of gathering the young dandelions needed for this recipe. They can be identified by their bright green narrow zigzag leaves. Arm yourself with a small knife and a plastic bag, and cut the plant off at the base of the leaves. Throw away the older,

A wonderful selection of eighteen different vegetables used in the spring salad coarser leaves and gather only from plants that have not yet flowered. If on the walk you happen to come across a violet or two, pick them to include in the salad dish.

Serves 4

300 g (10 oz) washed dandelion leaves
1 bunch fresh spring onions (scallions)
2 eggs
4 tbs virgin olive oil
2 tbs balsamic vinegar
salt and freshly ground black pepper
violets to garnish

Wash the dandelion leaves in several changes of water, making sure there are no bits of earth left. Wash the spring onions and cut each one lengthwise into four. Boil the eggs, shell them and cut each one into four.

Make a vinaigrette with the oil and vinegar and season according to taste. Mix the dandelion leaves with the vinaigrette, arrange the eggs on top and scatter with violets.

VERDURE IN PINZIMONIO
Crudité with Virgin Olive Oil

No one seems to know exactly where the word 'pinzimonio' comes from. The dictionary says it is a derivative of the words 'pinzicare' (sting) and 'matrimonio' (marriage)! In any case, this is a typically Tuscan recipe that brings together good fresh vegetables, Tuscan bread and the excellent virgin olive oil for which Tuscany is famous. It is a spring dish, to be made around May, when artichokes, celery, spring onions and fennel are at their best. It is an excellent way to start a meal, or is good as a simple snack.

Serves 4

4 small or 2 large artichokes
8 small spring onions (scallions)
2 bulbs of fennel
8 tender celery stalks
12 tbs virgin olive oil
4 tsp salt
1 loaf of wholemeal bread

Wash all the vegetables. Cut away all the tough leaves from the artichokes and cut off their tops, slice in half (if they are large, slice into quarters). Remove any choke. Cut the spring onions in half lengthwise. Quarter the bulbs of fennel,

removing any green stalks and discoloured parts. Split the celery stalks into two, lengthwise. Serve the vegetables in an earthenware dish (preferably standing in iced water). Make each person their own bowl of virgin olive oil, with 3 tablespoons of oil to 1 teaspoon of salt. Dip the vegetables into the oil and eat with the bread.

INSALATA DI FINOCCHIO
Fennel Salad

A bulb of fennel is a very versatile vegetable. Not only is it excellent cooked, but in its raw state it is good for every sort of salad. For those who like it, all you need do is eat it simply with good olive oil and salt and pepper. In southern Italy, little whole sweet fennel bulbs are eaten at the end of the meal instead of fruit.

Serves 4

2 medium fennel bulbs (they must be young and fresh), about 400 g (14 oz) cleaned weight
4 tbs virgin olive oil
salt and freshly ground black pepper

Keep a little of the green part of the fennel to scatter on the salad. Slice into very fine slices lengthwise so that each slice is held together by the stem.

Lay the slices out on a flat plate, pour over the virgin olive oil and season with salt and pepper.

INSALATA DI POMODORI E SEDANO
Tomato and Celery Salad

Meanwhile, summer has arrived – the season for those lovely ripe tomatoes with all the smell of the sun captured in them. Of course, I am talking about freshly picked Italian ones. You'll have probably noticed that in some Italian restaurants, the tomato salads are usually made with almost green ones. This is a new way of eating them, and even when green, they are quite tasty. However, I prefer them ripe.

Serves 4

4 large ripe tomatoes weighing 500 g (1 lb)
1 head fresh green celery
1 sweet large onion (white if you can get it or a red one, they are almost as sweet); alternatively, use large spring onions (scallions) with their green parts
1 clove garlic, finely chopped
6–8 fresh basil leaves
3 tbs olive oil (virgin if possible)
salt and freshly ground black pepper

Skin the tomatoes by immersing them in boiling water for a few seconds. Slice the tomatoes finely and lay them out on a large plate. Wash the celery and chop into small pieces including the tenderest leaves. Slice the onion. Chop the garlic very fine. Lay the sliced onion over the tomatoes, and sprinkle with the chopped garlic. Scatter the celery with the leaves over the plate and dress with olive oil, salt and pepper. I think the tomato contains enough acid so I don't add vinegar, but if you like it, go ahead.

INSALATA DI CAROTE E CORIANDOLO
Carrot and Coriander Salad

The carrot has a multitude of uses and is excellent raw as long as it is sliced finely. For this reason it is better to use large but young juicy carrots. Coriander used to be a frequently used kitchen herb and there seems to be a revival in the use of herbs like these. It is easily found in Greek and Indian stores.

Serves 4

4 large, peeled and finely sliced carrots weighing about 400 g (14 oz)
small bunch fresh coriander (about 3 tbs of leaves when the stalks are removed)
the juice of 1 lemon
4 tbs olive oil
salt and freshly ground black pepper

Grate the carrots on the largest-sized grater so that you get long strips of carrot. Remove the stalks from the coriander. Mix together and dress with lemon, salt, olive oil and ground black pepper just before serving.

INSALATA DI FAGIOLINI ALLA MENTA
French (Green) Bean Salad with Mint

What could be simpler than French (green) beans in a salad? This recipe can be eaten either hot or cold. It is important to have very fresh beans, without strings. The combination of the garlic and mint, along with the oil and lemon, gives a totally unexpected flavour.

Serves 4

320 g (12 oz) cleaned French (green) beans
salt
1 clove garlic
3 sprigs of mint
4 tbs olive oil
the juice of 1 lemon
freshly ground black pepper

Top and tail the beans. Boil them in plenty of salted water and cook until quite tender. Drain. Finely chop the mint and the garlic. Then mix them with the oil, lemon, salt and pepper and stir into the beans. Mix well and eat hot or cold.

INSALATA DI PATATE NOVELLE
New Potato Salad

This is one of my favourite salads in summer, when wonderful new potatoes are starting to appear. (I prefer the red-skinned ones, which remain waxy and al dente when cooked.) It is tasty on its own, and delicious with Scottadito.

Serves 4

600 g (1¼ lb) small waxy new potatoes
1 bunch spring onions
a handful of fresh mint leaves
4 tbs virgin olive oil
2 tbs red wine vinegar or balsamic vinegar
salt and freshly ground black pepper

Wash but don't peel the potatoes and boil in lightly salted water until they are just tender. Slice larger potatoes and leave smaller ones whole. Finely chop the spring onions (whites only), tear the mint leaves in small pieces and mix with the oil, vinegar, salt and pepper and the potatoes. Leave for an hour to cool and blend the flavours – though I prefer the salad warm.

CICORIA E RADICCHIO CON RUCOLA
Chicory (Belgian Endive) and Radicchio with Rocket (Arugola)

The flavour of the chicory and radicchio is slightly bitter, and combined with the rocket, produces a very appetizing salad.

In Italy the green chicory is used, cut very thinly. You can also use the white Belgian type, thus achieving a very Italian colour effect – the white of the chicory, the red of the radicchio and the green of the rocket.

Serves 4

200 g (7 oz) chicory (Belgian endive) heads
300 g (10 oz) radicchio heads
100 g (4 oz) fresh rocket (arugola)
the juice of 1 lemon
4 tbs olive oil
salt and freshly ground black pepper

After washing and drying the salad ingredients, cut the chicory and radicchio into strips and mix with the rocket. Serve with an oil and lemon vinaigrette.

INSALATA DI BIETOLE ROSSE
Beetroot (Beet) Salad

A winter salad, really very refreshing and pleasant. Try to find small uncooked beetroot with their leaves (you can use these as part of the filling for 'tortelloni di magro' with ricotta cheese). This salad is very easy to prepare and goes with almost any dish.

Serves 4

4 medium beetroot (beets) weighing 500–600 g (1–1¼ lb)
1 small bunch of spring onions (scallions)
the juice of 1 lemon
4 tbs olive oil
salt and freshly ground black pepper
some fresh parsley leaves

Cut off the leaves, leaving the stalks on the beetroot. Cook them in boiling water: if they are young, they take only 20 minutes.

Skin and slice Slice the cooked beetroot and lay the slices on a plate. Dice the onion and sprinkle it on the beetroot. Decorate with sprigs of parsley. Mix the lemon with the oil, salt and pepper and dress the salad.

INSALATA DI PORCINI CRUDI
Raw Cep Salad

Raw cultivated mushrooms make an excellent salad; however, using fresh ceps places this sophisticated delicacy among the finest dishes in the world. The ceps should be small and really fresh. I urge you to try them – they are incomparable. In Italy we use the 'ovuli reali' or Caesar's mushrooms for this purpose, but as these are relatively rare, I doubt that you'll be able to find them anywhere else.

Serves 4

300 g (10 oz) fresh ceps
1 tbs finely chopped fresh parsley
3 tbs virgin olive oil
the juice of half a lemon
salt and freshly ground black pepper

Clean the ceps well using a brush and a knife rather than washing them, and slice thinly. Dress with oil, lemon, salt and pepper. Scatter the parsley over them and serve as an antipasto on slices of toast made from white bread.

INSALATA DI CAVOLO VERZA
Savoy Cabbage Salad

In winter it is difficult to find fresh salad that hasn't been grown in a greenhouse. The Savoy cabbage, white and crisp, provides an ideal ideal to accompany roast meat.

I remember as a small boy, stealing a beautiful cabbage from a near-by field. One friend went home with an excuse to fetch the oil, one for the anchovies and one for the vinegar. We had found an old casserole with a broken handle. Behold, our own winter salad, eaten on a roof behind a warehouse in the chilly afternoon sun.

Serves 4–6

1 good crispy Savoy cabbage weighing 300 g (10 oz) without the darker outside leaves
6 anchovy fillets in oil
4 tbs olive oil
3 tbs wine vinegar
salt and freshly ground black pepper

Peel off the darker green outside leaves of the cabbage and with a very sharp knife slice the heart as thin as you can. Avoid the stalk. Chop the anchovies into small pieces and then in a bowl mush them together with the vinegar. When a smooth consistency, add the oil drop by drop. Season with freshly ground pepper and if necessary a little salt, but remember the anchovies are already contributing salt. Pour this dressing on to the cabbage, mixing well together so that every piece of cabbage is coated.

BAGNA CAUDA
Garlic Sauce with Crudité

When you eat bagna cauda don't make any social appointments for the day after, due to the effect the garlic has on your breath! It is a typical recipe from the Piedmont region, and is usually eaten in autumn or winter when the cardoon has undergone its first frost.

The bagna cauda is more than just a salad. It is a ceremony where friends participate and consume large amounts of good Piedmontese wine, which could be Barolo, Dolcetto or Nebbiolo. My sister-in-law taught me the trick of cooking the peeled cloves of garlic in milk in order to make it easier to digest, but still retaining its characteristic smell and flavour. The peeled cloves of garlic are cooked in milk before being used in the bagna cauda.

Serves 6

10 large cloves garlic
300 ml (½ pt or 1¼ US cups) milk
20 anchovy fillets
115 g (4 oz or ½ US cup) butter
4 tbs double (heavy) cream
2 red bell peppers
2 medium artichokes
2 fennel bulbs
2 carrots
4 celery stalks

Peel the cloves of garlic and put them in a small saucepan with the milk. Bring the milk to the boil, reduce the heat and simmer gently for 30 minutes or until the garlic is soft and beginning to disintegrate. Cut the anchovy fillets into small pieces and add to the garlic and milk. Cook together, stirring, to mash the anchovies with the garlic to form a paste. Add the butter in small pieces and stir until amalgamated. Remove from the heat and allow to cool a bit. Put the mixture through a sieve and then stir in the cream.

Wash and prepare the vegetables. Cut the red peppers lengthwise into strips 1 cm (½ inch) wide. Remove any seeds and pith. Remove the tough leaves of the artichokes and cut off their tops. Slice each artichoke into halves and make six slices from each half, cutting away any choke. Cut the fennel into halves and slice each half into six. Peel the carrots and cut each one lengthwise into six long sticks. Cut the celery lengthwise, each stick into four. Fill a large bowl with ice. Squeeze a little lemon juice on the ice and arrange the vegetables on top.

Serve the bagna cauda warm in a separate bowl for each person. To keep them warm, use little table heaters. Other vegetables can be eaten with bagna cauda: celeriac, hearts of cardoon and Jerusalem artichokes, preferably served raw, though you may blanch cardoon and celeriac.

INSALATA DI FAGIOLI BORLOTTI
Borlotti Bean Salad

Usually, this salad based on canned borlotti beans, is made with tuna fish and onions and is found in most Italian restaurants abroad. I prefer the Tuscan version with fresh borlotti beans that have just been cooked. Alternatively, use dried borlotti beans as long as they are not too old. The small amount of ingredients in this recipe aptly demonstrates that a minimum combination of flavours can produce a maximum result.

Serves 4

500 g (1 lb) fresh borlotti beans in their pods, or 200 g (7 oz) dried borlotti beans
4 tbs virgin olive oil
2 tbs wine vinegar
salt and freshly ground black pepper
1 tbs chopped parsley
1 clove garlic (optional)

If using the fresh beans remove their pods and boil in slightly salted water. Cook until tender – they take about 1 hour. If using dried borlotti beans, put them to soak in a large bowl of water for at least 12 hours. Drain and boil in fresh salted water until tender – they will take about 2 hours. When the beans are cooked, drain and, while hot, immediately pour over them the olive oil and vinegar. Season with salt and pepper and scatter with chopped parsley. Many people like garlic with their beans: crush one clove into some salt and add to the oil when dressing. Ideally, borlotti beans should be served with good Tuscan bread – wholemeal will do.

I FORMAGGI
CHEESES

The cheeses are brought to the table after il secondo, hopefully when there is a little red wine left. All sorts of cheeses are made in Italy with many regional variations. There are the famous ones: the hard cheeses such as parmigiano reggiano, the true Parmesan from Parma, and the more rustic pecorino, both of which are excellent eaten with pears; gorgonzola, the wonderful creamy blue cheese, is Lombardian and made with cows' milk; stracchino is very soft and mild, while fontina from the Aosta valley is semi-soft and is used for fonduta.

When I'm in Piedmont I love going up to Borgofranco to visit the balmetti, natural cellars hewn out of huge rocks where the farmers and peasants have been storing their wines in barrels for centuries. The local people go there in the late afternoon for a 'spuntino'. Spuntino is the Italian equivalent of high tea, only that instead of tea they drink wine and instead of cucumber sandwiches they eat slices of wonderful country breads with salamis and cheeses that are hanging from the ceilings. Sometimes by the end of the evening everyone is very merry and singing heartily.

Cheese is a very ancient food. It is made from cows' milk in the plains of Padana; goats' cheese is produced in the mountains, then there is sheep's milk cheese (more common in the south and in the islands) and even buffalo cheese. Some are high in fat, others have a fat content as low as 15 per cent.

This chapter surveys the different types of Italian cheese and then presents a handful of recipes based on cheese.

HARD CHEESES

Parmigiano Reggiano (Parmesan) True Parmigiano Reggiano is produced between April and November from cows' milk coming from the provinces of Bologna, Reggio, Mantova and Modena. Laws defining the manufacturing techniques of the cheese are very strict and a detailed description of the product must be clearly visible on the label. Only when you see this name printed on the cheese can you be sure of having bought the authentic matured product.

This cheese, one of the most famous in the world, plays an essential role in Italian cooking: it is usually grated on to various types of dishes – pasta, risotto, polenta, soups, for example. But it can also be eaten in chunks on its own, accompanied by some good bread and a glass of mature red wine. Parmesan is also excellent eaten with pears as a dessert.

A crumbly cheese, Parmesan belongs to the 'grana' (meaning grain) family, contains only 30 per cent fat, and is high in protein. It should never thicken, curdle or go stringy when it is added to hot food; if it sinks to the bottom of the plate, it is not the real thing.

Grana padano is a similar but slightly inferior cheese, industrially manufactured from milk coming from different regions outside the area where parmigiano reggiano is made. It is less matured than the real Parmesan, and therefore damper in consistency. I suggest you buy this only when you can't obtain the true reggiano type.

Both cheeses are made in circular shapes weighing 30–40 kg (66–88 lb) and matured for at least 18 months. (In some famous restaurants in Italy, minestrone is served in the hollowed-out Parmesan cheeses – as the soup is served the sides are scraped with a ladle, and some of the cheese is dissolved into the soup.)

Always buy both Parmesan and grana padano by the piece and grate it when you need it: pre-packed grated varieties are not recommended.

Pecorino Fresh pecorino (sometimes called 'caciotta') does not keep, but the matured pecorino, which keeps for some months, is used in the same way as Parmesan, grated on special pastas.

It is made from sheep's milk, from which it takes its name, in shapes weighing about 2 kg (some 4½ lb). It comes from central and southern Italy and two islands – Sicily and Sardinia. The two regions which both produce and use the most pecorino are Lazio (where they call the cheese pecorino romano) and Sardinia (where they call it pecorino sardo). The farther south you go, the spicier the pecorino becomes. The Tuscan version produced in Pienza, for example, is sweet and mature, while the Sicilian and Calabrian ones contain whole peppercorns and are very spicy. (I once saw some Sardinians devouring a very well-matured pecorino which seemed perfect except for the fact that it was crawling with maggots! Apparently this was considered a special delicacy.)

Roman pecorino is probably the oldest cheese produced in Italy, and it was served on the tables of the rich and poor alike; it is similar to the Sardinian pecorino – pale, almost grey in colour, and nearly always made in the characteristic round rush baskets and then air-dried. In Sicily the cheese is called 'canestro', after the baskets.

The Romans love to eat fresh pecorino together with very young broad beans and good bread: see the recipe for Pecorino con fave fresche, below.

Ricotta salata This is usually a derivative of pecorino, being made from its whey and then

Roman pecorino air-drying in rush baskets

dried, although it can also be made from goats' milk. It comes mainly from the south and is used grated on pasta. The flavour is similar to that of pecorino, but it is much less fatty.

Provolone The enormous pear-shaped cheeses covered in wax which hang from strings in Italian food shops are provolone. They come from the south of Italy and are produced in various sizes and flavours. The one most popular in the north is made with calves' rennet, is sweet-tasting and usually sold fresh, or no more than two to three months old. The cheese made with goats' rennet is spicy and suitable for maturing – the more matured it is, the spicier it becomes – and is preferred by people from the south.

Caciocavallo This cheese takes its name from the way it is hung to dry and mature – on 'horseback' over a pole. It is common in the south of Italy, as well as in the Balkans and in Hungary. It was already known in ancient Rome. Made from cows' milk sometimes mixed with goats' milk, its layered texture is similar to that of provolone, and its shape varies from oval to square. It has a pleasantly spicy taste if matured, and is sweet when fresh. It is eaten in slices or grated on some pasta dishes.

Toma Piedmont is famous for its toma, which is made from cows' milk in nearly every valley in the region. Each cheese usually weighs 2–3 kg (4½–6½ lb) and is sold in various stages of maturity – the maximum being two years. Most of the consumption of toma is local.

Eaten fresh, it has names like paglierina, tomella and tomini (see 'Fresh Cheeses', below).

SEMI-SOFT CHEESES

These cheeses are found all over the north of Italy. During the summer months the cow herds stay up on the high mountains where they graze on sweet aromatic alpine grass. This is what gives the region's cheese and butter its distinctive taste. In autumn there are never-ending processions of animals being brought down to the valleys for the winter. The cowbells round their necks clatter noisily and they are led by a festival queen, followed by her page – the youngest calf, wearing a tricolour scarf.

Fontina Fontina is made exclusively in the Val d'Aosta region. The genuine cheese bears a proper mark of quality with the inscription 'Fontina from the Val d'Aosta'. There are many imitations, but their quality and flavour do not come anywhere near the original, which is pale cream in colour and has a definite sweetness. Fontina is particularly good for cooking fondue and when eaten with good fresh bread. Each cheese is round and flat, weighs up to 15–20 kg (33–44 lb) and has a brick-red rind.

Bel Paese Translated literally, bel paese means beautiful country. It was developed in 1906 by Egidio Galbani to be produced in commercial quantities. The cheeses weigh 2 kg (over 4 lb) and are wrapped in wax to maintain their

Toma cheese drying in a protective cage

freshness. Bel Paese is very creamy in texture, and pale cream in colour; it is made from cows' milk, with a 52 per cent fat content. It can be eaten on its own or used for cooking. Galbani also produce an excellent range of factory-made products.

Asiago A cheese from the Veneto region made in the high plain of Asiago near Vicenza. It is made from semi-skimmed milk, and has a fat content of only 30 per cent. Each cheese weighs about 10 kg (about 22 lb) and is matured for two to six months, becoming spicier with age. It can be eaten on its own and can be used for cooking.

Taleggio Another cheese typical of northern Italy, probably the best-known one produced and distributed by the Galbani company. Each cheese is square, weighs 2 kg (some 4 lb) and is wrapped in a special paper to maintain freshness. It has a 48 per cent fat content and a soft, sweet flavour. It reaches maturity after only one and a half months, and is an ideal dessert cheese. I also use it in timballo di pasta and other dishes where the cheese should not go stringy.

Provola, provolini, burrini and ciccillo All of these cheeses are very similar – they have a fresh, creamy provolone base and are pear-shaped. Burrini are provola cheeses with unsalted butter in the middle; this gives a particular sweetness to the cheese, which is usually eaten on its own. Each cheese weighs about 500 g (1 lb) and is characteristically tied with a blade of straw.

SOFT CHEESES

Stracchino, crescenza and robiola At one time these cheeses were made almost exclusively from the milk of cows fed on hay in wintertime when they had come down from their alpine pastures. Stracchino, for example, takes its name from the world 'stracchi' which in the dialects of Piedmont and Lombardy means 'tired' – perhaps indicating how the cows feel in the wintertime. Originally, the cheeses were made in winter when the cold conditions enabled them to be stored for a while. Nowadays, of course, this is not a problem and they are available the whole year round. They are very soft rindless cheeses and are sold in specially wrapped portions ranging from 100 g (4 oz) or more to 2–4 kg (4½ to almost 9 lb) in weight. Their flavour is

deliciously fresh and sweet with a slight hint of sharpness. These typical dessert cheeses reach maturity in ten days, and can be spread on bread or crackers, but have few uses in cooking.

Gorgonzola and the veined cheeses
Gorgonzola is made from a base of stracchino, with the addition of the harmless fungus *Penicillium glaucum* which transforms it into the unique Italian blue cheese. It originated in the town of the same name, but nowadays it is made all over Italy. It has a 48 per cent fat content and a delicate buttery taste.

There are several variations. Apart from the sweet gorgonzola, there is a spicier, more mature one. The other erborinati – all the green- or blue-veined cheeses – are castelmagno, made at Donero in Piedmont; dolce verde which is sold in tubes; dolcelatte, especially popular in Britain; and lastly gorgonzola-mascarpone (also called Torta di San Gaudenzio), made of alternating layers of gorgonzola and mascarpone.

Gorgonzola has various uses, particularly as a dessert cheese and in sauces for fennel, pasta and polenta. I mix it with ricotta – see the recipe for Ricotta rifatta later in the chapter.

FRESH CHEESES

Mascarpone One of my boyhood dreams was of gorging myself on mascarpone, eating it in handfuls from a vast container. I was about twenty-five when I visited the Polenghi and Lombardo cheese factory in Milan on business. After being shown round the rooms where provolone, tome, grana and other cheeses were matured, I was taken to a small room full of steaming tables. This was where mascarpone – and my dreams – were made! It had just been spread very thinly on these tables to cool, and I was allowed to take a whole handful to taste. So dreams do come true sometimes – at least, in part!

This must be the fattiest cheese on earth: it contains 90 per cent fat. It is made from an extremely rich cream, slightly acid and whipped to an almost solid but very velvety consistency. Because it has a neutral taste it is used almost exclusively for making desserts and to enrich sweet sauces. It is also used in sauces for pasta.

My mother used to mix it with egg yolks and sugar to perk me up after the rigous of school. My own version of this is the recipe called tirami su.

Ricotta After Parmesan, ricotta is the cheese most frequently used in cooking. During a brief summer visit to Maratea in the province of Basilicata recently I had the good fortune to meet a friendly local shepherd willing to initiate me into the art of making authentic goat's milk ricotta. I was surprised to find that the process is very simple. First of all the cheese milk is skimmed to produce a full fat cheese (eaten fresh at this stage, it is called 'caciotta'). Then a small amount of fresh milk is added to the existing whey, which is then set to boil again. In no time at all small blobs of ricotta rise to the surface and are carefully fished out and put in the traditional basket or 'cestello', where they drip dry. A light cheese is formed, of exceptional taste and very low fat content.

Ricotta can be made with cows' and sheep's milk as well as that of goats, or from a mixture; the fat content varies according to the milk used, but is usually between 15 and 20 per cent. Ricotta is ideal used in many cooked dishes – crêpes with spinach, for example, and in ravioli. It is also widely used in desserts and cakes, as well.

There is also a semi-fresh ricotta that is eaten as a dessert cheese, and ricotta salata, mentioned above as a hard cheese, which is dried for several months and used grated on pasta in the same way as Parmesan.

When you are buying ricotta, make sure it is absolutely fresh and use it as soon as possible, because it quickly becomes acid and therefore useless.

Mozzarella This versatile cheese used in many dishes for its astounding melting quality was originally made only from buffaloes' milk, produced mainly on the plain of Aversa and in the area near Rome called the Agro Pontino. The original version is kneaded by hand while the whey is still very hot (a process that gives the cheese its characteristic 'layered' appearance), and is much more expensive than the factory-made type produced in the north of Italy from cows' milk. Although the cows' milk version is decidedly more rubbery in texture, it is nevertheless popular.

Various types of mozzarella exist, including walnut-sized bocconcini, 'pleats' of varying sizes, and the classic round mozzarella weighing about 200–300 g (7–10 oz) each. Good mozzarella should be very white and fairly elastic, and still be moist when sliced (the freshness can be gauged by the 'tears' of whey that emerge). When it is cooked it melts and goes very stringy. Mozzarella is an essential ingredient in pizza and Italians like to eat it in its natural state, uncooked and seasoned with salt, pepper and a trickle of olive oil, or in a salad with ripe tomatoes and a few fresh basil leaves. It is sometimes made into 'mozzarella in carozza' – fried between two slices of bread dipped in beaten egg – or a knob is put into the middle of potato croquettes, or 'suppli' (rice balls).

The use of mozzarella has grown enormously outside Italy, where it is often produced locally by non-Italian companies. Avoid the disgusting kinds made in Denmark and Belgium which bear no resemblance to the genuine mozzarella. The Italian type is exported in plastic bags which contain some liquid to keep them fresh. You should store mozzarella in the refrigerator, in a covered bowl of lightly salted water.

Also to be found in the markets and in good delicatessens is the smoked version of mozzarella, which is of a brownish hue and which is mainly eaten raw as an antipasto. I tried it on pizza with very interesting results.

Tomini and caprini As the name suggests, tomini are very small fresh toma cheeses. They are made from semi-skimmed milk and are round, about 4 cm (1½ inches) across and 2 cm (¾ inch) thick. They are eaten with freshly ground pepper, olive oil and vinegar. The best come from Chiaverano, a village near Ivrea; they are bottled in jars, with pepper, strong chili pepper, a few bay leaves and covered with olive oil, and can be kept for a long time. In Piedmont these tomini used to be called 'elettrici' due to their spicy flavour – they were given this name when electricity was first installed in people's houses. Nowadays progress has made its mark and they are called 'atomici'!

Caprini are the same as tomini, but are made with goats' milk and are more common in southern Italy and in Sardinia. The only type of this exclusively dessert cheese obtainable abroad is the one preserved in oil.

FONDUTA CON TARTUFI
Fondue with Truffles

A classic Piedmontese dish featuring the excellent fontina cheese from the Val d'Aosta with those jewels of nature – white Alba truffles. It is a speciality of great delicacy that will only succeed if the instructions are followed exactly. Whoever is lucky enough to get hold of some fresh truffles will enjoy a very special treat indeed. But fondue can also be eaten without truffles: it's good just with dipped bread or croûtons.

Serves 4

400 g (14 oz) fontina cheese
4 eggs
30 g (1 oz or 2 tbs) unsalted butter
300 ml (½ pt or 1¼ US cups) milk
1 small white truffle (optional)

Cut the fontina cheese into very small cubes and leave to soak in the milk for at least 4 hours. The milk should just cover the cheese. Thoroughly beat the eggs. In a double boiler melt the butter, add the beaten eggs, the cheese and a little of the milk that hasn't been absorbed by the cheese. Cook together over a very gentle heat, stirring all the time, until the cheese and eggs have amalgamated into a thick cream. Pour into a heated earthenware bowl and serve at once, adding thinly sliced truffle if you have one, or with croûtons of bread.

Previous page from left to right: Caciotta, Half-fresh pecorino, Pecorino with peppercorns.

Below: White truffles from Piedmont with a truffle-slicer.

PECORINO CON FAVE FRESCHE
Pecorino with Broad Beans (Fava Beans)

In Tuscany and Lazio, it is the custom to eat this speciality as soon as the fresh broad beans ripen. You need those small tender broad beans that can be found in late spring and early summer. Fresh pecorino, also called caciotta, should be absolutely fresh, but pecorino with peppercorns and slight aged pecorino are also suitable.

This dish makes an impromptu meal – it is tasty and can be eaten when one has not much appetite. It can also be eaten as an hors d'œuvre. The quantities used depend on how hungry you are. I would say about 150 g (6 oz) of pecorino and a dozen or so bean pods are sufficient per person. Of course, these should be accompanied by good home-made bread and a glass of white wine or a chilled young red wine.

Serves 4

600 g (1½ lb) pecorino
1.6 kg (3½ lb) young and fresh broad beans

Cut the pecorino cheese into thick slices. Put the broad beans in their shells on the table and let your guests pod them as they eat them. If you find them very small you can eat them whole.

RICOTTA RIFATTA
Remade Ricotta

This is a type of cheese created by putting two different cheeses together – ricotta and gorgonzola. These two cheeses complement each other perfectly, with the rough texture of the ricotta and the sharp taste of the gorgonzola. If you add some finely chopped parsley you will obtain an excellent creamy dessert cheese. Accompany with fresh celery stalks.

Serves 8

100 g (4 oz) gorgonzola, cut in small pieces
3 tbs milk
400 g (14 oz or 2 US cups) ricotta (preferably made with sheep's milk)
2 tbs finely chopped parsley
500 g (1 lb) celery stalks, cleaned

Mix the gorgonzola quite thoroughly with the milk. (If the gorgonzola you buy is very blue and strong, use a slightly smaller proportion of it. Now break up the ricotta cheese and add it to the gorgonzola mixture. Beat together until you have a creamy texture. Add the chopped parsley and arrange on a serving dish. Decorate the top with a fork and serve with celery stalks.

MOZZARELLA AFFUMICATA FRITTA
Fried Smoked Mozzarella

Smoked mozzarella, with its brownish smoky-flavoured skin and firm texture, is delicious in salads. This recipe makes a tasty antipasto or snack.

Serves 4

1 smoked mozzarella weighing about 280 g (9 oz)
1 egg, beaten
3 tbs flour
4 tbs dry bread crumbs
60 g (2 oz or 4 tbs) butter for frying

Slice the mozzarella into 4 thick slices. Dust each slice with flour, dip them into the beaten egg and then cover with the bread crumbs. Heat the butter in a heavy pan until it fizzes. Fry the mozzarella slices until crisp and brown on each side. It will take less than a minute to seal the overcoat. The cheese should hardly have melted, or the slices will fall apart. Serve with a lettuce salad.

PANZEROTTI CON MOZZARELLA
Croquettes with Mozzarella

These croquettes are delicious as a side dish or a snack. These were one of the things my mother would make a lot of to satisfy our hunger raids on the fridge on our return from school.

Serves 4

600 g (1¼ lb) potatoes
45 g (1½ oz or 3 tbs) butter
2 egg yolks
1 mozzarella, cut into fingers
salt and freshly ground black pepper
100 g (4 oz or 1 US cup) dry bread crumbs
2 eggs, beaten
oil for frying

Peel the potatoes and boil in lightly salted water. When cooked, drain and put back on the heat briefly before mashing. Add the butter, salt and pepper and mix well. When they have cooled a bit, add the beaten egg yolks and mix well to obtain a stiffish dough. Take some mashed potato in the palm of the hand and insert a piece of mozzarella in the middle. Seal up and roll into a sausage shape. Dip into the beaten eggs, then the bread crumbs. Heat enough oil in a deep fryer until very hot. Drop in the croquettes and fry until they are nicely golden and crisp. As they are bitten into, the mozzarella should go deliciously stringy.

MOZZARELLA IN CARROZZA
Deep-fried Mozzarella

The imagination of the Neapolitans has gone so far as to put the mozzarella in a carrozza (carriage) – one of the symbols of old Naples. It is a very easy, tasty recipe if cooked with a good stringy mozzarella and eaten right away. It can be eaten as a first or main course served with a green salad.

Serves 4

8 slices of thin white bread
200 g (7 oz) fresh mozzarella (try to buy the Italian ones sealed in water in plastic bags)
100 ml (¼ pt or ½ US cup) milk
6 tbs flour
2 eggs, beaten
salt and freshly ground black pepper
oil for deep frying – olive oil is best

Cut the crusts off the bread so that each slice measures 10 × 6 cm (4 × 2½ inches). Slice the mozzarella into 4 thick slices about 1 cm (½ inch) thick. Beat the eggs lightly and season. Dip the slices of bread on one side into the milk and then place a slice of mozzarella on the dry side. Season the mozzarella with salt and pepper and make a sandwich with the other slice of bread, milk-soaked side on the outside. Dust the sandwich with flour and then soak in the beaten egg. Heat the oil in a deep fryer, alternatively heat oil about 2 cm (¾ inch) deep in a pan. Fry the sandwich in the hot oil, turning it over if you are using a pan. The sandwich should be a nice golden colour, slightly crisp on the outside and the mozzarella filling should have begun to melt on the inside. Drain on kitchen paper and serve immediately.

LA FRUTTA &
I DOLCI
——————— FRUIT & DESSERTS ———————

Fresh fruit and the seasons are inseparable in my mind. That is why I feel uneasy about being able to buy grapes and strawberries all the year round. I spend the winter months longing for fresh fruit, and somehow that makes the first cherries or peaches of the season taste even better; the same in the autumn when you have the pleasure of looking forward to chestnuts, apples and pears.

When I was a child, it was my job to buy the fruit every day. As soon as I got home from school, I'd get on my bike and go off to buy fruit freshly picked from the trees. I knew exactly which farm grew the best peaches, the best plums, the best grapes. It felt good to be a wise buyer – the farmers respected me as a connoisseur from the day I refused to buy produce that was not perfect. We would usually eat everything I bought that day. If there was any fruit left over from our meal, it was stewed or made into preserves.

Although special desserts are generally reserved for special occasions, such as birthdays and Christmas, there are some superb Italian recipes – fruit tarts, baked peaches, pears in wine, puddings made of ricotta cheese, mascarpone eaten with stewed fruits. Wonderful fruit sorbets and icecreams are included in a meal or eaten at cafés in the heat of the day.

Some sweets and cakes are served only at Christmas or Easter – Pastiera di Napoli is made at Easter, for example, while Struffoli di Napoli, Cannoli alla siciliana and Panettone di Milano are all symbolic of Christmas.

Dessert wines are usually drunk with the sweet course, and there is a wide variety to choose from. My favourite, which is produced in the region I lived in when I was young, is Moscato d'Asti – slightly sparkling and tasting of muscatel grapes. Asti Spumante is the most famous sweet sparkling wine; others include Vin Santo from Tuscany (into which delicious almond biscuits called cantuccini are dipped), Lacrima Christi del Vesuvio, Malvasia from the island of Elba, Marsala, Torcolato from the Veneto region, Passito di Caluso from Piedmont and Monica di Sardegna.

Granny's lies

Sicilian Cahnoli

cherry

Almohds

lemon zabaglione

pricklx pear

pear

Ricotta Tart

Peach

Bomba

Amaretti

AMARETTI DI SARONNO
MARCA DEPOSITATA
LAZZARONI
ETTI DI SA

MANGO ALLO SCIROPPO DI LIMO
Mango in Lime Syrup

This is an exception to my rule of using only fruit in season. The mango, an excellent exotic fruit, is obviously imported from the Far East or Brazil. Unfortunately, it is picked while still green in order to keep it fresh during transport. Even so, some mangoes have an excellent flavour even when ripened in the packing case. The smaller Brazilian type is exquisite. But don't use canned ones.

Serves 4

2 ripe mangoes, or 4 if they are small ones
the rind and juice of 2 limes
100 g (scant 4 oz or ½ US cup) granulated sugar
2 tbs water
4 or 8 fresh mint leaves

Peel the limes and slice the peel lengthwise into very thin strips. Squeeze the juice and put this in a pan with the sugar. Add the water and heat for a few minutes until reduced to a syrup. Towards the end of this process, add the lime rind, mix to coat with the syrup and allow to cool.

Peel the mangoes with a very sharp knife. Cut them lengthwise as close as possible to the stone, which is flat, to obtain two caps. Slice these across the other way and, taking care to keep them together, arrange on a plate. Pour the syrup over including the strips of peel and decorate with a mint leaf before serving.

FRAGOLE AL LIMONE
Strawberries with Lemon Juice

This recipe uses beautiful fragrant strawberries when they are in season. I prefer to use wild ones, but it seems that they are rapidly disappearing from the wild. The ones that are force-grown in greenhouses are not the same. It is natural for Italians to eat strawberries with fresh lemon juice and sugar, just as other people eat them with fresh cream. The flavour of the strawberries is enhanced by the lemon juice. Naturally, the same applies for raspberries and all soft fruits.

Serves 4

500 g (1 lb) strawberries
the juice of 2 lemons
100 g (scant 4 oz or ½ US cup) castor sugar

Mango in lime syrup

Clean the strawberries, without washing them if possible. Put them in a dish. Pour the lemon juice on and then the sugar. Mix well and serve right away. The lemon juice has a very strong effect, so it is advisable to put it on just before serving.

PERE COTTE AL VINO BIANCO
Pears in White Wine

A few years ago, I was asked to write some recipes for a cooks' calendar. The dishes were to be photographed by my wife, a former professional photographer. Our kitchen was having work done on it, so my brother-in-law offered us his country house, putting his kitchen and private wine cellar at our disposal, and any wine we might need to cook with. One of the recipes was pears in white wine. I found that only the cellar containing vintage wines was open; the other, containing the ordinary wine, was locked. The 'cheapest' I could find was a Krug champagne. I can tell you that the recipe was a great success and the pears were quite delicious!

Serves 6

6 comice pears
200 g (7 oz or 1 US cup) granulated sugar
the rind of half a lemon
1 cinnamon stick, 5 cm (2 inches) long
1 vanilla pod, or 2 tbs vanilla sugar
enough wine to cover the pears in a pan – about 1 litre (2 pt) dry white
a further 200 g (7 oz or 1 US cup) sugar for the syrup

Peel the pears, leaving the stalk, and put in a pan. Add the sugar, wine, lemon rind, cinnamon and the vanilla and bring to the boil. Continue to cook, covered, on a low heat until the pears are cooked – about half an hour (when the point of a knife goes in easily). Take the pears out and put aside to cool. Add another 200 g (7 oz or 1 US cup) sugar to the juices and continue to cook the liquid fast and uncovered until it reduces to a syrup. This will take about 20 minutes. Pour this over the pears and serve when cold.

PESCHE RIPIENE AL FORNO
Baked Stuffed Peaches

A typical recipe from Piedmont where the peaches grow in abundance. For this recipe you need those lovely big ripe peaches with the yellow flesh. This dish can be made well in advance as baked peaches are excellent cold, but not straight from the fridge.

Serves 4

4 ripe peaches
2 tbs unsweetened cocoa powder
4 macaroon biscuits (amaretti), crumbled
2 egg yolks
2 tbs sugar plus 2 or 3 drops vanilla, or 2 tbs vanilla sugar
1 tbs pine nuts

Preheat the oven to 200°C (400°F or gas mark 6). Cut the peaches in two and remove the stones.

Scoop out some of the flesh from the middle of the peaches to make room for the filling. Mix the cocoa with the crumbled biscuits, the egg yolks, sugar, vanilla and pine nuts, blending well. Fill the cavities of the peaches with this mixture. Grease an ovenproof dish and put the peaches in it. Bake for 15–20 minutes. This excellent dessert needs a nice glass of Moscato d'Asti to go with it.

MELE COTOGNE SCIROPPATE
Quinces in Syrup

Quinces have a very distinctive flavour, but are good only when cooked. Quince jam and jelly are both delicious. An easy way to took them as a dessert is to stew them in water and sugar. This will become syrupy when cooked.

Serves 6

4 large quinces or 1 kg (2 lb) smaller ones
200 g (7 oz or 1 US cup) sugar
the rind and juice of 1 lemon
1 stick cinnamon, 10 cm (4 inches) long
10 cloves
water to cover

Peel, core and slice the quinces thinly. Put in a pan with the sugar, lemon and spices. Cover with the water and simmer on a moderate heat until cooked – about 1 hour. Remove the quinces from the pan and boil the liquid rapidly to reduce it to a syrup. Strain, pour over the quinces and serve cold.

SORBETTO AL DRAGONCELLO
Tarragon Fruit Sorbet

It is possible to produce any sort of ice cream or sorbet manually with the aid of a deep freeze. The trick is to turn a mixture of fruit juice or flavoured milk and the correct amount of sugar into a crystallized mass fluffy enough to be easily spooned. Care should be taken to whisk the ingredients just before they solidify to break down the crystals. This can be done by keeping an eye on the state of the sorbet or ice cream after an hour or so in the freezer. After whisking the mixture for a few seconds, it should be returned to the freezer. Nowadays, a sorbetière will do all this for you.

This is my newest recipe. I hope you like it.

Serves 4

2 tbs finely chopped fresh tarragon leaves
300 g (10 oz or 1½ US cups) sugar
750 ml (27 fl oz or 3¼ US cups) water
the juice of 2 large lemons

Boil together the tarragon, sugar and water and lemon juice for 2–3 minutes just to blend the flavour of the tarragon into the sugar. Cool the syrup, put in the freezer and proceed as above.

CROSTATA DI FRAGOLE
Strawberry Tart

This tart is wonderful when made with freshly gathered wild strawberries. Alternatively, any fruits such as blueberries, blackberries and raspberries are delicious made into this type of fresh fruit tart.

Serves 6–8

700 g (1½ lb) fresh strawberries
150 g (5 oz or ⅔ US cup) sugar
100 ml (¼ pt or ½ US cup) water
4 leaves gelatine (or equivalent amount of powdered gelatine)
the juice of half a lemon
For the pastry:
250 g (9 oz or 2¼ US cups) flour
100 g (4 oz or ½ US cup) unsalted butter
50 g (scant 2 oz or ¼ US cup) sugar
4 tbs dry sherry
a pinch of salt

To make the pastry, sieve together the flour, sugar and salt, add the butter cut into small pieces and mix together with your fingertips until the butter has completely crumbled. Add the sherry and mix lightly to make a dough. Cover and put aside in a cool place for at least an hour. Preheat the oven to 175°C (350°F or gas mark 4).

Roll out the pastry and line a tart tin 25 cm (10 inches) in diameter. Prick the surface and bake blind for 15–20 minutes or until the pastry is cooked.

Wash the strawberries and choose 180 g (7 oz) of the least good-looking ones. Cut into slices and put them in a small saucepan with the water, the juice of half a lemon, and the sugar. Bring to the boil and boil until the juice takes on some colour and becomes slightly syrupy. Remove from the heat, stir in the gelatine and leave to cool a little. Meanwhile, slice the remainder of the strawberries and sprinkle with a little lemon juice, keeping one beautiful strawberry aside for decoration. When the pastry and the strawberry syrup have cooled, spread a layer of the jellied syrup over the bottom of the flan. Arrange the fresh cut strawberries overlapping each other in a decorative way to make concentric circles. Place the whole uncut strawberry in the centre. Leave it to set before serving.

PERE COTTE AL FORNO
Pears Baked in Red Wine

Another very easily prepared recipe using cooked pears which can be found in many Italian restaurants. My mother used to make it in autumn when pears are plentiful and when the first wine has just been pressed. She would always make more than was needed; apart from being a dessert, it was also something special for us when we returned ravenous from school. The alcohol in the wine disappears when cooked, so the pears can be given to children.

Serves 10

10 conference pears
1 litre (2 pt) dry red wine
300 g (10 oz or 1½ US cups) sugar
1 cinnamon stick, 5 cm (2 inches) long
a few cloves
the rind of 1 lemon

Wash the pears and pack tightly, side by side, in a deep-sided ovenproof dish. Pour the wine over and add the cinnamon, cloves and lemon rind, then sprinkle half the sugar on the pears. Put into a cold oven and bring the temperature up to 200°C (400°F or gas mark 6). Cook, basting the pears every now and then with the juices. After 45 minutes sprinkle the remaining sugar on to the pears and cook for a final 10 minutes. Leave to cool before serving.

If too much liquid remains, reduce it a little by boiling it, then pour it over the pears before leaving them to cool.

BOMBA SICILIANA
Sicilian Bombe

From time to time it is acceptable to cheat a little to obtain a good recipe which would otherwise be too complicated. In the case of bomba siciliana, you would need to make two different flavours of ice cream first and then assemble the other ingredients. We start by buying good-quality ready-made ice cream, saving time, but still producing the real thing.

Serves 4

900 g (2 lb or 4 US cups) chocolate ice cream
300 g (10 oz or 1⅓ US cups) vanilla ice cream
225 ml (8 fl oz or 1 US cup) double (heavy) cream
75 g (3 oz) mixed candied peel and glacé cherries

Allow the chocolate and vanilla ice cream to become soft, not runny, by leaving it for an hour in the normal part of the fridge. Whip the cream until thick. Cut the candied peel into very small pieces and slice the cherries. Fold these into the whipped cream. Take a metal bowl 15 cm (6 inches) in diameter and 10 cm (4 inches) high. Line it evenly with the chocolate ice cream (which should be soft and workable) to a thickness of 2 cm (¾ inch): it is easy to do this if you use the back of a dessert spoon and have a bowl of warm water to dip it in to make a smooth finish. Put the bowl into the deep freeze to allow the chocolate ice cream to harden: this should take up to an hour. Now on top of this, spread the vanilla ice cream in a layer of the same thickness. The remaining cavity may be then filled with the whipped cream mixture. To complete the bombe, cover the top with a layer of chocolate ice cream.

Put the bowl in the freezer to solidify for at least 4 hours. Just before serving, put the bowl in hot water for a second or two to loosen the bombe. Turn out on to a plate. Cut into four with a knife that has been dipped in hot water and serve straight away.

TIRAMI SU
Pick-me-up

This is one of my favourite desserts made from that killer of a cheese – mascarpone. There are many recipes for Tirami Su, which translated means 'pick me up' or 'lift me up', due obviously to the large amount of calories in it! I developed this recipe using only a few ingredients. The result is stunning, judging by the reaction of the customers in my restaurant.

Serves 4

1 egg yolk
1 tbs sugar
½ packet (1 tsp) vanilla sugar
250 g (9 oz) mascarpone cheese
170 ml (6 fl oz or ¾ US cup) strong black coffee
1 tbs coffee liqueur (Kahlua)
10–12 Savoiardi biscuits
1–2 tbs unsweetened cocoa powder

Put the egg, sugar and vanilla in a bowl and mix gently to a creamy consistency. Add the mascarpone and fold in to obtain a cream. Put the coffee in a bowl with the coffee liqueur. Dip the biscuits for a second or two in the coffee mixture, letting them absorb just enough to keep firm but not fall apart. Starting with the biscuits, arrange in four individual dishes alternating layers of biscuit and mascarpone, ending with mascarpone. Dust with cocoa powder and put into the fridge to set and chill.

CROSTATA DI RICOTTA
Ricotta Tart

This tart is another cheese-based dessert with a superb result which my mother used to make from time to time as a special treat, usually on a Sunday. Ricotta is used all over Italy to make sweets. However, the ingredients and method suggest that this recipe comes from the south.

Serves 10

For the pastry:
250 g (9 oz or 2¼ US cups) flour
100 g (4 oz or ½ US cup) unsalted butter
50 g (2 oz or ¼ US cup) sugar
4 tbs dry sherry
a pinch of salt
For the filling:
40 g (1½ oz) candied orange peel
40 g (1½ oz) candied lemon peel
40 g (1½ oz) angelica
40 g (1½ oz) bitter dessert chocolate
2 egg yolks
150 g (5 oz or ¾ US cup) castor sugar
the zest of half a lemon, chopped
500 g (1 lb or 2½ US cups) very fresh ricotta

For the pastry, work the butter with the sugar, sherry and salt to a smooth consistency. Add the flour and work to obtain a stiffish dough. Put aside, covered, in a cool place for 1 hour.

The candied peel, angelica and chocolate should all be chopped into very small pieces about 5 mm (¼ inch) square. Beat the egg yolks with the sugar until creamy, add the chopped lemon zest. Beat the ricotta with a fork until light, then add it to the egg mixture. Finally, stir in the candied peel and chocolate pieces.

Preheat the oven to 190°C (375°F or gas mark 5). Line the bottom and sides of a cake tin with three-quarters of the pastry. Pour in the ricotta mixture and spread it evenly. Roll out the rest of the pastry and cut into strips 2 cm (¾ inch) wide. Make a lattice top on the tart. Put in the moderate oven. Bake until the top starts to turn brown – about 30–40 minutes. Serve cold.

CANNOLI ALLA SICILIANA
Sicilian Cannoli

This is a very typical Sicilian speciality using, once again, ricotta cheese. To shape the cannoli you need four or five cylinders 2.5 cm (1 inch) in diameter and 15 cm (6 inches) long. In Italy they use lengths of bamboo cane, and they also sell the equivalent in tin. If you ever go to Italy, don't forget to buy some of these moulds.

Makes 24 cannoli

For the pastry:
25 g (scant 1 oz or 1½ tbs) butter
25 g (1 oz or 2 tbs) castor sugar
150 g (5 oz or 1¼ US cups) flour
3½ tbs dry white wine
2 tbs vanilla sugar
a pinch of salt
1 beaten egg for sealing the cannoli
plenty of lard for deep frying
For the filling:
2 tbs orange water
500 g (1 lb or 2½ US cups) very fresh ricotta cheese
100 g (4 oz or ½ US cup) castor sugar
1 tbs vanilla sugar
50 g (2 oz) glacé cherries
50 g (2 oz) angelica
50 g (2 oz) candied lemon peel
50 g (2 oz) candied orange peel
80 g (3 oz) plain dessert chocolate
icing (confectioners') sugar for dusting

Beat the butter and sugar together until light and creamy. Add the wine, vanilla and salt and mix together. Fold in the flour and knead a bit to form a dough. Put the dough aside in a cool place for at least 2 hours. Roll out the dough with a rolling pin to a large sheet 5 mm (¼ inch) thick. Cut the sheet into 12 cm (5 inch) squares. Place a bamboo cane diagonally across the square of pastry and wrap the two opposite corners around the cane to form the cannoli. Seal the join by wetting the pastry with egg. Make three or four at a time (this number will probably be dictated by the number of cannoli moulds you have).

Now heat the lard in a large deep pan: the lard must be deep enough to cover the cannoli. When the lard is very hot, carefully put the cannoli in to fry. I find a long-pronged cooking fork is the best implement for handling the cannoli in the boiling lard. The cannoli are cooked when they have turned golden-brown. This will only take 1½–2 minutes. The pastry will puff up as it cooks, so the cannoli have a plump tube shape when ready. Lay the cannoli on kitchen paper to drain. Only remove the metal tubes or bamboo cane when the cannoli are cool.

To make the filling, beat the ricotta cheese with a fork, add the sugar, vanilla sugar and orange water. The ricotta should become creamier in consistency. Cut the peel, angelica and glacé cherries into small pieces. Chop the chocolate and mix these ingredients into the ricotta mixture. Fill each cannoli with ricotta mixture and line up on a plate. Dust with icing (confectioners') sugar and serve cool, but do not refrigerate.

A Moscato Passito di Pantelleria is the correct dessert wine to accompany this very delicious sweet.

PASTIERA DI GRANO
Wheat Tart

In Naples, Easter isn't Easter without this wonderful tart. It has, apparently, very old origins and it symbolizes wealth. Grain and ricotta cheese are the most basic of foods, and if you do not have them, it means you are very poor. Whatever Neapolitans may think of this, the tart is still a remarkable sweet. The important ingredient for it is whole wheat grain, which can even be bought in cans precisely for this purpose. I would suggest, though, that you buy the real thing. Allow plenty of time for preparing.

Serves 10 or more

For the pastry:
300 g (10 oz or 2⅔ US cups) flour
150 g (5 oz or ¾ US cup) castor sugar
150 g (5 oz or ⅔ US cup) butter or cooking fat
3 large egg yolks

For the filling:
200 g (7 oz) whole wheat to be soaked, or a 440 g (15 oz) can of cooked wheat called Gran Pastiera. Made by Chirico and obtainable from Italian delicatessens.
500 ml (1 pt) milk (if you are soaking your own whole wheat)
the zest of half a lemon and half an orange
1 tsp powdered cinnamon
2 tsp vanilla sugar
300 g (10 oz or 1⅓ US cups) ricotta cheese
225 g (8 oz or 1 US cup plus 2 tbs) castor sugar
4 large eggs (separated)
1 small wineglass orange water
150 g (5 oz) candied peel, chopped
icing (confectioners') sugar for dusting

The grain should have been soaked for 24 hours in several changes of water and needs to be cooked the day before the tart is made. Simmer the grain in the milk with the zest of half a lemon for 3–4 hours on a very low heat. When it is cooked, add a pinch of powdered cinnamon, a small sachet of vanilla sugar and the zest of half an orange. Cool and keep until the next day. Alternatively, use the canned ready-cooked grain, and add to it the zest of the lemon and orange, the powdered cinnamon and the vanilla sugar.

Make the pastry by working together the sugar, butter and the eggs until smooth, then add

Sicilian cannoli (left) and wheat tart (right)

the flour and make a smooth pastry. Put aside in a cool place for 1 hour or more. Preheat the oven to 190°C (375°F or gas mark 5).

To make the filling, beat the ricotta with the egg yolks and the orange water. Cut up the candied peel into tiny pieces, add them and the flavoured grain to the ricotta mixture. Beat the egg whites with the sugar and fold them very gently into the ricotta. Butter a large flan tin 35 cm (14 inches) in diameter. Press two-thirds of the pastry into the flan tin, covering the bottom and sides with an equal thickness. Pour in the filling. Roll out the remaining pastry and cut into long strips to form a lattice top to the tart. Put in the medium-hot oven and bake for about 45 minutes. Allow to cool and dust with icing (confectioners') sugar. The Neapolitans drink the locally produced wine, Lacrima Christi, along with this delicious tart.

MARZAPANE FRESCO
Fresh Marzipan

I asked many people who said they didn't like marzipan to taste the freshly made version, and all of them said it was delicious. There is an incredible difference between the factory-made type and the fresh. Try it and you will see. This is the basic recipe that can be kept in the refrigerator for some time until it is needed. You can either bake it or make it into different shapes, whatever is your fancy.

Makes 1.6 kg (3½ lb) marzipan

1,250 g (2½ lb) fresh almonds in their skins
400 g (14 oz or 2½ US cups) icing (confectioners') sugar
4 egg whites, beaten until stiff
extra icing (confectioners') sugar for handling

Put the almonds into a bowl of freshly boiled water for 5 minutes. Drain and shell them. Put through a fine mincer to obtain a fairly coarse flour. Mix with the sugar and fold in carefully the stiffly beaten egg whites. Work gently until you get a stiffish dough. Set aside to cool.

TORTA DI ELSBETH
Elsbeth's Cake

I remember my Aunt Dora sent us a cake for Easter made of fresh marzipan in the shape of a lamb. It was decorated with small caramellized aniseeds and little silver balls. She was living in Lecce at the time, where almonds grow in abundance. For us, Easter wasn't Easter without this 'sacrificial lamb'.

I made this cake for the first time for a very good friend of mine, Elsbeth Juda. It was a great success and I dedicated this recipe to her. I usually make the cake rectangular in shape, with two layers of filling, using as a mould a roasting tin that has sloping sides or a large pie dish at least 10 cm (4 inches) deep. The quantities in this recipe are for a finished cake that measures 30 × 20 cm (12 × 8 inches).

If you wanted to make a cake of more modest proportions, you could halve the filling and sponge cake ingredients and make only one layer. You would then need only 900 g (2 lb) marzipan and a pie dish or roasting tin measuring 20 × 15 cm (8 × 6 inches) as a mould.

Serves 15–20

1.5 kg (3¼ lb) fresh marzipan
200 g (7 oz or 1 US cup) icing (confectioners') sugar for dusting and rolling the marzipan
For the sponge cake:
6 medium eggs
300 g (11 oz or 1½ US cups) castor sugar
200 g (7 oz or 1¾ US cups) flour
For the filling:
500 g (1 lb or 2½ US cups) ricotta cheese
100 g (4 oz or ½ US cup) castor sugar
50 g (2 oz) candied orange peel, chopped
50 g (2 oz) candied lemon peel, chopped
50 g (2 oz) glacé cherries, sliced
the zest of 1 lemon
400 ml (15 fl oz or scant 2 US cups) double (heavy) cream
10 halves white peaches in syrup
half a glass strega liqueur

Preheat the oven to 190°C (375°F or gas mark 5).

Make the sponge cake first of all in this recipe. Beat together the eggs and sugar until they become light and foamy. Sift the flour and very carefully fold it into the egg mixture.

Butter a rectangular cake tin, approximately 25 × 20 cm (10 × 8 inches): the exact size is not vital, as the sponge will be cut up into pieces when the cake is being assembled. Pour in the sponge and bake in the moderate oven for 30 minutes or until it is firm to touch. Remove from the cake tin and allow to cool.

Dust your work surface and the rolling pin with icing (confectioners') sugar so that the marzipan does not stick. Roll out half of the marzipan into a large sheet to a thickness of 1 cm (½ inch). Sprinkle the icing sugar on the inside of the rectangular roasting tin (this stops the cake from sticking when it is turned out) and line this very carefully with a layer of marzipan. Trim the marzipan around the top and put the trimmings with the remainder. Cut the cooled sponge cake into thin slices and make a layer of sponge covering the bottom of the marzipan: use about half. Dilute the strega liqueur with double the amount of water and sprinkle a little on to the sponge, without wetting too much. Beat the ricotta with the sugar and add the lemon zest and chopped candied peel. Spread half of this ricotta mixture over the sponge. Slice the peaches and put them on top of the ricotta. Divide the remaining marzipan in two, and roll out one half to the same thickness as before. Cover the peaches with this second layer of marzipan. Now press down the mixture very gently with your fingers to push out any airholes. Use the remainder of the sponge to make a second layer. Sprinkle this with strega liqueur. Whip the cream and spread it over the sponge. Cover the cream with a second layer of peaches. Cover the peaches with the remainder of the ricotta mixture. You should have filled the baking tin by now. Roll out the final sheet of marzipan and lay it over the top to seal the whole cake, so that when turned upside down, no interior is visible. Leave the cake to set in a cold place for a couple of hours before turning out on to a serving plate. Dust with icing (confectioners') sugar. Cut the cake into slices and offer your guests Asti Spumante to accompany this wonderful treat.

TORTA CON NOCCIOLE
Hazelnut Cake

Yes, I like sweets as well! Foodwise, I really prefer to be called an all-rounder, as any type of food gives me satisfaction and pleasure. This cake is irresistible: it is a richer variation of the 'Crostata di ricotta' and the result is mouthwatering. I prefer to roast the hazelnuts before chopping them, as this gives a much nicer flavour.

Serves 6–8

100 g (scant 4 oz or ½ US cup) butter
25 g (1 oz or 3½ tbs) flour
125 g (4½ oz or ½ US cup plus 2 tbs) granulated sugar
4 large eggs
125 g (4½ oz) hazelnuts (shelled weight)
125 g (4½ oz) ricotta cheese
2 tsp grated lemon peel
6 tbs peach or apricot jam
1 tbs water to mix with the jam
25 g (1 oz) chocolate menier, or bitter chocolate, grated fine

Preheat the oven to 200°C (400°F or gas mark 6).

Lay the hazelnuts on a metal tray and roast them for 10 minutes in the oven: they should become a light, golden colour and their skins should be loose. Let them cool, then skin and chop finely. Butter a 25 cm (10 inch) flan tin. Grate the rind of the lemon. Soften the butter and beat it well with 70 g (3 oz or ⅓ US cup) of the sugar, add the egg yolks and continue to beat: the mixture should be soft and foamy. Fold in the sieved flour. In a separate bowl beat the ricotta with a fork until it is light, then add the chopped hazelnuts and the grated lemon peel. Add this mixture to the egg yolk and flour. Beat the egg whites until they become stiff, and fold in the remaining sugar. Fold very carefully the ricotta and flour mixture into the beaten egg whites.

Spread this mixture into the flan tin and bake in the medium oven for half an hour. Let the cake cool a little, then remove from the tin and place upside down on a plate. Dilute the jam with a little water and spread evenly over the top of the cake. Grate the bitter chocolate on the fine grater over the jam surface so that you have a light sprinkling all over. Serve with a glass of Passito di Caluso.

BUSIE D'LA NONA
Granny's Lies

A granny shouldn't tell lies, but these particular ones are sweet lies – made from strips of pastry that are then cut into ribbons and tied in bows by a patient granny.

This dish can be eaten after an informal dinner, or in the afternoon with a cup of coffee. Like the cannoli, they are better fried in pork lard.

Serves 6

60 g (2 oz or 4 tbs) butter
250 g (9 oz or 2¼ US cups) flour
1 large egg
2 tbs granulated sugar
5 tbs sweet Vermouth
a pinch of salt
pork lard for deep frying

Mix the butter with the flour, as for pastry; add the egg, sugar, salt and finally the Vermouth. Knead into a smooth dough; this takes 5 minutes or so – the dough should be fairly stiff. Alternatively, use an electric mixer that has a blade for dough making. Put the dough to rest in a cool place for 2 hours or more.

To make the 'busie', roll out the dough to a thickness of 3 mm (⅛ inch). If you have a pasta machine, you can use it to roll the dough out into long strips of the right thickness. With a jagged pastry wheel, cut the dough into strips 2.5 cm (1 inch) wide and 20 cm (8 inches) long. Gently tie the strips into bows. Heat the lard in a large deep pan and when the fat is very hot, fry the bows 2 or 3 at a time until golden-brown, remove and drain on kitchen paper and allow to cool. Pile them up and sprinkle with icing (confectioners') sugar.

BISCOTTI DI MELIGA
Polenta Biscuits

Meliga is the Piedmontese name for maize flour from which polenta is usually made. This basic ingredient is very common in Italy and one way to use it is in the making of sweets. For this recipe you will need a fairly coarse maize flour that can be found in any good Italian delicatessen. The recipe is very simple. These biscuits are usually found in Carmagnola, near Turin and also in the Aosta valley.

Makes 30–40 biscuits

200 g (7 oz or 1 US cup) unsalted butter
200 g (7 oz or 1 US cup) granulated sugar
300 g (10 oz or 1¾ US cups) maize flour (polenta)
100 g (scant 4 oz or 1 US cup) plain white (all-purpose) flour
salt
the zest of half a lemon
2 whole eggs plus 1 egg yolk

Preheat the oven to 190°C (375°F or gas mark 5).

Combine the flour with the polenta and the salt, add the butter, cut up into small pieces and the lemon zest, mix together to a soft bread-crumb consistency using your fingertips. Beat the egg, yolks and sugar together and then mix into the flour and butter to obtain a soft sticky dough. Butter a large flat baking tin. Using an icing bag with a large nozzle, 1.5 cm (½ inch) diameter, squeeze out 'S' shapes, circles and dots. Don't put them too close to each other as they will spread a little when cooking. Bake in the medium-hot oven for 15 minutes. The biscuits should be a wonderful gold colour with a darker brown rim. They are very crumbly and delicious.

FRITOLE DI LINO
Angel's Farts

We were celebrating my wife's birthday at la Trattoria da Lino in Soligheto, near Treviso. Course succeeded delicious course and we would not have thought ourselves capable of another mouthful when our host Lino and his wife produced an enormous heap of puffs as a special surprise. They were so perfectly delicious that we ate every one. When I came to make Lino's recipe myself for this book, it seemed to me that there was only one way to describe their heavenly lightness – and now our name for them is 'angel's farts'.

Serves 6–8

100 ml (¼ pt or ½ US cup) milk
100 ml (¼ pt or ½ US cup) water
50 g (2 oz or ¼ US cup) granulated sugar
15 g (½ oz or 1 tbs) unsalted butter
a pinch of salt
200 g (7 oz or 2 US cups) plain white (all-purpose) flour
4 medium eggs
2 tsp Lievito Bertolini (baking powder with vanilla)
olive oil for frying
For the cream filling:
2 medium eggs
1 tbs vanilla sugar or 2–3 drops vanilla essence
150 g (5 oz or ¾ US cup) sugar
500 ml (18 fl oz or 2¼ US cups) milk
100 g (scant 4 oz or 1 US cup) flour

Put the milk, water, sugar, butter and salt into a saucepan and bring to the boil. Sift in the flour and baking powder, stir briefly – the mixture will become very stiff. Remove from the heat and allow to cool, then knead in the eggs one by one. You will probably need a friend to help you scrape the sticky dough from your hands, otherwise you will wash it all away.

Fill a pan with olive oil about 2 cm (¾ inch) deep. Heat the oil. When it is hot, drop in a teaspoon of dough. The dough will almost immediately start to swell, as it swells it becomes perfectly round and surprisingly turns itself over in the hot oil so as to gently brown on all sides. The balls of dough will increase four times in size during cooking. Remove from the oil and put aside to drain but keep warm. When you have discovered how these balls grow, fry them 2 or 3 at a time, according to the size of your pan. Don't let the oil get too hot: the slow puffing up of the dough, which takes about 2 minutes, is essential to the texture of these delicacies. When biting into the fritters, the outside should be crisp and the inside practically hollow. Fill this hollow with the following cream, or with warm zabaglione (see next recipe).

For the cream filling, beat together the eggs, the sugar and the vanilla sugar until light and frothy, fold in the flour and then slowly the milk, stirring all the time. If using vanilla essence, add a few drops. Put the mixture in a heavy-bottomed pan and heat slowly on a low flame, stirring all the time, until you have a smooth cream. Allow to cool a bit, though best not cold.

Make a small incision in your fritter balls and push a teaspoon of cream into the hollow.

ZABAGLIONE AL MOSCATO
Zabaglione with Muscatel

Zabaglione is one of the best-known Italian desserts. You will find this delicious recipe, based on eggs, in nearly every Italian restaurant, both in Italy and abroad. Marsala wine is normally used along with the sugar to produce the fluffy consistency. The use of a good Moscato Passito instead of Marsala gives it a fresh flavour. If you don't have a special round copper pan, you can use a round bowl standing in a large pan of hot water.

Serves 4

4 medium egg yolks
100 g (scant 4 oz or ½ US cup) castor sugar
170 ml (6 fl oz or ¾ US cup) Moscato Passito

Beat the egg yolks with the sugar until the sugar is dissolved. Add the wine and beat for a few minutes more. Put in the bain marie over a low heat, and using a whisk, beat until a firm, foamy consistency is obtained. Pour into individual glasses and serve with very delicately flavoured biscuits.

Overleaf: Desserts from left to right, polenta biscuits, hazelnut crunch, granny's lies, angel's farts.

BONET PIEMONTESE
Piedmontese Bonnet

This is a typically Piedmontese dessert which, when translated, means 'cap' or bonnet. Don't ask me why. It is a richer version of crème caramel, with its distinctive burnt sugar flavour.

Serves 6

For the cake mixture:
6 eggs
150 g (5 oz or ¾ US cup) sugar
2 tbs cornflour
4 tbs unsweetened cocoa powder
400 ml (15 fl oz or 2 US cups) double (heavy) cream
600 ml (20 fl oz or 2½ US cups) milk
15 crumbled amaretti biscuits
a small glass dark rum – about 50 ml (2½ fl oz or ¼ US cup)
For the caramel:
50 g (scant 2 oz or ¼ US cup) sugar
2 tbs water

Preheat the oven to 160°C (325°F or gas mark 3).

To make the cake mixture, whisk the eggs, the sugar, the cornflour and cocoa until creamy. Add the cream, the milk, the rum and the crumbled amaretti and mix. To make the caramel, put the sugar and water in a pan and heat until the sugar caramelizes and changes colour. Pour the caramelized sugar into the bottom of individual soufflé dishes. Pour the cake mixture on top and put them in the oven in a dish filled with water. Bake at a low heat for about an hour. Remove, cool and put in the refrigerator for 2–3 hours. Turn upside down on to plates and serve with more amaretti biscuits.

TARALLUCCI DOLCI
Sweet Tarallucci

In Naples, when you say that something is going to end 'a tarallucci e vino', it means that there will be a happy ending. This could mean a row being reconciled by getting together and having a few tarallucci and some wine. I would like to see international political disputes solved in this manner. It would be very civilized indeed!

The tarallo is a ring-shaped biscuit and is usually found in many of the southern regions of Italy. It could be savoury or sweet, as in this recipe. Taralluccio is the smaller form of tarallo.

Serves 8–10

350 g (12 oz or 3½ US cups) plain white (all-purpose) flour
3 medium eggs
75 g (3 oz or ⅓ US cup) granulated sugar and 1 tbs vanilla sugar, or a few drops vanilla flavouring
2 tbs strega liqueur, or Anisetta
1 tsp powdered cinnamon
1 tsp aniseed (optional)
olive oil for frying
1 beaten egg for sealing the rings

Beat the three eggs in a bowl with the sugar, add the cinnamon, the aniseed, the liqueur, vanilla and flour and work the mixture until you have a dough. Put it aside in a cool place covered with a cloth for 1–2 hours.

To make the tarallucci take a small piece of dough about the size of a plum and roll it into a sausage with your hands. The sausage should be about 1 cm (½ inch) in diameter and about 15 cm (6 inches) long. Form each sausage into a ring by crossing over the ends and pressing together. Seal the join with a little beaten egg.

In a small pan heat up the olive oil. The oil should be at least 2 cm (¾ inch) deep in the pan. Deep-fry the rings two or three at a time. Half-way through frying, after half a minute, take out the tarallucci and make an incision with a sharp knife along the top so that when you return them to the hot oil, they split open a little. Fry until golden-brown, remove and drain on kitchen paper. Any wine is suitable to patch up a Neapolitan row!

STRUFFOLI DI NAPOLI
Neapolitan Struffoli

If Naples can't celebrate Easter without the pastiera, then it is even more unthinkable to celebrate Christmas without struffoli. It is a must. My mother used to make these for Christmas, and they were subsequently devoured by us. In many families they will be made as presents for friends and relatives.

Serves 10

500 g (1 lb or 4½ US cups) flour
5 medium eggs
3 tbs granulated sugar
grated rind of a lemon and of an orange
a pinch of salt
1 tbs pure alcohol (if not available, strong vodka will do)
oil for deep frying
For the caramel:
250 g (9 oz) honey
100 g (scant 4 oz or ½ US cup) sugar
2 tbs water
For decoration:
50 g (2 oz) angelica
25 g (1 oz) silver balls

To make the dough, beat the eggs with the sugar, then mix in the flour, adding the zest of the orange and lemon, the salt and the alcohol. Knead well for 3 or 4 minutes, make into a ball and cover. Leave to rest for 2 hours in a cool place.

Take a little bit of dough at a time and roll into sausage shapes with your hand to a diameter of 1 cm (½ inch). Cut the sausage into small pieces 1 cm (½ inch) long. Make quite a few. It is quite laborious rolling out these sausages and will take you some time.

Heat the oil in a small pan so that the oil is 2 or 3 cm (about 1 inch) deep. Fry the struffoli quite a few at a time in the hot oil until slightly brown, remove and drain on absorbent paper. Continue this way until all the dough is used up.

To make the caramel, use a heavy-bottomed pan and heat up the sugar and honey with 2 tbs water until the liquid becomes clear. At this point, add the struffoli and the chopped angelica, stir carefully until all the struffoli are coated with caramel. Arrange on a plate in the form of a crown. Decorate with silver balls (not too many) and leave to cool. It will taste delicious.

CROCCANTE DI NOCCIOLE
Hazelnut Crunch

Almost every Christmas, I make this sweet and put it into little individual cellophane bags to give as presents to friends and relations. I like to make them a couple of weeks before Christmas and store them in an airtight jar to keep them crisp. A little care is needed when making them, as the liquid sugar used to make the hazelnuts stick together is extremely hot and will mean many a burnt finger!

Makes 1.25 kg (3 lb) hazelnut crunch

700 g (1½ lb) hazelnuts, shelled
700 g (1½ lb) sugar
6 tbs good-quality honey
peel of half a lemon and half an orange
about 10 sheets of rice paper
half a lemon

Preheat the oven to 230°C (450°F or gas mark 8).

Put the hazelnuts in a flat ovenproof pan and roast in a hot oven until the skins remove easily and the hazelnuts remain pale in colour. If you shake the roasted nuts in a sieve, most of the skins will come off. Cut the peel off the lemon and orange and slice into fine strips, and then into cubes. Put the sugar in a heavy-bottomed pan along with the honey on a medium to strong flame. Stirring most of the time, cook until the sugar and honey have become liquid and turn brown in colour. This takes about 10 minutes. At this point add the peel and the nuts to the caramel in the pan. Stir, keeping the pan on the heat until all the nuts are well coated. Remove from the heat.

Now lay out the sheets of rice paper and make little heaps of the hazelnut caramel using 3–4 tablespoons for each heap. The nuts tend to stick up from the caramel: wait till you reach the bottom of the pan and use the remaining caramel to fill up any gaps around the nuts. Flatten the heaps by patting down with half a lemon – take care, as they will still be very hot. Leave to cool a bit, but when still warm, cut with a large knife into 2 × 3 cm (1 × 1½ inch) pieces: if the caramel is cold the knife will shatter rather than cut the pieces. Store in airtight jars.

I VINI

——— WINES ———

I was brought up in Monferrato, which is one of the best wine-producing areas in Italy. Later on I attended various courses to train as a sommelier and then spent many years dealing in wine. Over the years I have heard some very fanciful descriptions of wines, and have come to a very simple conclusion: a wine is good if you like it.

Of course, with the help of a good guide you can develop a more refined palate. Price alone does not determine the quality of a wine; nor does the snobbery connected to labels. On the other hand, not all wines made at home by countryfolk are good and genuine, as we are often led to believe. I have tasted some very bad home-made wines.

Italy is the largest wine producer in the world. The Italian wine industry is not only producing vast quantities of wine, but – despite the sins of the past – wines of excellent quality, too. And the number of companies making exceptional wines that can be ranked with the finest wines in the world is growing. (One of these companies, Antinori, has just celebrated 600 years of uninterrupted wine production with the introduction of three new wines called Tignanello, Sassicaia and Solaia.)

'Wine can be made from grapes, too', says an old Italian proverb. To put a stop to any shady practices and to protect the consumer, in 1963 the Italian government brought in a law that forces the wine producer to declare the origin of its grapes and to meet very stringent requirements before receiving the 'Denominazione di Origine Controllata' (DOC), a mark of quality similar to France's 'Appellation Contrôlée'. There is a higher classification – 'Denominazione di Origine Controllata e Garantita' (DOCG) – which is awarded only to the very best wines. They include Barolo, Barbaresco, Chianti, Vino Nobile di Montepulciano and Brunello di Montalcino. (Tignanello, Sassicaia and Solaia, even though excellent wines, do not carry any mark of quality; being new, they are waiting to be given a classification, which I suspect will almost certainly be DOCG.) About 200 wines bear the DOC classification. The Chianti classification is the only one divided into two: some bottles have a black cockerel ('Gallo Nero') label on their necks (this is the premier wine, Chianti Classico, grown in a small area between Florence and Siena), while the others, from six surrounding

Chianti Classico

7176017

Chianti Putt

N° 7200239

B   B

ROCCHIANTI VGERI

Barbera

BARBERA   ASTI

591917

MARCHESI INCISA DELLA ROCCHETTA

SASSICAIA

1982

TENUTA SAN GUIDO

BOLGHERI

Imbottigliato all'origine dal produttore
C.I.T.IA.SpA Bolgheri (07 LI)
Distribuito dal M.SI.L&P,Antinori, FI

VINO DA TAVOLA DI SASSICA

ITALIA   12.5%vol

Frascati

D N° 1053941

Valpolicella

CLASSICO

M780648 1

D.O.C.

areas, carry a cherub ('Putto') label and are called after the locality.

Apart from DOC and DOCG wines, there are, of course, countless other local wines which are not generally known outside their own regions. Italians tend to drink the local wine. It would be hard to find a good Barolo in Sicily or a Nuragus di Sardegna in Lombardy, although that is changing a bit now. On the other hand, a vast range of Italian wines from nearly every region can be found abroad. The export of Italian wine grows by 20 per cent every year.

Most of the wine consumed in Italy is everyday table wine. Although big wine drinkers, the Italians usually drink it only with meals, and sometimes as an aperitif. In bars in the Veneto region, you often hear someone ask for an 'ombra', which means a glass of dry white wine. In summer wine is usually diluted with mineral water, but not good Barolos or Brunellos, of course. Even a humble wine drunk on holiday will often taste like the best in the world!

Italians used to drink vast quantities of French champagne. But lately some Italian companies, particularly in the Veneto region and Conegliano, have been producing dry sparkling wines which are comparable to the French product. I usually decant dry sparkling wine into a carafe, as is the custom in Veneto. This reduces the amount of carbon dioxide and prevents the bottle 'sweating' when placed in an ice bucket.

Every region in Italy produces its own distinctive wines, be they red, white or rosé, and the characteristics depend on soil constitution, the position of the sun, the vintner's skill and the mixture of grapes used. The following is a broad outline of the major Italian wines, and an idea of which wine to drink with a particular type of dish. For an in-depth discussion of Italian wines, I suggest that you read *Viva Vino 200: DOC and DOCG Wines and Wine Roads of Italy* (1985) by a friend of mine, Bruno Roncarati, who is one of the great connoisseurs of Italian wine.

Wine and food must be in harmony with each other. Generally speaking, the choice of wine depends on how the food is prepared, and how strong a flavour it has. It is pointless to serve a good wine with vinegar- or lemon-based dishes such as some antipasti or salads, or with citrus fruits. White wine goes well with seafood salad or cold antipasti; a rosé or light red wine (perhaps chilled) is good with hot antipasti. White meats such as chicken require a light wine, but if cooked with aromatic herbs and spices, then a wine of more robust nature is acceptable. Red meat, without a doubt, needs a full-bodied red wine; mature vintage wine is ideal for game dishes. The same rule applies for cheese. If the cheese is fresh and delicate, then a light wine is preferred; a stronger red one can be drunk with strong cheeses such as mature pecorino or Parmesan. Dessert wine is of prime importance, too. Asti Spumante goes well with zabaglione and other light desserts, and Passito with cakes and fruit tarts.

As a rule, you should not use more than four types of wine, even if the meal consists of more courses.

WINES AS AN APERITIF

Vermouth is an Italian invention and is simply wine with the addition of an infusion of herbs. It is excellent served with ice, as are the following wines which have a natural aromatic flavour of their own: Traminer, Verduzzo, Tocai, Terlano, Prosecco, Vernaccia, Lacrima Christi. They should be served at a temperature of between 8° and 10°C.

WINES TO ACCOMPANY ANTIPASTI

As this is the first wine to be drunk at a meal, it should not be a heavy one. Many antipasti contain fish of some sort, and so need to be acompanied by a light, dry wine. The antipasti found at most seaside locations contain seafood and are consequently served with the local dry white wine, under the rule 'local food, local wine'. The best wines for seafood and oysters are the following:

Pinot Grigio from Friuli and Trentino; Vermentino di Gallura from Sardinia; Muller Thurgau dell'Alto Adige; Cortese di Gavi and Erbaluce di Caluso from Piedmont; Blanc de Morgex from Val d'Aosta. Also, Lugana della Lombardia; Orvieto; Verdicchio di Jesi and Rapitala from Sicily.

For shellfish I would choose the following: Riesling Renano, Corvo di Salaparuta Siciliano, Nuragus di Cagliari; Vernaccia di San Gimignano, Pinot Franciacorta from Lombardy; Greco di Tufo, Soave del Veneto and Epomeo d'Ischia.

Various salami can be eaten with light red or rosé wines which, of course, can be served chilled. I would suggest Rosato di Bolgheri, Kalterersee (a wine from Caldaro in Alto Adige) or Grignolino Piemontese.

WINES TO ACCOMPANY FIRST COURSES

You might not think that there are good wines to accompany pasta or soup courses, but here are my suggestions. Obviously, if you have started a Pinot Grigio or Soave with the antipasto, then you can use the same along with a clear soup. First courses can be divided into three groups:

Wines for clear or vegetable soups might include a good-quality Trebbiano di Romagna, a Tocai Lombardo or a Sylvaner del Trentino. In Piedmont, some countryfolk add a half glass of red table wine to soup. I've heard that the French in Périgord do the same. Buon appetito and cheers!

For risotto or pasta with a fish sauce, I'd suggest a Grave del Friuli; Prosecco di Conegliano or a Gavi dei Gavi. In short, any good-quality wine, not forgetting Bianco di Custoza.

For risotto and pasta with a meat sauce, light red wines should be served: Sangiovese di Romagna, Dolcetto di Dogliani or Cabernet del Friuli. There are two wines from the Veneto region that are perfect along with the classic meat sauce – Valpolicella and Bardolino. Cannonau di Sardegna is excellent also. And if the sauce is cooked in the oven in the Sicilian style, then a Corvo Rosso should accompany it. My favourite wine for drinking with risotto with truffles is a young, slightly chilled Barbera d'Alba.

WINES TO ACCOMPANY FISH

Fish is a very delicate food and is rarely cooked in highly spiced sauces, so accompany it with dry white wine chilled to a temperature of between 8° and 10°C.

Carema, a wine-producing town in the Aosta Valley

Falerno, which comes from the Campania region, is one of the great wines for fish. Excellent Tuscan varieties are Pomino di Frescobaldi and Bianco di Pitigliano. Also good are the Roman Est Est Est, Frascati and Marino, and the white wines of Friuli and Trentino such as Riesling Italico and Cabernet.

If the fish is more highly spiced and aromatic, as it might be when grilled, I would suggest an excellent rosé wine from Puglia called Five Roses, produced by Leone de Castris. It should be served very cold. Be careful though – it has a 13 per cent alcohol content!

WINES TO ACCOMPANY MEAT, POULTRY AND GAME

We now come to a more complex class of wine. We need to divide the meat into groups as before.

Let's start with the white meats – veal and chicken. For these, we require a red wine with a full, but not heavy, flavour. Piedmont produces excellent wines to accompany meat of this category: Fara Novarese, Sizzano, a young Carema, Ghemme and Donnaz. From Veneto come Merlot and Breganze.

For red meat we can go a step higher. Again from Piedmont, we have Nebbiolo, Carema Riserva, Boca and Barbera del Monferrato. Tuscany produced Nipozzano, Nobile di Montepulciano and Carmignano. Torgiano comes from Umbria, Rosso Piceno from Marche, and Aglianico del Vulture and Cannonau come from Sardinia.

Highly flavoured game dishes demand the highest quality of wine that the Italian wine industry can produce. Barolo and Barbaresco can be described as the male and female of wines. Barbaresco is slightly more delicate, but has a

great character. These are de luxe wines and need to be matured for four to five years at least.

Vino Nobile di Montepulciano, Brunello di Montalcino, Sassicaia, Tignanello and Solaia are the great wines of Tuscany. Grumello comes from the Valtellina and is a good-quality wine. In Naples, they drink Taurasi.

WINES TO DRINK WITH CHEESE

Some of my friends' wives are reluctant to invite me to dinner because they think I would be difficult to cook for! This must mean I have awkward tastes. In fact nothing could be farther from the truth. I am quite content if presented with a good cheese served with tasty bread and washed down with a glass of good wine. Cheese is one of my favourite foods. In fact, it is a food that is never really enjoyed to the full, being nearly always served after a meal, when one is more than full from the preceding courses. Sometimes I decide to indulge myself in this luxury and buy a selection of cheeses, such as a mature toma from the Val d'Aosta, a piece of stracchino or some Sardinian pecorino with peppercorns. The bread I'd choose would be the tasty Pugliese type; the wine might be a fine

bottle of Barbera d'Asti home-made by an amateur wine maker. If all these fine things are shared with good friends in a pleasant atmosphere, then the pleasure would be hard to beat.

Wines for soft, fermented cheeses should have a special character – not full bodied, but well balanced with not too high an alcoholic content. The ideal ones would be Santa Maddalena from the South Tyrol, or St Magdalener as they say in German. Going further south, we find Pinot Nero dei Colli Orientali del Friuli, then on to the Val d'Aosta where we find Donnaz. In Piedmont there is the Grignolino and in Veneto the Bardolino. Both are excellent companions for cheese.

To serve with hard, matured cheeses, we find we need wines with a fuller-bodied quality, but not necessarily with a high alcoholic content. Carema, Nebbiolo, Spanna and most of all Barbera d'Asti are perfect accompaniments to toma and Parmesan; while provolone and pecorino are best served with wines from the central southern parts of Italy, such as Chianti, Rosso di Cerignola or Cannonau di Sardegna.

WINES TO ACCOMPANY FRUIT

There really are no special wines to accompany fruit. Because fruit has a high acid content, it does not go well with wine. For stewed fruit or cooked pears, I would suggest a Brachetto d'Acqui, a Freisa d'Asti from Piedmont or, naturally, a Lambrusco di Sorbara from Emilia. I would not recommend drinking wine with grapes or any type of citrus fruit.

DESSERT WINES

Dessert wines are sometimes treated as the 'poor relation' among wines. I do not know why this is, but it is certainly a pity. At grand banquets their qualities are appreciated. They are never consumed in large quantities, but are taken in small liqueur glasses to accompany sweets of every description.

The most famous sparkling dessert wine is Asti Spumante which comes from the highly aromatic Muscatel grape. It is a pleasant drink to have between courses to quench one's thirst, as long as it is well chilled. It is a wine for special occasions, and is consumed most at Christmas to accompany the famous panettone or other cakes. Another sparkling wine, but slightly dry, is the Prosecco di Valdobbiadene.

Fruit tarts and special sweets such as cannoli alla siciliana and sfogliatelle call for a sweeter, liqueur-type wine. Italy has many of them. The ones that I would recommend are: Torcolato, Picolit, Malvasia di Castelnuovo Don Bosco, Moscato Naturale d'Asti, Vin Santo di Gambellara and Sciacchetrà. It is traditional in Tuscany to dip cantucci, which are almond biscuits, into Vin Santo. Aleatico di Gradoli, a sweet wine from Lazio; Aleatico di Puglia, Moscato di Trani, Primitivo di Manduria, Malvasia di Lipari, Moscato di Noto, the latter originating from the island of Pantelleria; Giro di Cagliari, Malvasia di Cagliari, Monica di Sardegna, Nasco di Cagliari, and Vernaccia di Oristano: judging by the huge range available, it is obvious that Italians enjoy ending a meal with this special type of wine.

Wines from Carema

INDEX

Author's Acknowledgments

To the following people go my profound
and unconditional thanks for
having in one way or another contributed
to the book:

Flo Bayley
Grazia Bolzoni
Nina Burgai
Anna Carluccio
Carlo Carluccio
Rosalba Carluccio
Caroline Conran
Penny David
Giulio Gallo
Rose Gray
Christine Hanscomb
Liz Hippisley
Bernard Higton
Elsbeth Juda
Susan Mitchell
Jean Moncrieff
Lucinda Montefiore
Carey More
Lucy Patrick
Dr. Bruno Roncarati
Dora Santarlasci
Zimmie Sasson
Lino da Soligheto
Carol Smith
Mary Trewby
Colin Webb

I would like to thank the following
shops and dealers which patiently put up
with my often unusual requests:

Camisa and Son (Groceries)
Parmigiani e Figlio (Groceries)
Lina Stores (Groceries)
Richards (Fish)
Cecil (Fish)
Bifulco (Meat)
Robert Bruce (Vegetables)
Fenn (Poultry)
La Fornaia (Bread)
Sue Graham (Salads)

Styling:

David Mellor
4 Sloane Square London SW1

The Conran Shop
77–79 Fulham Road London SW3

Heals
Tottenham Court Road London W1

Gallery of Antique Costume & Textiles
2 Church Street London NW8

Robert Young Antiques
68 Battersea Bridge Road London SW11

Photograph on p.6 by David Brittain
Author's photographs on pages 7, 14, 15, 17 (top), 21
(left and bottom), 188 (bottom), 189 (bottom)